Legacy of Freedom

GEORGE CHARLES ROCHE III

LEGACY

OF

FREEDOM

ARLINGTON HOUSE NEW ROCHELLE, NEW YORK

THIRD PRINTING, OCTOBER 1970

SBN 87000-065-9

Library of Congress Catalog Card Number: 79-93456

MANUFACTURED IN THE UNITED STATES OF AMERICA

To My Family

❦❦❦❦❦❦❦❦❦❦❦❦❦❦❦❦❦❦❦❦❦❦❦❦❦❦❦❦❦❦❦❦❦❦❦❦❦

Acknowledgments

❧❧❧❧❧❧❧❧❧❧❧❧❧❧❧❧❧❧❧❧❧❧❧❧❧❧❧❧❧❧

Permission to quote material from the following sources is hereby gratefully acknowledged:

Barrow, R. H. *The Romans*. London: Penguin Books Ltd., 1949.

Berlin, Isaiah. *Two Concepts of Liberty*. Oxford: The Clarendon Press, 1958.

Brinton, Crane. *Ideas and Men: The Story of Western Thought*. Englewood Cliffs, N.J.: Prentice-Hall, Inc., 1963.

Chamberlain, John. *The Roots of Capitalism*. Princeton: D. Van Nostrand Company, Inc., 1965.

Chesterton, Gilbert K. *St. Thomas Aquinas*. New York: Sheed & Ward, Inc., 1933.

Corwin, Edward S. "The 'Higher Law' Background of American Constitutional Law," *Harvard Law Review*, Copyright 1928 by The Harvard Law Review Association.

Dawson, Christopher. *The Dynamics of World History*. New York: Sheed & Ward, Inc., 1956. (Permission granted by The Society of Authors, London.)

Dawson, Christopher. *The Making of Europe*. New York: Sheed & Ward, Inc., 1952. (Permission granted by The Society of Authors, London.)

Dawson, Christopher. *Religion and the Rise of Western Culture*. New York: Sheed & Ward, Inc., 1952. (Permission granted by The Society of Authors, London.)

Eckermann, Johann. *Conversations of Goethe with Eckermann*, translated by John Oxenford, edited by J. K. Moorhead. New York: Everyman's Library, E. P. Dutton & Co., Inc., 1930.

Ferrero, Guglielmo. *The Principles of Power*. New York: G. P. Putnam's Sons, 1942. (Permission granted by Nina Ferrero Raditsa.)

Fertig, Lawrence. *Prosperity Through Freedom*. Chicago: Henry Regnery Company, 1961.

Hamilton, Edith. *The Greek Way*. New York: W. W. Norton & Company, Inc., copyright 1930, 1943, W. W. Norton; copyright renewed 1958 by Edith Hamilton.

Hamilton, Edith. *The Roman Way*. New York: W. W. Norton & Company, Inc., copyright 1932 by W. W. Norton; copyright renewed 1960 by Edith Hamilton.

Hardy, W. G. *The Greek and Roman World*. Cambridge, Massachusetts: Schenkman Publishing Company, Inc., 1962.

Hart, Jeffrey. "The Rebirth of Christ," *National Review*. December 28, 1965. New York, 150 East 35th Street.

Joad, C. E. M. *Teach Yourself Philosophy*. London: The English Universities Press, 1965.

Jouvenel, Bertrand de. *On Power: Its Nature and the History of Its Growth,* New York: The Viking Press, Inc. Copyright © 1948 by The Viking Press, Inc. Reprinted by permission of The Viking Press, Inc.

Kirk, Russell. *The Conservative Mind*. Chicago: Henry Regnery Company, 1960.

Krutch, Joseph Wood. "If You Don't Mind My Saying So," *The American Scholar,* Autumn, 1966.

Lewis, C. S. *Christian Reflections*. Grand Rapids, Michigan: Wm. B. Eerdmans Publishing Company, 1967.

Lewis, C. S. *The Discarded Image*. New York: Cambridge University Press, 1964.

Lewis, C. S. *The Great Divorce*. New York: Macmillan Company, 1946.

Lewis, C. S. *Mere Christianity*. New York: Macmillan Company, 1952.

Lewis, C. S. *Miracles*. New York: Macmillan Company, 1947.

Maritain, Jacques, "St. Augustine and St. Thomas Aquinas," an essay appearing in *A Monument to Saint Augustine*. New York: Sheed & Ward, Inc., 1945.

Molnar, Thomas. "Imperial America," *National Review*. May 3, 1966. New York, 150 East 35th Street.

Molnar, Thomas. *Modern Art as an Expression of Our Times*. Bryn Mawr, Pennsylvania: Intercollegiate Studies Institute, Inc.

Morley, Felix. *Freedom and Federalism*. Chicago: Henry Regnery Company, 1959.

Niebuhr, Reinhold. *The Nature and Destiny of Man: Human Nature*. New York: Charles Scribner's Sons, 1964.

Nock, Albert J. *Our Enemy the State*. Caldwell, Idaho: Caxton Printers, 1946.

Noüy, Lecomte du. *Human Destiny*. New York: David McKay Company, Inc., 1947.

Ortega y Gasset, Jose. *The Modern Theme,* New York: Harper Torchbooks, Harper & Row, Publishers, Inc., 1961.

Ortega y Gasset, Jose. *The Revolt of The Masses*. New York: W. W. Norton & Company, Inc., copyright 1932 by W. W. Norton; copyright 1960 by Teresa Carey.

Peterson, William A. *The Private Sector and The Public Sector: Which is Which and Why*. Bryn Mawr, Pennsylvania: Intercollegiate Studies Institute, Inc.

Peterson, William A. *The Wonderful World of Modern Economics*. Bryn Mawr, Pennsylvania: Intercollegiate Studies Institute, Inc.

Rushdoony, Rousas J. *This Independent Republic*. Nutley, New Jersey: Presbyterian & Reformed Publishing Co., 1963.

Saint-Exupéry, Antoine de. *Wind, Sand and Stars*. New York: Harcourt, Brace & World, Inc., 1949.

Schoeck, Helmut and Wiggins, James. *Relativism and the Study of Man.*
Princeton: D. Van Nostrand Company, Inc., 1961.

Schumpeter, Joseph A. *Capitalism, Socialism, and Democracy.* New York:
Harper & Row, Publishers, Inc., 1950.

Steinbeck, John. *America and Americans.* New York: The Viking Press,
Inc. Copyright © 1966 by John Steinbeck. All rights reserved. Reprinted
by permission of The Viking Press Inc.

Vivas, Eliseo. *The Moral Life and The Ethical Life.* Chicago: Henry
Regnery Company, 1963.

Weaver, Richard. *Life Without Prejudice.* Chicago: Henry Regnery Company, 1965.

Weaver, Richard. *Visions of Order.* Baton Rouge, Louisiana: Louisiana
State University Press, 1964.

Preface

It is unlikely that this book would ever have been written without the encouragement of Leonard Read and the remarkable staff he has assembled at FEE. The editorial assistance and wisdom of Paul Poirot has been especially helpful throughout. My gratitude is also due Miss Vernelia Crawford for her indexing of the manuscript. To my secretary, Mrs. Muriel Brown, go special thanks for her unfailing energy and enthusiasm in all stages of the book's preparation.

Much of whatever merit *Legacy of Freedom* may possess is owing to all the help which has been so generously provided by everyone at FEE— the rest of the book is my own responsibility.

G. C. ROCHE III

Introduction

ᴥᴥᴥᴥᴥᴥᴥᴥᴥᴥᴥᴥᴥᴥᴥᴥᴥᴥᴥᴥᴥᴥᴥᴥᴥᴥᴥᴥᴥᴥᴥᴥᴥᴥ

ALBERT JAY NOCK ONCE WROTE, "SOME DAY I should like to write an essay on the subject, 'How can one tell one is living in a dark age?'" Surely we are living in the most deeply troubled century within human experience. War, the threat of war, man's inhumanity to man, the readiness of some human beings to exercise tremendous coercive force over other human beings . . . this may indeed prove to be the darkest of dark ages. It is the thesis of this book that these problems arise because Western man has departed from his heritage.

We live in an age in which we hear on every side, "It does not matter what a man believes." This book is written in the fervent belief that it matters a very great deal what each of us believes. Not everyone may be a philosopher, but one can scarcely hope to order his life or find meaning in the world around him unless he has some idea of the underlying problems of the universe and of the human experience, some guiding rationale which serves to provide a pattern and purpose to his existence. I believe that most persons in this nation still harbor within their hearts many of the ancient verities. As a people, or at least as individuals composing our society, we believe in God, in right and wrong, in individual dignity and decency, and in the necessity for individual freedom. Unfortunately, a new "intellectual" class has arisen in the modern world whose purpose seems to be leading men away from these beliefs. As the result, the ancient truths and the heritage of our civilization are under heavy attack in our time. The individual citizen, the layman, the "average" man, is unprepared to deal with this attack and comes increasingly to question his own heritage because of his inability to defend it.

Such a failure of belief and such a lack of understanding is doubly unfortunate, because the defenders of the Western tradition are active, thoughtful, and very much on the scene in the mid-twentieth century. Yet mass communications, public school education, and public entertainment consistently reflect the values of the "intellectuals" who would destroy the tradition of our civilization. Therefore, there is all too little contact between those who would defend the ancient verities and those who would appreciate that defense if they only knew of it. This book is written in the hope of introducing some of those laymen to the heritage of their civilization and to the defenders of that heritage.

This, then, is a book about the history, personalities, and ideas which have distinguished Western civilization. This civilizing message of the Western heritage touches upon, among many other things:

1. The Greek realization of individual potential;

2. Socrates' insistence upon a fixed value system;

3. Plato's and Aristotle's development of the idea of a "controlling intelligence";

4. Plato's insistence upon the importance of forms, of values beyond exclusively material concerns;

5. Aristotle's development of the ideals of constitutionalism and limited government;

6. The Stoic assertions of individual dignity and responsibility, nearly achieving the moral framework of Christianity;

7. The tremendous success of the "Old Roman Character" founded upon self-responsibility, family, and honor, and the tragic results leading to the fall of Rome when the old Stoic heritage was denied;

8. The moral impact of the Judeo-Christian heritage, *making explicit* the concept of a fixed moral framework premised upon the existence of a Creator outside the natural order;

9. The teachings of the Church Fathers and St. Augustine, emphasizing such human potentialities as *memory* to set individual man apart from the natural order as the one creature in the world with the spark of divine personality;

10. The development of the Christian ideal through the triumphant reassertion of the entire heritage of a God-oriented universe of fixed values, as set forth by St. Thomas Aquinas.

The heritage of value which constitutes Western civilization has had a number of distinguished defenders in the modern world as well, consistently emphasizing the individual, the divine origins of personality, a fixed system of right and wrong, and the related ideas of limited government and free moral choice. But an alien tradition, stemming partially from the Renaissance and the Enlightenment, and epitomized in the modern world by the French Revolution, the totalitarian state, and the welfare state, has risen to challenge these traditional values, offering an alternative system in which government replaces God, relativism replaces a definite right and wrong, and the mass-man replaces the individual person.

Only a return to the standards upon which our civilization is based, the standards reflected in the American Revolution—fundamental belief in God and a fixed value system—can correct this substitution of coercion in place of volitional action, of power in place of right. It is precisely this heritage, in all its facets, that Western civilization provides for us so richly.

Of course, there have been all sorts of errors made by Western man along the way. Contradictions, confusions, different approaches to the same problem abound in the record of our civilization. This is understandable when man "sees through a glass darkly." The meaning of the universe is not necessarily a readily discernible fact. Yet the common thread of a God-oriented universe, of a fixed right and wrong, and of an emphasis upon individual dignity, does exist in Western civilization, if we but have the wit to see it.

Lord Acton, the distinguished historian of nineteenth-century England, gave advice to would-be writers of history: "Don't." Lincoln once commented, "It is better to remain silent and be thought a fool than to speak out and remove all doubt." Perhaps Acton and Lincoln both had the same idea in mind. But a Hebrew sage of ancient times perhaps set forth the viewpoint most clearly when he wrote, "In a place where one is unknown, one is permitted to say, 'I am a scholar.'"

All of these men had in mind the same central point. A writer analyzing complex ideas is embarking on a difficult venture. No man nor any combination of men ever has a monopoly on an understanding of any truth. And even if a man did completely understand any situation, he could not fully express it, since every expression of truth is to that very extent a limitation of truth. The best that anyone can hope to do is to express the sense of the understanding which he possesses.

The sense of my understanding is easily expressed. The heritage of Western civilization and of this nation is deep and abiding. This book is written in the hope that it offers a small introduction to a large and vitally important subject, a subject that the reader will be prompted to take up and carry much further than this author has been able to do.

Contents

❦❦❦❦❦❦❦❦❦❦❦❦❦❦❦❦❦❦❦❦❦❦❦❦❦❦❦❦❦❦

Legacy of Freedom

1

The Modern Malady

❧❧❧❧❧❧❧❧❧❧❧❧❧❧❧❧❧❧❧❧❧❧❧❧❧❧❧❧❧❧❧❧❧❧❧❧

SOMETHING IS WRONG

SOMETHING IS DEEPLY WRONG WITH THIS WORLD OF OURS. IN AN age so enamored with science and scientific terminology, it might be said that something is "out of phase." Most individuals seem to adhere to one set of values, while the society they comprise seems to follow an almost diametrically opposed value system. Evidence of this confronts us on every side in a world in which force or the threat of force limits human creativity, a world in which men actually seem to believe that coerced action is more productive than volitional action. Indeed, this coercion is not only the working premise on which much of modern society seems to proceed, but it now is increasingly presented to men as though it were *morally justified.*

No, this is not another treatise on what's wrong with the Communists. We scarcely need look to them for examples of coercion and repression of human creative capacity when we have such painful examples so much closer to home. Instead, we might profitably examine *our own assumptions and attitudes.* Though painful, such examinations often reveal some startling viewpoints.

Most people, for example, if we were to consult them as individuals, would emphatically deny their willingness to use coercion to achieve their individual goals. Yet if we take a number of these individuals and call them a society, we find them quite willing to use coercion to achieve their "social" goals. To understand this peculiar dichotomy, this ability of so many of us simultaneously to value the individual and disparage him, we need to turn to our past and examine the sort of thinking that has been *done for us* by people who have concerned themselves with such problems. The force of ideas is often underestimated, as Lord Keynes warned us fully thirty years ago, in *The General Theory of Employment, Interest and Money:*

> The ideas of economists and political philosophers, both when they are right and when they are wrong, are more powerful than is commonly understood. Indeed the world is ruled by little else. Practical men who believe themselves to be quite exempt from any intellectual influences are usually the slaves of some defunct economist. Mad men in authority who hear voices in the air are distilling their frenzy from some academic scribbler of a few years back.

Ultimately then, all of us are deeply concerned with the quality and truth of the ideas that find acceptance in the age in which we live. It is the writer's conviction that we have increasingly abandoned ideas of strength, vitality and truth, and have stood by unknowingly while ideas have been substituted that are both incorrect and dangerous. If we sincerely wish to correct the evils that face us in our time, we can only do so by retracing our steps from error to truth, from folly to wisdom, from coercion to freedom. Such a retracing would necessitate a consensus on certain fundamental values recognized by Western man; yet agreement as to what constitutes these fundamental values no longer exists. Some restatement and re-evaluation is therefore more urgently required than ever before in our history. Equally vital is a frank examination of the ultimate justification which serves as the basis for these ideas.

Too many of us who recognize that all is not right with the world retreat into a mere reassertion of ideas which have become platitudes. However well-founded such platitudes might be, the truths they contain must be re-examined and properly understood before they can become effective.

As a modern social critic has suggested, "Our task is much like finding the relationship between faith and reason for an age that does not know the meaning of faith."[1] Like a modern St. Thomas, we must be willing to re-examine the foundations of our faith, and of our reason, to discover the relationship between them.

The story has often been told about the argument that developed between the philosopher and the theologian in which the theologian chided the philosopher, saying: "You philosophers are like a blind man in a dark room looking for a black cat that isn't there."

The philosopher replied: "What you say may be true, but it is you theologians who say you *find* the cat."

Especially in our modern age, anyone who presumes to examine the past of Western man and emerge with a solid core of defensible ideas capable of standing on their own merits is likely to be accused of having found that black cat. Yet, the attempt must be made, because the cat is surely there.

This discussion is not intended as an exhaustive treatment of the intellectual history of the West; rather it is intended as a demonstration of the assumption that throughout the history of Western man a consistent theme of individual human dignity has gradually developed, based upon a very real view of man as at once a child of the physical universe and a spiritual being. This theme in both its physical and spiritual components has been increasingly ignored by modern man at his great peril.

THE DECLINE OF THE WEST

In the nineteenth-century world of ideas, the dominant conception was that of perpetual progress. But since the time of World War I, the idea of the decline of Western culture has increasingly invaded our consciousness. Even amidst our prosperity, the assumption of the decline of Western civilization seems to persist, an uneasy feeling in the air.

If one chooses to assume that decline and not progress is the order of the day for the Western world, there is an abundance of evidence to which he can turn. Never has force been more exalted. Coercion is King; coercion, the ultimately destructive force, is rampant throughout the world today. It is not merely that coercion has become commonplace. Worse yet, it has become acceptable. It would seem that the nineteenth-century progress of science has produced the twentieth-century decline of politics. The tremendously increased possibilities of coercion of man by other men through methods coming from the world of science may well have produced this result. As one wit has expressed it: "The superman built the airplane, but the apeman got hold of it."

These possibilities of coercion are not limited to the destructive weapons of war that have been produced in our time. The world of modern communication and transportation has set the stage for the age of coercion. In the less scientifically advanced world of our forefathers, the education of children, the care of the sick and aged, the keeping of the peace, and the production of the means of sustenance were activities engaged in by the individual citizen, close to his own home. In the age of science this is no longer true. Increasingly, we find the individual citizen living more by television than in the real world. If we know more about what the world is doing, as individuals we seem to play less and less part in that doing. Modern man increasingly seems to feel that if things are not right with the world, surely that is not the responsibility of the tiny little individual. As James Burnham phrased it in his *National Review* column, speaking as he imagined a resident of the new "global village" might speak, "Surely no one could expect us to provide the food and houses and medicines and cars and planes and computers and rockets that our village needs, or blame us for the crimes and wars and riots and revolutions."

If the individual citizen is so divorced from reality by the gadgets of modern science that he no longer feels responsibility for the conduct of himself and his immediate world, the modern state is quick to fill this responsibility-gap. Perhaps we should not blame the modern state so exclusively, however. It seems that states, or political principalities under whatever name, have always been willing to assume this function for man. It is, however, an encouraging sign that throughout history usually some men complained about the process. The story is told of a peasant, standing before the grand vizier of Egypt thousands of years ago, who found the courage to say, "Thou hast been set as a dam to save the poor man from drowning, but behold thou art thyself the flood."

A millennium later St. Augustine, writing in *The City of God*, summed up the complaint of the individual against the encroachments of the state, represented in this case by Alexander the Great:

"Excellent and elegant was the pirate's answer to the great Macedonian Alexander who had taken him in. The king asking him how he darest molest the seas so, he replied to Alexander with a free spirit, 'How darest thou molest the whole world? But because I do it with a little ship only, I am called a thief; thou doing it with a great navy art called a conqueror.' "

Coercion, however reprehensible in the individual, seems to become acceptable if only committed on a grand enough scale. The traditional protection which mankind has erected against such coercion, when committed on the grand scale, has been a spiritual bulwark, insisting that the rationality and the dignity of the individual stems from inalienable rights given us by our Creator and not by the state. When we have departed from this view of the individual as derived from the Stoic and Christian heritage, when we have failed to insist that the code which applies to the individual must also apply to society as a whole—in short, when we have failed to recognize that freedom derives its meaning from a concept of higher law—we have allowed ourselves to create political regimes exempt from the restraints of reason and understanding. Such political regimes have ruled on the basis of expediency alone.

Modern man has carried this to unbelievable lengths and insisted that not only the state but society as well must be without higher values and guided solely by expediency. The search for truth has been replaced by the search for facts. Moral values have been replaced by "social organization." In such a situation, it should not be surprising to discover that the individual has been submerged in society.

When the individual thus comes to be controlled by society and society by the state, mankind is due for trouble on an unprecedented scale. Human creativity and growth come from the unpredictability of voluntary human action and yet it is this very freedom of action which cannot be allowed in a coercively oriented society. In short, man has now progressed to the point where he can stifle all progress. As Friedrich Hayek has phrased it:

> There can be little doubt that man owes some of his greatest successes in the past to the fact that he has not been able to control social life. His continued advance may well depend on his deliberately refraining from exercising controls which are now in his power. In the past the spontaneous forces of growth, however much restricted, could usually still assert themselves against the organized coercion of the state. With the technological means of control now at the disposal of government, it is not certain that such assertion is still possible. At any rate it may soon become impossible. We are not far from the point where the deliberately organized forces of society may destroy those spontaneous forces which have made advance possible.[2]

In the words of C. H. Waddington, a contemporary scientist: Freedom ". . . is a very troublesome concept for the scientist to discuss, partly because he is not convinced that, in the last analysis, there is such a thing." Apparently, man has now progressed to the point where man himself is no longer necessary, at least not in any meaningful sense of human personality.

Before the repudiation of the spiritual side of man, the state had extended its claims over only a part of human life. The modern state accepts no such limitation and has extended its authority over the individual citizen in his total existence. As this new state has arisen in the modern world, with it has come a new type of social unrest. Western man has always had his political disturbances, but it is only in our time that political revolution has adopted the character of a religious crusade. This is a natural enough progression because, if man exists only by and through the state, if his total existence indeed is encompassed by political coercion, what outlet can one have for his energies but the field of political coercion?

The pseudo-religious impulse behind such social movements as the anarchism, socialism, and Marxism of the nineteenth century and the totalitarian experiments of the twentieth century is essentially destructive rather than constructive; if society is based on no principle of justice and no ideal end, and is therefore the mere embodiment of material force, what other possible ends can come from such means except the use of further coercive, destructive force?

How does a society essentially negative in character continue, then, to exist? Hilaire Belloc's water beetle, which flabbergasts the human race, provides the answer:

> By gliding on the water's face
> With ease, solarity and grace.
> But if he ever stopped to think
> Of how he does it, he would sink.

The growing threat of warfare to end all civilization, the growing financial difficulties, the growing poverty in the face of prosperity, these and all the other troubles which face our world, both East and West, are beginning to lead a few people to wonder just what *is* holding this process together.

Perhaps we should not be surprised that the modern coercive state is having increasing difficulty in keeping its head above water. As in the case of Dr. Johnson's "Lady-Preacher," we should instead feel that "such a creature is like a dog walking on its hind legs; we do not expect the thing to be done well, but are surprised that it is done at all."

We might expect that the total state, depending as it does upon coercion, should pioneer a new development in the outstanding form of coercion, war. It is instructive that the concept of total war has awaited so-called "modern" and "enlightened" times. If there is no place for the individual personality in the monolithic mass of the coercive state, then surely there can be no room for qualms about what happens to individuals in time of war: thus the concept of total war. As Richard Weaver has described it:

One was considered to be like one, and one like all, and this equalitarianism was followed by many corrolaries asserting the right and liability to equal treatment. If men are no different from animals, females no different from males, the young no different from the old, philosophers no different from fools, it is easy to proceed on to say that non-combatants are no different from combatants. They are all now fused into one element which is treated as a unit for the purposes of war—by the country as well as by the enemy.[3]

Thus coercion breeds the total state and the total state breeds total coercion. Since coercion cannot release creative action, we should not be surprised that it releases destructive action instead.

HYBRIS

As we look at our world to determine how this coercion has come upon us with such great force in our own time, we might note that man was creating his own slavery to material goods and machines before the modern coercive state began to enslave him. We live in an age that worships *things;* we have granted power to things of our own creation and in the process what should be our servant has sometimes become our master. If man indeed has two sides, a spiritual and a material, a higher and a lower, we should remember that a worship of the merely material is a downward pull. To merge man with material reality destroys his dignity in the process, because the dignity of man ultimately rests on his orientation to something higher than himself, something which man has not created.

Man has been promised for the past several hundred years that he need only conquer nature to achieve a heaven on this earth. Thus, as science advances, modern man has expected this heaven to become easier and easier of attainment. Modern science has told man that there is nothing that he cannot know and modern politics tells him there is nothing he cannot have. In a very real sense modern man has become, in Richard Weaver's phrase: "A spoiled child who has not been made to see the relationship between effort and reward . . . . The truth is that he has never been brought to see what it is to be a man. That man is the product of discipline and of forging; that he really owes thanks for the pulling and tugging that enable him to grow. This concept left the manuals of education with the advent of romanticism. This citizen is now the child of indulgent parents who pamper his appetites and inflate his egotism until he is unfitted for struggle of any kind."[1]

Thus it is the peculiar triumph and tragedy of modern culture to be responsible for the greatest advances in the understanding of nature and the greatest failures in the understanding of man. There is reason to believe that a very real connection exists between these positive and negative aspects of this modern culture. This growing gap between our technology and our morality increasingly imperils Western civilization.

It may well be that man's progress in the understanding of nature has produced a state of mind which causes him to misunderstand the total world of both man and nature. Once man comes to believe that he need merely exercise his reason upon the external world to understand it and ultimately to control it, he begins to envision an ideal world in both the physical and political realms; and he comes to believe that this ideal world constitutes the true reality. Soon a gap opens between this ideal world and reality. But once man has elevated his reason above all other considerations, he comes to believe that this conflict between his ideal and reality will always be resolved in favor of his ideal. Modern man does not seem to understand that science can harbor illusions on the image of nature and thus mislead. This misleading tendency becomes doubly dangerous when it serves to discredit the possibility of a spiritual side to man's nature, as it has done in the modern world.

If the price man pays for this confusion seems high, it may be recalled that the sin of pride in man's imagined self-sufficiency has throughout history produced disastrous results. Man has seemed to be at his worst when unwilling to recognize the weakness and dependence of his existence on earth, and when he has grasped after power out of proportion to his virtue and knowledge. The Biblical definition of the ultimate sin is the unwillingness of man to recognize his dependence upon God and to assume instead that the natural world over which man presides constitutes all reality. As Reinhold Niebuhr has expressed it:

One aspect of this human pride is man's refusal to acknowledge the dependent character of his life. Thus Egypt exists by the beneficences of nature in terms of the Nile's rhythmic seasons, but according to Ezekiel, she imagines herself the author of this source of her wealth: "Behold, I am against thee, Pharaoh, king of Egypt, the great dragon that lieth in the midst of his rivers, which hath said, My river is mine own, and I have made it for myself" (EZEKIEL 29:3). One might write pages on the relevance of this prophetic judgment upon the self-sufficiency of modern man whose technical achievements obscure his dependence upon vast natural processes beyond his control and accentuate the perennial pride of man in his own power and security.[4]

The sinful nature of man in his seeking to make himself God is perhaps expressed most clearly by St. Paul: "Professing themselves to be wise, they became fools and changed the glory of the incorruptible God into an image made like to corruptible man . . ." (I ROMANS 22–23)

The rapid development of the material aspects of Western civilization aggravated this weakness of modern man. As a cascade of new scientific discoveries and inventions poured forth upon mankind, little attention was given to the solving of the human equation. Soon this flood of material things became mistaken for reality itself. The minds of most men had been exposed to such error by the philosophy of the past several hundred years in its questioning attitude toward man's traditional beliefs:

> Without becoming much more intelligent men had learned to employ the tricks of rational thought. An infinitely seductive tool, a new toy, had been put in their hands and they all had the illusion that they knew how to use it. This tool had obtained sensational results which gradually transformed their material life and raised unlimited hopes. It was natural that the respect heretofore bestowed on the priest should be transferred progressively to those who had succeeded in harnessing the forces of nature and in penetrating some of her secrets.[5]

Such an approach, turning from free will and moral responsibility to a view of the individual as only a collection of living matter scarcely different from the animals of the earth—leading, in short, to a view of man without spirituality—paved the way for the de-humanization of man and for the creation of the amoral framework necessary for the rise of the totally coercive state in its modern form.

The Greeks called the sin of pride hybris. But the really prideful attitudes had to await modern man. It took a modern poet, Algernon Swinburne, to write:

> The seal of his knowledge is sure,
>   the truth and his spirit are wed; . . .
> Glory to Man in the highest!
>   for man is the master of things.

The story of the sorcerer's apprentice immediately comes to mind, in which the apprentice, not really understanding the sorcerer's art, learns a trick or two and fancies himself master of material things. Yet, as you recall, material things soon demonstrated to the apprentice how little he really knew. Like Kipling's orangutan with "too much ego in his cosmos," man has now equated discovery with understanding and understanding with power.

In "The Last Department," Rudyard Kipling wrote:

> Twelve hundred million men are spread
> About this earth and I and you
> Wonder when you and I are dead
> What will these luckless millions do?

When we hear an individual spout such egotistic nonsense, we recognize it for what it is. Yet, when we talk about man as a whole, we are quite willing to depart from reality and from any standard of objective truth and retire into the comfortable, although deceptive, world of relativism within which, "Man is the measure of all things." Man's sin of pride, his unwillingness or inability to recognize any standard above his own, leads him to think entirely in terms of finite means and ends. Yet, there is more to man than these finite conceptions. He forever reaches for the stars and is never satisfied. He makes the attempt, as Bishop Sheen has commented, to multiply the finite into the infinite only to discover that he is multiplying zeros. The sort of individual personality and human variation that would justify a man's resisting his descent into the mass of cyphers which composes the citizenry of the coercive state has no validity until he encounters the Infinite; until he sees his higher side. Nowhere is the futility of man's prideful departure from the Infinite more immediately apparent than in the scientific world itself. As Alfred North Whitehead has commented: "Scientists who spend their life with the purpose of proving that it is purposeless constitute an interesting subject of study." Or, in the words of Lecomte du Noüy: "There is nothing more irrational than a man who is rationally irrational." When man views himself as capable of stating a final truth, especially a concept of truth in which man is the measure of all things, he is primarily demonstrating how ignorant he is of his own ignorance.

"Not the least pathetic is the certainty of a naturalistic age that its philosophy is a final philosophy because it rests upon science, a certainty which betrays ignorance of its own prejudices and failure to recognize the limits of scientific knowledge."[4]

When we see the cocksure man in daily life, we recognize him as the ignorant man. Yet when we see the cocksure man in the area of philosophy, we fail to apply that same commonsense judgment. On an individual or a social basis, as Socrates pointed out long ago, the wise man is he who realizes his limitations.

St. Paul, remember, defined sin not as ignorance but as pride. John Calvin described the result in *The Institutes of the Christian Religion:*

> They worship not Him, but figments of their own brains instead . . . Professing themselves wise they become fools . . . They become vain in their imaginations.

Since modern man's hybris is the sin of pride, the ultimate sin, it is easily traceable in nonreligious areas as well. Writing well over 100 years ago, Nathaniel Hawthorne produced a short story entitled, "The Birthmark," in which he emphasized that an exclusively scientific view of life ultimately destroyed human values, replacing them with intellectual arrogance, a demand for material perfection here and now that ultimately debased human existence in the pursuit of a heaven on earth.

Once man begins this dangerous, prideful game, he is less and less willing to allow anything to remind him of the values from which he has departed. Consider much of what passes for art in the modern world. Previous to our own era, art was viewed as a means of representing and expressing the beauties of the real and the ideal world in which we lived. But now even art must represent man's creation of his own reality:

> Abstract art illustrates a moment in the history of the human race when man does not believe in a higher reality but desperately searches for a substitute reality of his own creation. No human enterprise, whether in politics or art, can resist such a stress, can sustain such a burden, since the enterprises of man are not autonomous. They refer to something beyond: Genuine art never was created for its own sake, it was always a means of worship, an

affirmation of belief, an aspiration pointing beyond itself. The beauty of art is reflected beauty.[6]

The notion that reality is fixed, that truth and beauty conform to objective standards, is one that makes modern man extremely uncomfortable. One hundred fifty years ago the German poet, Goethe, pointed out something that each of us can confirm in his own experience if he will but think about it. Eras in a state of decline, eras in the process of dissolution, throughout history have tended to be subjective in their view of the world. Examine your own moods. Which are more constructive? Which are healthier? Those turning inward and feeding upon themselves—or those reaching outward into reality? All creative action is a product of *self,* but it is a product of self as it moves outward into reality to create a new reality. An inward turning of self ultimately stifles the creative, expansive powers of which the self is capable. Judged by these standards the subjective tendencies of our age indicate sickness in the extreme.

The total intellectual climate of our times is therefore the problem. As the German theologian, Karl Heim, has remarked: "All world views ultimately reduce to one of two alternatives, personal theism or secular materialism." Surely we live in a world of secular materialism—a world in which all that seems to matter is the present, evident, temporal world. In philosophy, logical positivism attempts to eliminate value judgments and replaces these judgments with the worship of scientific method. In the so-called "social sciences" modern behaviorists have concerned themselves with almost totally quantitative measurements, as though man were solely a collection of reflexes and appetites that could be measured by strictly animal standards. In fact, we live in an age in which the application of the methodology of natural science to human affairs is the order of the day. The very term "social science" reeks of such misuse, assuming that man is a measurable quantity within the natural universe, and nothing more.

Man has been injured in this process by not one, but two wrong turnings. First, through the sin of pride, human reason was elevated to the be-all and end-all of evaluation. This was reflected through the methodology of natural science through which man was to know and therefore control all reality. But man became the subject of his own methodology of natural science. In the process, human reason joined human spirituality in the discard. Man was told that he himself was to be de-humanized.

Once men had removed God from their thinking and elevated themselves to the role of gods, they then assumed an infallibility that expressed itself through the exercise of power over others as a means of achieving the heaven on earth they envisioned. The exercise of that power toward that goal led to the rise of a new concept of the state and of a new belief in the *moral justification* of the coercive power of the state. Thus the individual human being was exposed to the most destructive and repressive exercises of coercion imaginable. And modern politics was born.

INDIVIDUAL DIGNITY

The French novelist, Antoine de Saint-Exupéry, was riding aboard a European train when he chanced to see two peasants of the lowest possible human condition. With these two people, whom life had left neither dignity nor animation, was their young son, a beautiful, intelligent, and unspoiled child. The sight of such a child in the company of such parents stimulated Saint-Exupéry to a flight of fancy which tells us a great deal about human striving:

> A golden fruit has been born of these two peasants. Forth from this sluggish scum had sprung this miracle of delight and grace. I bent over the smooth brow, over those mildly pouting lips, and I said to myself: This is a musician's face. This is the child Mozart. This is a life full of beautiful promise. Little princes in legends are not different from this. Protected, sheltered, cultivated, what could not this child become?

> When by mutation a new rose is born in a garden, all the gardeners rejoice. They isolate the rose, tend it, foster it. But there is no gardener for men. This little Mozart will be shaped like the rest by the common stamping machine. This little Mozart will love shoddy music in the stench of night dives. This little Mozart is condemned.

> I went back to my sleeping car. I said to myself: Their fate causes these people no suffering. It is not an impulse to charity which has upset me like this. I am not weeping over an eternally open wound.

Those who carry the wound do not feel it. It is the human race and not the individual that is wounded here, is outraged here. I do not believe in pity. What torments me tonight is the gardener's point of view. What torments me is not this poverty to which after all a man can accustom himself as easily as to sloth. Generations of Orientals live in filth and love it. What torments me is not the lumps nor the hollows nor the ugliness. It is the sight, a little bit in all these men, of Mozart murdered. Only the Spirit, if it breathe upon the clay, can create Man.[7]

Man's fate has been to sense the promise of the human spirit and yet so often fail to achieve that promise. Yet perhaps man's nature is best expressed in the attempt rather than in the fulfillment. With Robert Browning, we should believe, "A man's reach must exceed his grasp, or what's a heaven for . . . We must try and try and try . . ."

It is the trying, even in the face of defeat, that distinguishes man from animal. Describing his exertions in the face of supreme physical hardship following a plane crash in the North African desert, Saint-Exupéry could write, "I swear that what I went through, no animal would have gone through."

The reason for this human quality, this ability to stick to the job when all hope of fulfillment or all capacity to go on has been exhausted, is man's faith (and when faith is gone, man's innate knowledge) that he has more than his animal capacities on which to draw. It is a sentiment expressed repeatedly throughout man's literature that, "When you have done your utmost, something will be given to you."[8]

Man's evolving nature would seem to contain at once a spiritual and an animal side. What is this instinctive recognition of man that he has a spiritual as well as an animal nature, except a restatement, under other names, of the old Biblical division of the affairs of this world into the province of God and the province of Satan, the province of Good and the province of Evil? Schweitzer's remark that we find in man a union of spirit and nature reminds us that a complete view of human personality cannot ignore man's spiritual yearnings and assumptions, because failure to recognize man's spiritual side is in effect failure to recognize his creative side; it is to "murder the child Mozart" in man. Real value must always be created and the act of creation presupposes the extension of individual effort. Like most of the expressions of folk wisdom, which usually contain a simple rendition of a fact of life (or common sense, if you prefer), the statement, "You get out of life just what you put in," remains as true today as ever. Extension of individual human effort is the *sine qua non* of progress, both individual and social. Modern man, in his social as well as his political programs, is overly inclined to expect authority to determine beforehand what course of action should be pursued. In reality, of course, all meaningful action ultimately is the spontaneous, personal reaction of individuals to the circumstances of the particular situation. Even in the physical universe, not to mention the moral realm, those who presume to direct the affairs of the world do not know what is going to happen from one day to the next. Yet, by some flight of fancy these same would-be social planners presume themselves capable of predicting and regulating the marvelously diverse and mysterious capabilities of the human mind, which contains not only all the subtleties of the natural universe, but the magic source of individual creativity as well: *Free Will.*

To interfere with that free will, with that individual creativity, with that marvelous human capacity for individual difference, is to stumble into the error that the poet Blake describes: "One law for the lion and the ox is oppression."

Even those of our age, so enamored of scientism as to recognize no value not measurable within the physical universe, are confronted with a strange phenomenon. The material of a freely working universe, working independently and *without purpose,* would in effect slowly dissipate its energy. Purposeless change in the natural order thus could only produce extinction, could only be *devolutionary,* not evolutionary. Yet in the evolution of man we find not the dissipation but the consolidation of energy, working toward a higher and higher purpose and creativity. So even if we were to take modern science literally at its word, we find that the laws of nature apply to all of nature, except man. Man alone in the physical universe has this choice of reaching upward or downward, of reaching toward spiritual development or material decline.

Throughout history the philosophers have sensed this choice available to man. Plato, for example, called a strictly materialistic existence "an exercise in dying." The nonmaterial side of human nature can scarcely be said to have evolved from the material order. If it had evolved from the merely material order, the difference between an Einstein and a monkey would be only a difference in degree of technical intelligence. But there is more to the matter than that. In the words of Reinhold Niebuhr, "It is the quality of the human spirit . . . to lift itself above itself as living organism and to make the whole temporal and spatial world, including itself, the object of its knowledge."[4]

This idea of man being the only resident of this material universe who has the capacity to transcend that universe, including self-transcendence, is difficult to grasp in an age so filled with naturalistic assumptions. The idea is hard to grasp because it is hard to visualize. It is hard to visualize because vision itself is in the sensory order and therefore is a poor tool to further the understanding of a phenomenon not of the sensory order.

Once man arrives at this understanding of the human capacity for self-transcendence, he is ready to begin to discuss the unique qualities of the individual, because it is in that self-transcendence that the individual exercises his powers of judgment necessary for the use of his free will. And it is in the exercise of that free will that human freedom becomes a reality. In this world only man, in his ability to stand outside himself, is capable of the virtually endless variation of impulse and decision that makes up human personality. It is the exercise of this faculty which *guarantees* that no two individual humans will be identical, no matter how similar their natural environment and heredity. It is this individual difference, this capacity to choose to be different, that has enabled man to understand his physical universe and that has made possible his spiritual evolution. In short, it is man's capacity for individuality that distinguishes him from the animal kingdom.

When modern philosophy denies the existence of capabilities not measurable by the methods of natural science, it ultimately denies man his capacity for self-transcendence, thus denying him his free will, his individuality, and his basis for the exercise of individual human freedom. The friends of freedom thus must begin the return to the values they espouse through recovery of "... the lost vision of the person as a creature of both intellect and will."[9]

Modern philosophy has promised man freedom from the "myths and superstitions" of the past and has promised that man will come to exercise the role of God within the universe, but the promise has not been fulfilled. On the contrary, the widening of the spiritual horizon of man is the means for the development of his individual personality and freedom. Spiritual development, that is, the capacity for self-transcendence in human nature, alone can free man from the chains in which modern naturalism has bound him. Even man at his worst proves the point. When man reaches his most wretched imaginable state, we still sense a difference between man and animal; what we are still willing to call a "state of nature" when applied to animals, we call "wretchedness" when applied to man. This presupposes a view of human personality diametrically opposed to modern naturalism.

With Ovid, all mankind senses:

> While the mute creation downward bend
> Their sight, and to their earthly mother tend,
> Man looks aloft and with expectant eyes
> Beholds his own hereditary skies.

Man alone engages in sport, in the uneconomic depletion of energy for a goal without tangible purpose. All creative human action, all feats of heroism, all the actions of those whom men have called saints, are a demonstration of this essentially uneconomic effort. The concepts of giving one's all, of risking everything on a single throw of the dice, of refusing to compromise in the face of certain extinction, are attributable only to human personality. Only man is willing to set aside his material good for a *higher goal.* Self-sacrifice requires self-transcendence, an action of which only man is capable.

The only meaningful evolution of the human personality, therefore, must be spiritual in nature, through the exercise of free will. For this, freedom is essential.

TRUTH

"Ever learning, and never able to come to the knowledge of the truth." In these words, St. Paul defined man's condition in this life. (II TIMOTHY 3:7) Man is indeed ever learning, and yet never seems to arrive at final truth. Perhaps man is looking in the wrong place for his truth. Truth, after all, is more than a mere demonstration of logic. When man equates truth with what "works" or with what "makes sense," he may be finding a pragmatic, logical explanation of truth. But if truth can be defined as an explanation of the meaning of life, surely logic alone is unequal to such a task. Once, in a moment of reverie, Goethe phrased the idea thus: "I will tell you something, by which you may abide during your future life. There is in nature an accessible and an inaccessible. Be careful to distinguish between the two; be circumspect, and proceed with reverence."[10] By accessible and inaccessible, Goethe did not mean that which could be known and that which had to be doubted. By the inaccessible, he meant only a different category of knowledge, not amenable to the same standards of human judgment. While Goethe pointed out that we could not use the same tools to discover the inaccessible, and thus had to doubt our knowledge of the inaccessible, he went on to insist ". . . there is no permanence in doubt; it incites the mind to closer inquiry and experiment—from which, if rightly managed, certainty proceeds; and in this alone can man find thorough satisfaction."[10] Put another way, if man would reach the inaccessible, he must first doubt that the tools of this world, observation and logic, are in themselves capable of such a discovery. And from that doubt, and the resultant meditation upon the limitations of human knowledge, an understanding of the inaccessible can in fact emerge. When man evades the moral obligation of achieving convictions and goals as a guide to his life, he is failing to be a complete individual, an individual capable of meaningful existence.

Worse yet, even after the individuals who make up a society have decided upon acceptable standards for the conduct of a truly human existence, it seems necessary that the truth must be rewon over and over again, since error is endlessly preached among us. To date, in fact, judging from the popular press, the schools, and most of the actions and institutions of men, error seems to prosper a good deal better than truth. What's more, error can usually marshal a large majority on its side whenever we choose to put the question to a vote. Error, in fact, is so prevalent, as to what does or does not constitute truth, that men have become afraid to make judgments and to employ terms of value. This at least limits the problem of defining truth, because if we abandon all standards, then no one can be wrong! This is what the modern world offers to man as a substitute for truth. Yet, a world unwilling to make judgments or to define truth can only become a world in which no truth is admitted. Carried to its logical conclusion, such a world would surely be another form of Hell.

Thus, despite all the doubt that has grown up around the concept and all the opprobrium sure to be heaped upon anyone who presumes to discuss the possibility of the existence of ever-lasting and unchanging truth, the problem of its definition must be met head-on by the political philosopher who would offer his society more than mental pabulum. Such a man must never presume to dictate what people must think, but he should be willing to make judgments between conflicting values, to go beyond the realm of mere questions of fact. Unless such a man has values which seem to him worthy of defense, he can scarcely suggest an outline of a society worthy of being judged as a whole. Such a man often will best serve his society by opposing its majority will. We live in an age in which the definition of truth has become what the majority decides it should be. And the first truth, which the political philosopher might need to espouse as he leads this society from the wilderness, could be the positive statement of the fact that truth has no necessary relation to what the majority says it is, and that, in fact, the majority would seem in modern times to be more often wrong than right. As Friedrich Hayek has suggested: "There is . . . never so much reason for the political philosopher to suspect himself of failing in his task as when he finds that his opinions are very popular."[2]

A man willing to judge "truth" on its merits is the true realist, because he is able to understand that the structure of reality is independent of his own desires. He grasps the fact that the world was created before he arrived and will still be here when he, in his earthly form, has departed. He understands that there is more to the world than its physical manifestations and that there is more to man than his physical forms. Because he understands that there is more to reality than the physical world, he comes to know the unknowable. He comes to recognize that it cannot be changed arbitrarily at his will, that truth is subject not to his definition, but to his understanding.

Once this understanding of truth has been achieved, man measures his success in this life by his capacity to live in conformity to human nature at its best. As man progresses toward such an understanding of truth and of human nature, he finds that the progress he has made is lasting and meaningful, and not subject to the whim of any current majority.

Meanwhile, the men who measure all things by themselves and who recognize no ultimate truth and no higher law, are constantly busy making over the world—and, so they think, truth—in their own image. That they bring disaster to themselves and to their world is not difficult to understand.

One of the best weapons in the arsenal of the opponents of truth is the production of a flood of words that pours over modern man in such great quantity as to make coherent ideas increasingly difficult to retain. All too many modern men seem satisfied if they have words that can be passed as current, whatever the content and meaning of those words might convey. Our age seems to have taken the advice of Mephistopheles:

> Mind, above all you stick to words,
> Thus into the safe gate you will go
> Into the fane of certainty;
> For when ideas begin to fail
> A word will aptly serve your turn.[10]

Truth is, of course, more than words. Thus truth can scarcely be derived from a "dialogue" that denies first premises and engages instead in an endless proliferation of ill-considered ideas, each more fatuous and ill-founded than the last.

Modern man, drenched in his flood of words, finds himself unable to accept the idea of unchanging truth and is likely to suggest that man cannot "turn back the clock." This concern for rushing onward without ever looking behind to see where we have been, or pausing to examine where we are, reveals a philosophic bankruptcy. Surely truth must not be affected by the passage of time; if it were, truth itself would become impossible.

Yet, the modern world flees from the idea of a fixed truth. Richard Weaver has compared the modern pursuit of "facts" and "dialogue" to the efforts of a drunken man, who sensing his loss of balance, tries to regain his equilbrium by fixing firmly upon certain details. "With the world around him beginning to heave, he grasps at something that will come within a limited perception. So the scientist, having lost hold upon organic reality, clings the more firmly to his discovered facts, hoping that salvation lies in what can be objectively verified."[1]

Thus modern man is told that if he cannot have truth, at least he can have "facts." Each of us can easily recall from his own experience people who became increasingly unproductive as they occupied themselves with larger and larger quantities of technical minutiae. The sort of intellectual tail-chasing that takes place in a concern for "facts" and "dialogue" when conducted by the individual, is equally a sign of nonproduction when engaged in by an entire society. Even when the facts are correct, modern man has so scientifically analyzed the world around him into its component parts that he has forgotten what the question was that he originally set out to solve. In short, he fails to see the forest for the trees and forgets that the whole is a great deal more than the sum of its parts.

Such is the modern climate of opinion. Again drawing from personal experience, most people, I believe, would readily assent that in the subjects in which they, as individuals, are well versed, most discoveries have been made and most error corrected by men who ignored or challenged the prevailing "climate of opinion." With C. S. Lewis we must condemn ". . . the uncritical acceptance of the intellectual climate common to our own age and the assumption that whatever has gone out-of-date is on that account discredited. *You* must find out why it went out-of-date. Was it ever refuted? And if so by whom, where, and how conclusively? Or did it merely die away as fashions do? If the latter, this tells us nothing about its truth or falsehood. From seeing this, one passes to the realization that our own age is also a 'period,' and certainly has like all periods its own characteristic illusions. They are likely to lurk in these widespread assumptions that are so ingrained in the age that no one dares to attack or feels it necessary to defend them."[11]

This ingrained assumption of our age which no one examines and yet which serves as the basis of so much of our thinking is that all values must have their origins in the strictly measurable physical world as apprehended by the methodology of natural science. The hybris of a scientific age made the original mistake, but the sensory perception of each of us in his everyday life further compounds the error. The difficulty in nature, of course, is to discover not what is readily apparent to us, but what is concealed from our view. In nature, if we will but stop to think of it for a moment, there are many things which contradict our senses and yet are perfectly true. In relation to the earth, the sun stands still; it does not rise and set; rather it is the earth that moves. Each of these three statements is perfectly true, yet each contradicts the senses. If even our material world is so capable of misleading our "common sense," why should we hesitate to admit that our powers of observation drawn from the sensory order would lack the power to tell us about nonmaterial qualities? Yet every day all of us reinforce the scientistic tendency of our age by accepting, *unexamined*, the assumption that reality equals matter. Thus, each of us is guilty of what Richard Weaver has described as the replacement of an "aristocracy of form. . . by the democracy of matter."[3] At a time when all the world is too imbued with the spirit of naturalism, we must reach behind that spirit to get the truth for ourselves or learn to do without truth.

Such a process of self-education is far more difficult than any of us might expect at first glance. Naturalistic assumptions, unproven by any knowledge, and resting only on a faith in the absence of faith, confront us on every hand. Nature herself misleads us simply because she always gives her evidence in terms of the questions we ask of her. Again in the words of C. S. Lewis, "What we learn from experience depends on the kind of philosophy we bring to experience." Thus, if we bring unexamined materialistic assumptions to our study of nature, we find these assumptions only strengthened by the evidence we are willing to accept. Modern man has become so involved in his materialistic assumptions that he has included his transcendental assumptions in the same package; and, finding that the transcendental does not fit within the material, he has rejected the transcendental. Our first duty in the rediscovery of truth, then, is to drive a wedge between the material and the transcendental.[1] Man loses too much by his marriage to the strictly material. He begins with the assumption that nothing makes sense except matter; then discovers that matter (if not measured by a higher standard than itself) also comes to have no meaning. Thus, ultimately, all man's powers, including not only his spiritual side, but also his strictly rational side as well, come to be denied by the modern world.

One hundred years ago, modern man presupposed that his science was revealing a world of rational and predictable function that he could come to understand and master. More recent scientific developments now begin to suggest precisely the opposite idea: Modern man now doubts that the workings of his universe make any sense at all. In the words of the German theologian, Karl Heim, ". . . this willingness to downgrade reason, i.e., not to expect the universe to make sense, is a necessary by-product of the materialistic world view, because the exercise of reason demands a confidence in the existence of an ultimate Mind to support ultimate meaning."

The naturalistic assumption of our age first did away with truth in the name of reason and has now done away with reason in the name of science. Of course, to do away with truth and reason is to do away with man, and thus to rob all existence of meaning, no matter how scientific it may be.

If naturalism has robbed modern man of his reason to be, relativism has completed the destruction of man's values in the ethical realm. After attacking faith, relativism itself has developed into a new faith. If ultimate truth is beyond our reach, at what point is it possible to stop without reaching the opinion that one belief is quite as good as another? As one critic of the new faith of relativism has phrased it: "Is there any real need for us to consider seriously any aspect of things in general that might lacerate our feelings? Why face any of the so-called facts that we do not like? (Ultimately, they may turn out not to be facts!) Since we lack absolute coordinates, should not a belief, a cultural complex, or a moral or ethical system be judged on its own terms, and is not one of them just as good as another? These questions show the evasive value of relativism and we can see from them how easily the belief can be distorted to a point where it can obscure a great deal of valid information."[12]

Making a faith of the principle that man can have no faith is what modern man has done. One modern relativist, Bernard Berenson, writing in *Aesthetics and History,* has described his position: "Human values depend on our physical makeup, on the way our brain, belly, and members act, and on the demands made by the needs, appetites, and impulses they give rise to." Surely if modern man believes that all human values arise from man's physical makeup, from man's animal nature, we can scarcely be surprised when the same men act like animals.

The original scientific intent of relativism was a good deal more honorable than this corrupted position. Max Weber's idea of "value-free" science, *Wertfreiheit,* was intended to limit science to the avoidance of value judgments, since ultimate ends could only be sheer personal preference not subject to rational argument. Weber was really only saying that facts are the proper realm of scientific inquiry. He was perfectly correct; but the modern relativist often has become *absolutely relative* and now uses absolute negatives to refute absolutism. Applying his doctrine not to the area of science but to the area of human personality and ethics, the modern relativist has in effect come to say, "All generalizations are wrong, including this one." The modern relativist has thus made honest skepticism into an absolute doctrine and then has extended an honorable scientific idea into the realm of human values where it has no place. Thus, all human values are now supposedly to be judged by a mistaken standard, mistakenly applied.

In the modern relativist's lust for "facts," he has overlooked one fact so basic that any human being who stops to consider the problem can immediately recognize the omission. Every creature in the world with the exception of man acts as it must act, as a creature of the animal kingdom. Man alone, at least part of the time, acts as he "ought." Considering this one unique quality of man's actions, we can legitmately ask why he and he alone can resist the pull of expediency which governs all nature when he senses an obligation to do what he considers "right."

None of us would suggest that a fish ought to live on land, that apples ought to fall up, that charging elephants ought not to hurt whatever happens to be in their paths, because we know that the actions of things and animals within the physical universe are determined by their nature and by their circumstances.[14] The use of the word "ought" applies only to man's conduct in recognition of a sense of moral obligation and in recognition of the capactiy of free will to decide in favor of fulfilling that moral obligation. As the German philosopher, Immanuel Kant, phrased it, "Ought implies can." Man alone is free to choose, and man alone has the basis upon which to make a moral choice. That is, man has free will and man has available to him a fixed concept of truth which provides the guidelines of right and wrong within which he exercises his free will. When modern naturalism and relativism assault the concepts of free will and truth, they assault the dignity of man.

Science itself must assume the existence of something like truth. If it failed to do so, there would be no difference between science and the merest superstition. Thus, man must begin his search for truth by first finding faith.

> For we are saved by hope: but hope that is seen is not hope: for what a man seeth, why doth he yet hope for?
>
> But if we hope for that we see not, then do we with patience wait for it. (ROMANS 8:24,25)

Once man understands that faith is a prerequisite of coming to the truth, it is easy to make the next step. Truth, after all, is that which clarifies, not confuses. Truth, therefore, is the expression of universality in human affairs. There is no reason why this universality should necessarily be clear to man in all its details. While everything demonstrable is true, there is no reason to assume that everything which is true is necessarily demonstrable. Since man often cannot demonstrate the truth to his own satisfaction, he sometimes makes the mistake of assuming that truth therefore does not exist. This is rather like an ignorant man reading a book whose meaning he does not understand, then saying that the book has no meaning, rather than drawing the proper conclusion that he has no understanding.

Unless we are to abandon all standards to the nihilism of the modern materialist and relativist, we need to face squarely this question of why the truth is so difficult for man to know. One way to begin the approach to the problem is to understand that there are two levels of rationality, two methods by which reason and order can be comprehended within the universe. The first kind of rationality is what we achieve in an accountant's well-kept set of books or in an engineer's well-drawn blueprints. The second kind of rationality, to which the human mind aspires but does not always attain, is in the more abstract realm of truth. It is man's fate to live between these two worlds of rationality. We are children of nature and children of the spirit at one and the same time. We are faced with the absolutes, the framework provided by God within which man operates, and yet find that circumstances of time, place, and condition necessitate a relative application of those absolutes. This dilemma is not new. St. Thomas grasped the importance of custom and relativity in human society and urged a minimum interference with man's traditional ways of doing things. It is the task of an absolute ethical system to provide the guidelines within which the decisions of man's relative circumstances can best be made. A meaningful ethical system then is at once absolute and relative.

A system that is simultaneously relative and absolute is not mere double talk. In Max Weber's methodology for the social sciences, he insisted that the attempt must be made to keep separate: (1) Statements relating to empirical facts; and (2) Statements relating to evaluations of those facts. This corresponds to the religious ideal of evaluating the circumstances of a situation and deciding to do the "right" thing, according to a fixed moral code. The point is that this does *not* make the moral code relative, it only makes the "circumstantial decision" relative. After all, conscience is a *decision-making* act of will, evaluating changing factual situations in terms of unchanging right and wrong. Indeed, there can be no notion of good until evil is recognized, because a man's choice of good does not become good until it is the conscious expression of a preference over an evil alternative. It is the individual's power to make a choice, to exercise his power of free will, that lends the moral tone to his actions.

This then is the answer to the modern assertion that no rules can exist to be universally applicable for all times and places, presumably because moral choice must be an internal, individual matter. And it is true that man makes his choices dependent upon circumstances; but it also is true that circumstances may change, whereas the principles of right and wrong remain the same.

Man's morality and man's view of truth thus appear to be changing; but it is man who is in motion, not the concept of truth. Man, in the different stages of his life, in the variances of his perspective, becomes a different person. As Goethe phrased it: "We see the world one way from a plain, another way from the heights of a promontory, another from the glacier fields of the primary mountains. We see, from one of these points, a larger piece of world than from the others; but that is all, and we cannot say that we see more truly from any one than from the rest."[10] Thus it is man's perspective of reality that changes. Reality and truth remain forever the same. Truth is fixed and absolute, yet *comprehended* differently by each of us. To say that truth changes because we change is to return to modern man's sin of pride.

> Time flies, you say; Ah no!
> Time stays, *we* go.

GOD

In the physical universe man stands with one foot in the material and the other in the spiritual. He possesses the knowledge which transcends the merely sensory order and yet does not reach a full intuition of the spiritual order. Some men escape this halfway house of human existence and apparently see the spiritual order with far more clarity than most of us can achieve. Such men are called mystics.

The mystic, of course, is extremely rare; yet even in our most materialistic of ages, the man who sees only self-assertion and sensual satisfaction as his goals in life remains almost as rare as the mystic. As the historian Christopher Dawson describes it:"The normal man has an obscure sense of the existence of a spiritual reality and a consciousness of the evil and misery of an existence which is the slave of sensual impulse and self-interest, and which must inevitably end in physical suffering and death. But how is he to escape from this wheel to which he is bound by the accumulated weight of his own acts and desires? How is he to bring his life into vital relation with that spiritual reality of which he is but dimly conscious and which transcends all the categories of his thought and the conditions of human experience? This is the fundamental religious problem which has perplexed and baffled the mind of man from the beginning and is, in a sense, inherent in his nature."[13]

It is this age-old religious problem that man continues to face despite all of his scientific and technological progress. In fact, some scientists are beginning to suspect that what they call the evolution of man's rational processes is really only an evolution toward the ethical conclusions reached by the major religions several thousand years ago. Thus, it would appear that what is evolving is man's capacity to perceive and understand a moral order which has always existed.

What we describe as moral values, such concepts as right, goodness, and duty, since they are nonmaterial concepts, must manifest themselves through the human mind. "Just as there could be no beauty in this world without matter, wood or stone or sound or paint or steel or film or trees or flowers or sky; just as there could be no truth without the propositions of history and science, and logic and mathemetics so there could be no manifestation of moral goodness in this world without human minds and wills and emotions to serve as its medium."[14] If mind is necessary for morality, and man's mind, as opposed to his intuition, has only lately begun to perceive this morality, then some universal mind already in existence before the evolution of the human mind must be responsible for the concept of morality independent of human mind, will, and emotion.

If this world were the product of a creative mind which had established both this earth and its moral order, man's intuition of moral values, gradually evolving toward a knowledge of those values, would be a natural result. But if the world were mindless and the product of chance, as the naturalist and relativist would have us believe, then this human intuition of a moral code and this human evolution toward a knowledge of that code would be a very unlikely chance indeed.

If such a mind is the Creator of the universe and the original source of moral values, those moral values may be the means through which the nature of that Creator is revealed to this world. "On this supposition, just as happiness and goodness are manifested in particular human minds, truth in particular propositions, beauty in particular physical things, so God's nature is manifested in the universal values, happiness, goodness, truth and beauty."[14] Thus man's acceptance of a moral order in the universe, first dimly perceived by his intuition, and subsequently more completely understood by his evolving consciousness, is the means by which man recognizes his Creator. To deny the moral order, on the other hand, is to deny the will of God.

This act of denial by modern man, this sin of pride by which man thinks himself the measure of all things, ultimately cuts man off from the source of his dignity and creativity. Even many of those people who would insist that they still espouse religous values seem to base their ideas on the premise that God has withdrawn into silence and inactivity since Biblical days and has placed man on his own feet to do as he will in this world. Such people allow God a place in strictly "religious" matters, but assume that in matters of science or art, all achievement is the product of nothing but human capability. Yet is human capability enough?

> Let anybody only try,with human will and human power, to produce something that may be compared with the creations that bear the names of Mozart, Raphael, or Shakespeare. I know very well that these three noble beings are not the only ones, and that innumerable excellent geniuses have worked in every province of art, and produced things as perfect. But if they were as great as those, they rose above ordinary human nature, and in the same proportion were as divinely endowed as they. And after all, what does it come to? God did not retire to rest after the well-known six days of Creation, but is constantly active as on the first. It would have been for Him a poor occupation to compose this heavy world out of

simple elements, and to keep it rolling in the sunbeams from year
to year if He had not had the plan of founding a nursery for a world
of spirits upon this material basis. So He is now constantly active
in higher natures to attract the lower ones. . . . That is what I call
the omnipresence of the Deity, who has everywhere spread and
implanted a portion of His endless love, and has intimated even in
the brood, as a germ, that which only blossoms to perfection in
noble man.[10]

If God offers man the opportunity to expand in dignity and
consciousness, and capability, he also leaves man free to choose
instead a withdrawal into self, into a tinier and tinier package of
conceit, thus denying himself the sources of human dignity. Perhaps this withdrawal into self, this denial of human self-transcendence, is the condition that man describes as Hell. As C. S. Lewis
has phrased it, "A damned soul is nearly nothing: It is shrunk, shut
up in itself. Good beats upon the damned incessantly as sound
waves beat on the ears of the deaf, but they cannot receive it. Their
fists are clenched, their teeth are clenched, their eyes fast shut.
First they will not, in the end they cannot, open their hands for
gifts, or their mouths for food or their eyes to see."[15] When man
denies his dignity and his powers of creativity by turning from his
spiritual side and insisting that no final moral code and no Creator
exists that human nature should accept as a final authority, he has
divorced himself from reality, as perceived both by his intuition
and by his evolving consciousness. The worst offenders in this sin
of pride are not those who come to the subject with a skeptical eye;
such men often can be persuaded that they have overlooked important values. Worse offenders are those who remain within religion and yet somehow make God a province of their personality,
rather than making their personality a part of the province of God.
"There have been men before now who got so interested in proving the existence of God that they came to care nothing for God
himself . . .as if the good Lord had nothing to do but *exist!* There
have been some who were so occupied in spreading Christianity
that they never gave a thought to Christ. Man! You see it in
smaller matters. Did you never know a lover of books that with
all his first editions and signed copies had lost the power to read
them? Or an organizer of charities that lost all love for the poor?
It is the subtlest of all the snares."[15]

The sin of pride is equally offensive whether man chooses to ignore God entirely, or to make God over in man's image. For all of modern technological and scientific progress, the human race still awaits evidence that it is capable of solving all the problems of the universe. Man might be much better disposed if he could comprehend enough of the Incomprehensible to find his place in the scheme of things and then devote himself to fulfilling the duties of his place, rather than pretending that he has the power to control and, indeed, remake the entire framework as he would choose. The reason of man proves to be a very different thing indeed from the reason of God.

Modern science increasingly finds itself arriving at the same conclusions of a Controlling Intelligence such as man's intuition has always perceived. After all, what we call the "laws of nature," or science, are in reality only an examination of the laws of probability. That is, science is based upon the assumption that nature behaves the same way when we are not watching her as she does when we are watching her. In other words, if the scientist were to assume that the action of each particle of matter in the universe were unpredictable, all probabilities, and therefore all scientific "laws," would become meaningless. The atomic composition necessary for life, even in its simplest form, is infinitely too complex to have occurred by chance. Science itself tells us that such an occurrence is fantastically improbable. Thus, in the material realm, as we have already seen in the ethical realm, some controlling intelligence is necessary to explain the workings of the universe. A controlling intelligence which has supplied such a framework, giving man both an animal nature and a spiritual nature, in effect also gives man free will because it gives him a choice between following his animal side or his spiritual side, thus providing the variety of human experience that causes man alone of the elements within the physical universe to evolve in a potentially higher direction.

Man becomes confused about the scheme of things because his scale of observation is so limited. As we have already seen, a man tends to recognize in the world what he was expecting to find there. The nature of the scientific investigation of that world of which man is capable is such that he sees details without being able to see the entire picture. The faulty and flawed close-up available to man that the naturalism of our age tells him is reality is due to man's myopia in the spiritual realm. Ultimately, the materialistic system fails to explain much. Belief in a Creator enables man to see a view of a cosmic order on its different spiritual and material levels at one and the same time.

Traces of the spiritual side of the universe are discernible to all of us if we will but take the time to look about in our everyday experience. For example, God is revealed to us in our contact with other personalities. The people whom we meet and with whom we work are obviously creatures of such freedom and uniqueness that mere external analysis of the behavior of man would fail to provide the essence of their personality, thus not only obscuring that essence, but actually falsifying it. The naturalism and relativism suggesting that there is nothing to man but the animal side and nothing to the universe but its physical characteristics, imemediately runs into all kinds of practical difficulties when it comes to the concept of the human mind. In the words of Dr. Wilder Penfield, head of the Neurological Institute at McGill University, "It is much easier to explain all the data we have regarding the brain if we assume an additional phenomenon, 'mind,' than it is to explain all the data if we assume only the existence of the brain." In a word, there is more to mind than the mere workings of the animal brain of man.

Of all the elements within the physical universe, only man is capable of standing *outside himself.* This capacity for self-transcendence leads man to search for God. In the words of St. Augustine, "I dive on this side and on that as far as I can see and there is no end. . . I will pass beyond this power of mine which is called memory; yea I will pass beyond it that I may approach unto Thee."Yet in this search man is limited in his quest for God since the idea of God can only be conceptualized on a material level. It is hardly surprising that God's existence cannot be measured on a merely material level and that therefore such a view of God tends to be disappointing. Man's capacity for abstraction beyond that level is limited, and thus the nature of his knowledge of God is limited. But as long as man realizes that what is real must be intelligible and that the universe is not intelligible without the concept of a Creator, he will move toward God in his intuition and in his rationality, although his understanding can never be perfect in this life.

Ultimately man returns to God by any route which he follows. In the words of one modern theologian, Michael Novak, "The terrifying thing about the discovery of God is that one comes to see that He has been there all the time. He is not dead; we have been dead."

HISTORY AND TRADITION

Thomas Carlyle once asserted: ". . . the thing a man does practically believe (and this is often enough *without* asserting it even to himself, much less to others); the thing a man does practically lay to heart, and know for certain, concerning his vital relations to this mysterious Universe, and his duty and destiny there, that is in all cases the primary thing for him and creatively determines all the rest." Philosophers through the ages have spoken of the connection between life's mysteries and man's capacity for individuality and creativity. Aristotle, for example, noted the close link between man's ability to think in abstract, philosophic terms and his ability to conceive the idea of myth. Philosophy in this sense, then, is the story of the adventures of the soul in its discovery of the cosmos; it is the pursuit of spiritual adventure.[14] We should not think of myth as that which is contrary to reality, because in the best sense of the word myth *is* reality. The most important aspects of man's existence are often perceived by man through his capacity for *feeling*, rather than in his rational capacity. It is the modern coercionist who destroys reality in his attempted destruction of myth. The possibility of the existence of an *idea* that cannot be coerced is too painful a possibility for his ego to tolerate. The revelation of God to man is such a myth, that is, an idea too large to be tolerated by the modern ego. The revelation is at once individual, as it is directed to the innermost self of each person, and socio-historical, as seen through man's past experience.[4] Without God's revelation to the individual through intuition, the social and historical revelation of God to man would not be understood. Without the social and historic revelation of God to man through history, man's individual intuition of God would have no external reality to serve as a guideline for understanding that intuition. Few of us can reach far enough back to remember a moment in our childhood when the idea of God had not already penetrated our consciousness. It is this consciousness that tells us what to look for in man's historical record, what guidelines we must recognize. Yet it is history that shows us how man has built upon this intuition to evolve in his consciousness of God and of the spiritual elements of human personality.

History is important because man is a creature of reflection. As man constructs his myths upon which to reflect, he has only the past upon which to build. The present is only a perpetual instant, with no depth of its own. The future is only a screen upon which we project images drawn from our past. Thus history, man's past, man's myths, are the source from which we must derive values as a determinant for present and future action. ". . . The chief trouble with the contemporary generation is that it has not read the minutes of the last meeting."[1]

Historical continuity therefore is absolutely necessary to, "Assert eternal Providence, and justify the ways of God to men." This sense of the importance of history is a distinguishing characteristic of Western civilization, a characteristic which usually has not been found in non-Western culture. Western man has consistently believed that his capacity for self-understanding can grow most surely by an examination of the dawning consciousness of man throughout his recorded history. The concept of individuality which has also grown up within Western civilization is closely tied to this same historic sense, because the dignity of the individual self is expressed primarily through the human capacity for self-transcendence, that is, the individual's capacity to stand outside the physical world, himself included, and sense the course of events. Thus a belief in the individual is based upon a belief in man, which in turn is based upon a belief that man must have a meaningful history if man himself is to be meaningful.

The exercise of individual human personality in history, the exercise of man's free will, has been increasingly obscured by the naturalistic interpretation of history, treating as it does all of man's historical development as the mere workings of "scientific laws." Western man has generally insisted upon the importance of timeless myth, of a significance to history that presupposes a human pageant and human values far more important than a mere collection of the random results of the laws of probability. Modern man's inability to comprehend this importance of myth and history has resulted in a shriveling of his consciousness. All too many of us no longer seem able to comprehend that kind of knowledge represented by myth and history. Yet, man's expansion of consciousness, if it is to occur at all, must be in the direction of transcendental ideas, since man's concept of the individual as a creature of dignity lies in that direction.

To the extent that the world and our society are still capable of functioning creatively, that creativity is largely due to "inherited moral capital," that is, due to living within the norms derived from man's history even though we no longer recognize the validity of those norms. Modern man is cut off from his roots and has the choice of returning or dying. Like the plant that blooms after it has been cut from its roots, we are even now blooming, but it is the bloom of ultimate and certain death, not unlike that of Rome during its decadence.

Ortega y Gasset has speculated that each generation must have its historical mission, a mission to develop those capacities unique to itself. But he goes on to suggest that generations, like individuals, often fail in their efforts and leave their mission unaccomplished. Ultimately, such generations are disloyal to themselves. They fail to advance, and live instead in a world provided by other generations, a world to which the derelict generation adds nothing. Ortega continues, "It is obvious that such a dereliction of historical duty cannot go unpunished. The guilty generation drags out its existence in perpetual division against itself, its essential life shattered. I believe that . . . the present generation is of this derelict type. Seldom have men lived in greater mental confusion. . . "[16]

The Bible warns us, "He that troubleth his own house shall inherit the wind. . . ." The record of modern man reveals that he first went so far in his self-love and hybris as to imagine himself God, to imagine that he could know all. But since then modern man has discovered that the one sure point of his knowledge is that he knows very little. Modern man was thus first swollen to a great size, only to be later reduced to the vanishing point. This disaster has come about because modern man has thought himself superior to the workings of history and isolated himself from his own tradition. No period in history has known so much about so many different things, and yet known so little about the nature of man.

What modern man has forgotten and what history might easily have told him, had he been willing to listen, was that human nature remains always the same. So many of the masters of the "new knowledge" and the "new technology" are so assured of their capacity to mold human nature, that they foolishly promise a bright future. Suggesting that such modern men might profitably consider man's past and begin by an examination of human nature as described by Homer nearly 3,000 years ago, Joseph Wood Krutch has pointed out, "Many readers are no doubt too young to remember that thirty years ago we went through something rather like this once before. That time it was Marxism and the rise of Communist Russia that were making all the ideas and all the culture of the past obsolete and were creating a new socially oriented man, while those who clung to the cultural traditions of western Europe were already anachronisms. Lincoln Steffins, who was then in his I-have-seen-the-future-and-it-works phase, paid me the compliment of analysing my attitudes as typical of those who were fast disappearing, and John Strachey devoted considerable space in his *Literature and Dialectical Materialism* to an analysis of me as a representative of a dying culture. Acquaintances, who failed to convert me, took me aside to suggest that, since people whose attitudes were like mine would soon be liquidated, it would be prudent of me to cast my lot with the new men even if I would prefer not to do so. Homer, as well as other portions of the culture of western Europe, has survived while most of the socially conscious proletarian literature of the 30's is forgotten."[17] Only the sweeping scope of history will tell us what man's nature actually is, as expressed in time. At different times and places he has revealed himself in different lights, and only by taking account of the total picture of these revelations, can we have a knowledge of human nature that even remotely approaches completeness. One of the most oft-repeated quests of the modern world, filling our literature, is modern man's so-called "search for identity."

Modern man's loss of that identity is due precisely to his unwillingness to turn to history as the revelation of human experience.

Historian Page Smith recalls the story of a hunter deep in a forest. Hopelessly lost and despairing at his position, the hunter is confronted by an ugly old crone who tells him that beyond a nearby stream lies her homeland, a veritable paradise. She promises to lead the hunter to this paradise, but he must carry her across the stream in return. Skeptically, the hunter agrees, but when the old lady climbs onto his back she is so heavy that he is scarcely able to move. Yet, true to his bargain, he pushes out into the stream and finds that at each step, the weight of the old lady grows less and less. By the time they reach the other side, the old lady has become a beautiful princess. Together, the hunter and the princess enjoy paradise.

The old lady is tradition, the stream is history. The idea is simply that man must carry tradition forward with him, into the living stream of history. If he does so, he will discover the answer to the futility of his lost existence in the endless woods of life, gaining purpose, meaning, and direction. As St. Paul urged the Romans, ". . . knowing that tribulation worketh patience; and patience, experience; and experience, hope," (ROMANS 5:3-4) mankind can be redeemed.

Science, the popular discipline of the modern age, concerns itself with the exactly measurable qualities of the physical universe. This is not true with history, which is the chronicle and measurement of human existence. History, unlike science, must not be the mere measurement of precise quantities. Man, unlike matter, has understanding, and seeks more understanding, especially understanding of self. It is this capacity for self-knowledge that is unique with man and that is available to him only through history. Man can only envision a future when he has sufficient faith that the values which he espouses have found meaning and expression in history. The historical view presupposes that the universe makes sense; that it contains purpose and meaning, whether or not we are able to grasp that meaning fully.

The unique quality of man is his ability to make a choice. To make such a choice, it is first necessary to discover where life is leading. To discover where life is leading, it is necessary to understand where life has been. Thus, the human capacity for choice is closely bound up in the idea of history. The task that confronts all of us as we must make our choices is, therefore, closely connected with a return to the contemplation of history. We must reflect at length upon the moral order which lies at the base of human dignity and upon the duties which such a moral order imposes.

To side with history and presuppose that there exist external values and a higher side to the nature of man, reaffirming a definite idea of right and wrong, is a dangerous decision in this age. To be free of present-mindedness is to recognize modern man's tendency toward self-destruction. This is a tendency of which he does not like to be reminded. Yet, freedom from such present-mindedness is necessary if man is to be honest with himself. That freedom is sufficient justification for the study of history and literature. Eternal reality is not subject to a simple definition. As C. S. Lewis has phrased it, "Time itself, and all acts and events that fill Time are the definition, and it must be lived."[15] It is history that provides the dimension of time within which man can study eternal reality.

History, however, is not an almanac within whose pages all the answers to life's problems appear. Though history reports successes, it also reports failures. The expansion of man's consciousness is at best an unfinished undertaking. Yet, the guidelines for the continuation of that undertaking are present in the record of man's strivings to date.

The ideas treated in this introductory chapter are intended as no more than the expression (hopefully in a reasonably clear and intellectually defensible form) of intuitions deeply held within our society and Western civilization. The thoughtful reader will recognize that such a chapter tends to be all assertion and no proof, all generality and no specifics, all broad concepts and no detail or supporting information. However, it will have served its purpose if it makes clear the issue that has grown up between the traditional view of human nature and the modern view. Such problems ultimately concern us all in our immediate practical affairs and in any consideration of the future of Western civilization.

If the issue has now been clearly drawn, we can turn to an examination and an analysis of the development of Western thinking along these lines during the past 2,500 years, tracing what some of the outstanding thinkers of Western civilization have thought and felt on the subject and what the total picture of our intellectual heritage has been. Only when we fully understand that intellectual heritage can we understand the danger of departing from it. If this chapter has introduced this larger problem, it has served its purpose.

2

The Greeks: The Search Begins

❧❧❧❧❧❧❧❧❧❧❧❧❧❧❧❧❧❧❧❧❧❧❧❧❧❧❧❧❧❧❧❧

WESTERN MAN'S SEARCH FOR AN UNDERSTANDING OF HIMSELF and of his universe began with the Greeks in the sense that they gave the greatest impetus to the classical search for man's identity.

PHILOSOPHY

To the Greeks, the word philosophy meant "world view." This "world view," unlike our modern definition of philosophy, had a very broad meaning and included scientific study. It is in the area of what we would call science that the Greeks first excelled. Thales, a Greek who lived six hundred years before Christ, devoted himself to this scientific portion of the "world view," and is generally regarded as the "Father of Philosophy." He was the first in a long line of inquiring minds, including, among others, Pythagoras, Heraclitus, Anaxagoras, Democritus, and the famous Hippocrates, the "Father of Medicine," in whose name today's medical men still pledge their skills. Ancient knowledge of the physical universe was so slight by our standards as to be almost meaningless. Yet these pioneers are important to us, not for what they knew, but for their curiosity toward what they didn't know. They epitomized the "inquiring mind" and operated on the principle that man *can* learn about his universe. Perhaps the best term

to describe these early Greeks would be "the physical philosophers."

If these Greeks were doing a little original thinking about
their "world view" in the scientific realm, they also had time to
do some very original thinking in political matters. They conceived the idea of the *polis*, the Greek city-state. In fact, our words
"political" and "politics" have their origin in this Greek idea.
Many of the words by which Western man has done his political
thinking were originally used by the Greeks. They tried a variety
of forms: monarchy, oligarchy, tyranny, democracy, aristocracy.
They fared best under direct democracy—a system by which informed and concerned individuals took the responsibility of meeting to discuss the problems faced by the city-state and how to
resolve them. In their political forms, as in their scientific thinking,
the Greeks placed a high priority upon the *informed, responsible
individual.*

In artistic endeavor, the Greeks were also turning out some
highly original thinking. The epic poetry of Homer in the *Iliad* and
the *Odyssey* is filled with beautiful language and exciting adventure
and concerns man's perpetual problems concerning the *who?
what? where?* and *why?* of human experience. The Greeks also
gave us the drama. While they pioneered in this new art form, in
the tragedies of Aeschylus, Sophocles, and Euripides, and the
comedies of Aristophanes, they also probed deeply into those
perpetual problems of man.

In all these endeavors, the Greeks would have been the last
to say they had final answers. But at least they pointed the way
for Western civilization, emphasizing the need to look beneath the
surface of everyday human experience if man wishes to learn and
grow.

In addition to their scientific, political, and literary efforts,
early Greek contributions in art and architecture also laid a substantial base for the building of Western civilization. By about 500
B.C., the Greek city-states, with Athens leading the way, had built
well upon two basic principles: responsible, informed individualism, and the inquiring mind. But like any number of other societies
both before and after them, their faith in their own ideals seemed
to weaken as they grew more prosperous. After a series of wars,

first with the Persians and then among the Greeks themselves, the concepts of the individual and the inquiring mind came to be viewed even by the Atheneans as a "threat to the safety of the state." A Socrates who thought for himself was now viewed as undermining the youth of the city-state.

The rest of the story is quickly told. A young prince in nearby Macedonia had been tutored by Aristotle and believed that his mission was to carry the Greek message to the world. This young prince, Alexander the Great, like many "message carriers" since, thought that the method for getting this message across was to conquer the world with his army. Starting with the Greek city-states, he did just that. At least, he conquered the then-known world around the eastern end of the Mediterranean and even marched his armies as far as India. Like most "conquerors," Alexander agreed with the people who called him Great. He saw himself as a patron of the arts, and was especially interested in philosophy. The story is told that while traveling with his entourage, Alexander was confronted by one of his ministers who rushed up to him to announce breathlessly, "Sire, Sire, just beyond the next hill is the greatest philosopher in all your realms!" Alexander himself hurried over the hill to discover Diogenes, lying on his back on a grassy knoll and sunning himself while he contemplated some philosophic puzzle or another.

"I am Alexander the Great, master of the world," the young ruler announced. Alexander continued, "I am also patron of the arts and can give you anything you wish . . . You have merely to state your desire."

Now that was a generous offer, and Diogenes didn't respond immediately. But when he did his answer was right to the point. "Please move, Sire, you are standing between me and the sun." At least one of those individualistic Greeks with an inquiring mind was still around, and one may hope that Alexander got the idea. After all, the Greek philosophy he admired so much was based on the very antithesis of the political patronage he was offering. And there is no record that Diogenes was executed as "an enemy of the people."

The empire of Alexander soon crumbled, as do most programs based on coercion. But Alexander's interest in Greek thought and culture did spread those ideas throughout the Mediterranean area. The Greeks were finished as leaders in their city-states; Hellenic culture was gone. But in its place, Hellenistic culture, culture based on Greek ideas, yet espoused by others than the Greeks themselves, arose to pass along the best of those ideas to the next generations of Western civilization.

The most important part of this Greek contribution lies not in the scientific, artistic, or political forms of the Greeks, but in the Greek view of man and his meaning, in the Greek assumption that man's past, present, and future posed problems worthy of an inquiring mind. Yet for all that penetrating analysis, the Greeks were a practical people and usually managed a sense of humor. Thales, the "Father of Philosophy," a man who knew enough astronomy to predict successfully an eclipse in 585 B.C., often has had the story told at his expense that once he gazed so intently into the heavens while out for a walk that he fell into a well. But he was a long way from being either an absent-minded professor or an impractical man. One year he noted that the next olive crop promised to be a large one, so he picked up options on all the olive presses on the Isle of Lesbos. Thales cornered the market and made a handsome profit when the inevitable rush for olive oil came at the end of the season, thus demonstrating that even philosophers can make a living.

A similar story is told of a friend of Socrates who was bankrupted by one of the wars leading to the decline of the great city-states. He not only was broke, but he had fourteen female relatives on his hands. The Greek polis was no welfare state. It was far too individualistic for that. So Aristarchus, Socrates' friend, was bemoaning his fate when the practical philosopher suggested that there would always be demand for clothes and that Aristarchus should buy wool and put the women to work spinning and making garments. He did so, and soon everyone was making a nice living, including the fourteen female relatives. But Aristarchus quickly developed another problem . . . now the women were accusing him of living in idleness while they worked! He returned to Socrates for a bit more advice. What he got is both a demonstration of Greek practicality and a suggestion that the entrepreneural function is a very old idea indeed. Socrates advised, "Tell them of the story of the sheep who complained that the watchdog did nothing."

These stories of Thales and Socrates are not mere entertainment. They also demonstrate that the Greeks were extremely practical people who did their thinking with a hardheaded sense of reality. Often the men who are most genuinely practical also prove to be those most willing to search for answers beneath the surface of events. Because of that Greek belief that the individual *can* discover such answers, and because some Greeks made the attempt to do so, the largest of the Hellenic contributions to Western civilization lies in the analysis of man and his purpose, in the determination of right and wrong, and the relationship of that right and wrong to human nature and human institutions.

The problem of right and wrong in human concerns began to play a dominant role in Greek thought in the fifth century before Christ. Such studies centered not on the physical universe, but on man's relationship to man, that is, upon *ethical* considerations.

At that time in Athens there arose a group of teachers who advertised themselves as capable of teaching the science of improved personal relations between the individual and his associates. This new group of teachers tended to emphasize ways of persuading one's neighbor to a different viewpoint. For example, courses were offered in how to plead one's case before a jury. This early emphasis on "How to Win Friends and Influence People," was offered to the public by a group of men who came to be known as Sophists (men of wisdom).

Many Greeks did not approve of this approach to teaching. As a number of them, Socrates included, pointed out, these teachers seemed not to be searching after truth, but only looking for immediate results. What standard could remain for truth if all things were judged only by how well they work? Socrates must have been persuasive in criticizing the Sophists for their failure to make truth their guide; because even today, after twenty-five hundred years, the word "sophistry" suggests not only fallacious reasoning, but dishonest reasoning as well.

Actually the Sophists varied widely among themselves. Some were only what today would be called speech teachers, while others went far beyond the mere teaching of technique to insist that the usefulness of any doctrine was the only reliable guideline, since no possibility existed of the establishment of absolute truth. Some Sophists carried their viewpoint to an attack upon the state, while others tried to uphold the existing political format. In the *Republic*, Plato sarcastically describes the Sophists, Protagoras and Prodicus, who, he said, felt they had ". . . only to whisper to their contemporaries: 'You will never be able to manage either your own house or your own State until you appoint us to be your Ministers of Education'—and this ingenious device of theirs has such an effect in making men love them that their companions all but carry them about on their shoulders." Yet other Sophists were what we would call anarchists, men who thought law was based on fraud and "put over" on the people through the misleading tenets of religion.

Protagoras, perhaps the most outstanding of the Sophists, asserted that he was the wisest man in the world and insisted that anyone who came to him as a student could develop the same skills. As a sort of money-back guarantee, Protagoras even promised that any student who studied under him was guaranteed to win his first trial in court or his tuition would be refunded. It was Protagoras who first said that "man is the measure of all things," which in effect made the definition of reality relative to each man's view of that reality. This reduced truth to the level of opinion and denied objective reality.

Gorgias, another of the most distinguished Sophists, carried these relative standards to the definition of virtue, thus developing the theory of moral relativism. Such definitions of reality, truth, and virtue contain within them a number of implications: ". . . an individual's perceptions and judgments are relative; universal truth valid for all men is denied, each man being the sole judge of what seems so, and therefore true to him; there is no authority higher than man to weigh and decide between conflicting opinions; and since man is constantly changing his mind, truth is not only a matter of the individual, but of the individual at that moment."[12] The standards adopted by the Sophists sound quite familiar to our modern ear. In fact, similar statements confront us every day from our communications media, our schools, and even our pulpits.

While the Sophists directed their attention to analyzing the feelings and impulses which they saw governing the decisions made by individual men, and therefore saw no purpose or guiding direction to man's activities except that in accordance with the necessity of nature, Socrates recognized that man's importance rested not upon that physical side of his nature, but upon his insight, an insight into his own nature and that of his universe that provided an objective standard for the estimation of men and their actions. Socrates thus resisted the current of his age in an effort to discover a standard of truth and a definition of reality that gave man a greater dignity than the Sophists' view of human nature permitted. The short, bandy-legged, ugly man whom the Greeks knew as Socrates possessed the sort of character perfectly capable of standing against the spirit of an age. His principal biographers, Plato and Xenophon, dwell at great length on his amazing powers of physical endurance and the excellence of his record as a fighting man. Not the least of the demonstrations of his physical vigor was that, at the time of his death at the age of seventy, Socrates left two small children, one a babe in arms. A man of extreme simplicity in his habits of eating and drinking, and yet with a reputation for being able to drink heavily with no apparent effects, Socrates wore the same simple clothing winter and summer and habitually went barefoot, even in the midst of a winter campaign.

Socrates was beloved as a teacher rather than as a man of affairs. He wrote no treatises, taught in no classroom; his only classroom was the street in Athens, where he would stop a citizen and start a conversation. What we today call the Socratic method, the process of question and answer, is at once the best and the most difficult of all teaching methods. Only a man of exceptional intellectual capacity, and, more important, with a highly developed moral sense, could have successfully used such a method. Once one of his students admitted at the end of a Socratic dialogue, "I cannot refute you, Socrates."

Socrates replied, "Ah, no! Say rather . . . that you cannot refute the truth, for Socrates is easily refuted."

Yet, that truth was sometimes hard to discover, as Socrates would have been the first to admit. Once when a young man was introduced to Socrates as being a student of brilliant promise, the old teacher said that he felt sure the young man must have thought a great deal. The boy answered, "Oh, no—not that, but at least I have wondered a great deal."

"Ah, That shows the lover of wisdom," Socrates said, "for wisdom begins in wonder."

For Socrates, and ultimately for Western man, wisdom did indeed begin in wonder. The knowledge of the truth is only revealed to those who are first willing to admit its existence and begin to ponder its content. As Socrates, and after him, Plato and Aristotle, pointed out, the person who believes that all truth is subjective and is a matter only of opinion, must finally concede to one who believes that truth is an objective reality. If Protagoras or another relativist insisted that one man's opinion was equally valid with another's opinion, then he could not deny the validity of the opinion of a Socrates that such a thing as objective truth exists. Socrates thus began with the assumption that truth is a matter of objective reality, and that it is error which is subjective and relative, since it exists only in the mind of the individual person. The means by which such error was to be avoided was to come to a knowledge of the truth. That which is true is that which is good; thus knowledge equals virtue in the Socratic equation. What was the source of this knowledge? Ultimately, self-knowledge was most valuable since knowledge of the truth, and therefore knowledge of virtue, only had meaning when practiced through the self-control of the individual. Thus the Socratic injunction, "Know thyself."

Socrates never committed anything to paper, and what we know of him is based primarily on the reports of his principal student, Plato. Plato used Socrates and his dialogues as a literary device to convey the philosophy of Plato himself, as well as the ideas of his teacher. Thus, it is impossible to say precisely which ideas belong to each. Yet, the direction which Socrates was pointing is clear. Since he believed that goodness and truth were basic realities and that only lack of knowledge would cause man to pursue anything but truth and virtue, he spent his life attempting to open his own eyes and the eyes of those about him to the realization that a knowledge of virtue and truth was man's only road to happiness. He preached no dogma and insisted upon no fixed set of beliefs, saying simply, "Although my mind is far from wise, some of those who come to me make astonishing progress. They discover for themselves, not from me—and yet I am an instrument in the hands of God."[18] Man's happiness was to be found deep in the heart of the individual as he came to understand his own nature and to strive to live in accordance with the best of that nature. Here, five hundred years before Christ, much of the idea of self-transcendence was already beginning to take shape in the mind and heart of Socrates.

Though Socrates never pretended to erect a philosophic system, his thinking was consistently directed toward an ethical frame of reference. He deeply felt the need for a fixed system of truth to provide a framework within which man made his decisions.

"Know thyself." Some very vital ideas are contained within that simple advice. If man is indeed capable of knowing himself, such self-knowledge would demand the most rigorous rationality. True knowledge could scarcely be taught, but could only be understood by each man through his own efforts. Man's intelligence alone is capable of the creation of abstract ideas. Thus man's rationality allows him to perceive his spiritual personality and allows an understanding, a self-knowledge, attainable by no other being within the natural order. Even long before Socrates, the Greeks had come to understand nature as a never-ending process of birth and growth, what they called *Dynamis*, a maturation and discovery of the treasures written deep within the nature of mankind. It was Socrates' contribution to recognize that such development toward a higher goal could only be achieved by man if that higher goal were fixed, and not dependent upon man's nature in itself.

The Greeks at their best had emphasized the individual and the inquiring mind. Socrates' special addition to these concepts was the idea of a fixed right and wrong, giving order and purpose to the cosmos and pointing the way toward man's discovery of what that order and purpose might be.

Socrates never developed a complete philosophy. Throughout his long life he perceived the concept of absolute good, searching his own inner experience and that of others for proof that such absolute good existed. He admitted late in life that he had not found the answer that he was seeking. Yet he, more than any other, pointed the way for later fruitful consideration of the possibility of man's self-knowledge and for the development of man's higher side in accord with fixed moral principles.

AN IDEA TAKES ROOT

Socrates was not the only teacher of his time to insist that fixed standards of right and wrong existed independently of man. Within one hundred years of Socrates' lifetime, Buddha, Confucius, and Zoroaster, each in his own respective civilization of India, China, and Persia, had also insisted that man could prosper only in terms of a fixed code of conduct. Thus, even though life in some form had existed on this earth for over a billion years and human life for over a million years, it was only within the past twenty-five hundred years, in man's most recent moment of existence, that the human mind had begun to look about it and consider its nature, its origins, and its future. Even then, most of this thinking seemed to be occurring in the minds of a very few men indeed. It is the period of time marked by the beginning of their thinking, roughly 600 B.C. to 400 B.C., that may properly be spoken of as the beginning of Western civilization, since the civilizing influence of these ideas became effective as it was channeled through the Western experience.

Despite the fact that the first great outburst of energy devoted to the study of the nature and purpose of man occurred about twenty-five hundred years ago, we should not forget that some such moral sense, however poorly understood and enunciated, had actually been in existence for five thousand years. As long before the time of Socrates as Socrates' own time is before our days, Egyptian scribes were recording advice to rulers and heads of families concerning the moral obligations of right conduct which these men of responsibility owed to those about them. Man had long realized, or at least suspected, the existence of some such moral code.

Still, the great outburst of energy occurring almost simultaneously in China, India, Persia, and Greece pointed the way toward Western civilization and toward man's first systematic thoughts in terms of an underlying cosmic cause which gave meaning to all existence. Buddha's attempts at Nirvana (the total emancipation from the material life), Zoroaster's preaching of the never-ending struggle of good and evil and light and darkness in this life, and Confucius' insistence upon the ethics of personal self-control leading to righteousness and wisdom as man's source of happiness, all were beginning to make the ethical assumptions which presupposed a higher order of meaning than a merely material universe.

The battle of definition between mind and spirit, the definition which had to be worked out to distinguish man from the animal world and to enable him to know the truth which would give him his place in the universe, was beginning. In St. Paul's later assertion that the things which are seen are temporal and the things which are not seen are eternal, we can sense what difficulty the early moral thinker had in his attempts to define the realm of the mind and the spirit.

Another primary influence upon the developing ethical system that was to serve as the basis of Western civilization was the developing world view of the Hebrew people. With the Hebrews, for the first time history became more than mere chronology. God, a fixed ethical system of right and wrong, and a discussion of man's failures to measure up to such a system, together with an accounting of the high price which man paid for such failings, were all elements of Jewish history as it developed. The Old Testament is at once the history of man's tribulations in this life and the promise of his redemption from those tribulations. In fact, it was the opinion of the brilliant nineteenth-century historian of liberty, Lord Acton, that the Jews in their federation and in their strictly limited view of political power, were giving the world an early demonstration of the achievement of human liberty by placing man under Divine authority, rather than human authority.[19] Another student of liberty, Henry Grady Weaver, saw in the history of the Jews the evolution of a moral code. Weaver makes clear that this moral code was a demonstration of man's striving after a higher reality in line with his spiritual nature.[20]

Yet, all of man's earlier strivings for the first several thousand years, as exemplified by the Egyptian attempts, by all of the moral teachings in the work of Confucius, Buddha, and Zoroaster, by all of the moral framework and the development of the idea of a human history as produced by the Hebrews, only achieved their focus and direction and formulation when developed by the Greeks and subsequent Western man. Thus Western civilization is the heir to a tradition that extends far back in human history and encapsules the best of these early strivings to pass them on toward modern man. Other Greeks than Socrates were concerning themselves with the same problem. The plays of Euripides demonstrated that a natural moral order exists. Again and again, as, for example, in *The Trojan Women*, Euripides made clear that an act of injustice or impiety carried within itself the seeds of destruction that would inevitably bear bitter fruit with the passage of time. In *Works and Days*, Hesiod also presupposed a moral order in the universe, a code of conduct to which all men were subject even when they attempted to violate it.

Yet it is Socrates who was the true spokesman for the first positive statement of such a program. He, more than any other, was most emphatic that the individual man could achieve his own salvation. If Buddha wished for the annihilation of material life, Socrates was willing to enjoy its blessings. If Confucius would have had men guide their conduct only by tradition, Socrates thought that man could evolve toward a *higher understanding* building upon such a tradition. If the Hebrews had insisted that man could not grasp truth unless that truth were given him by God, Socrates insisted that man's striving of spirit and intelligence was also the means whereby man might come to improve his comprehension of that truth. Thus the whole problem of ethics, as a problem with which man could work, was first clearly presented as a field of human endeavor by Socrates.

For all the originality of Socrates' contribution, we should not forget the impact of the unique Greek matrix from which he grew. It was the Greeks who first influenced the Western world in its course, destined to be so uniquely different from the Eastern world. Consider the change wrought by the Greeks as described by Edith Hamilton: "The ancient world, insofar as we can reconstruct it, bears everywhere the same stamp. In Egypt, in Crete, in Mesopotamia, wherever we can read bits of the story, we find the same conditions: a despot enthroned, whose whims and passions are the determining factor in the state; a wretched, subjugated populace; a great priestly organization to which is handed over the domain of the intellect. This is what we know as the Oriental states today. It has persisted down from the ancient world through thousands of years, never changing in any essential. . . . This state and this spirit were alien to the Greeks. None of the great civilizations that preceded them and surrounded them served as model. With them something completely new came into the world. They were the first Westerners; the spirit of the West, the modern spirit, is a Greek discovery and the place of the Greeks is in the modern world."[18]

The earlier moral teachers had turned away from the world. Buddha, Confucius, and Zoroaster, while offering much of sound moral value, largely believed that such value could be achieved by turning from this life. It was the Greeks who began the valuable idea implicit in Western civilization which emphasizes the place of the individual and the importance of a fixed moral order *without* neglecting this life and this world.

GREEK DECLINE

Why did the Greeks ultimately decline? What happened to a people with such faith in the individual, with such a desire to learn and grow, with such tremendous creative capacity in every phase of human endeavor? The answer lies, it appears, in evils which have led a number of other civilizations, Rome included, down the road to dusty death: war, centralization, decline of old values and honorable traditions, and unwillingness to allow the free play of the individual. Each of these tragic causes and effects is readily apparent in the history of Greece as it declined.

Most of the accomplishments of what we call "The Greeks" were really the accomplishments of the citizens of one particular city-state, Athens. One of the neighbors of Athens, Sparta, in fact pioneered in all the repressions of the individual with which we associate the modern totalitatrian state. The young Spartan was trained from birth to maintain an obligation to the power of the state and to ignore or destroy everything which did not serve that obligation. All creativity, all dignity, all human aspiration, had purpose only as it served Sparta. As Plutarch described the citizens, "In Sparta, the citizens' way of life was fixed. In general, they had neither the will nor the ability to lead a private life. They were like a community of bees, clinging together around the leader and in an ecstasy of enthusiasm and selfless ambition belonging wholly to the country."

Of course, it was not this Spartan society that produced the creativity and the divine spark of human dignity which we sense in ancient Greece. Athenian democracy was the home of that human progress. In Athens the state took no responsibility for the individual and the Athenian thought of himself as one of a union of individuals free to develop his own powers and pursue his own life. This freedom was to be limited by self-control. And in that freedom and self-discipline, the heights of Athenian creativity and dignity were reached. But when the Athenians were no longer willing to exercise that self-discipline in their political affairs or in their personal lives, Greece declined. As Thucydides tells us, "The cause of all these evils was the desire for power which greed and ambition inspire." Thus the Greeks ultimately failed through their inability to discover *why* and, ultimately, *how*, political power should be limited.

The Athenians were the only people of antiquity who grew great through the exercise of democratic institutions. But when those democratic institutions came to be corrupted, and when the people of Athens no longer recognized any limitation to their power except their own appetite, ". . . No force that existed could restrain them; and they resolved that no duties should restrain them . . . In this way the emancipated people of Athens became a tyrant . . . They ruined their city by attempting to conduct war by debate in the market place. Like the French Republic, they put their unsuccessful commanders to death. They treated their dependencies with such injustice that they lost their maritime Empire. They plundered the rich until the rich conspired with the public enemy, and they crowned their guilt by the martyrdom of Socrates."[19] Thus an excess of democracy proved to be the death of democracy. Once the desire to rule, or any other human appetite, becomes so strong that it accepts no restraint, and once it begins to insist that man is the measure of all things and that no standard of right and wrong should limit the exercise of his power, the way is paved for the decline of faith in the individual, the destruction of creativity, and the reign of coercion.

As Greece lost her way politically due to a collapse in the standards of her morality, the same declining standard of morality also wrought havoc with the standards of Greek society. Traditional Greek morality had been based on the cardinal virtues of justice, wisdom, self-restraint, and courage. The doctrine of self-discipline in conformity with a higher moral law was an accepted standard. The rise of relativism in the Fifth Century B.C. that produced the Sophists turned the old standards topsy-turvy. Why, talk of justice or virtue if we no longer know what these qualities mean? Standards began to decline. And if Greek creativity and individual genius began to decline as well, that was due to "environment" or "the system," never to the individual's departure from a high moral standard. If these arguments have a peculiarly modern ring to our ears, we might remember that if the Greeks pointed the way for us when they were right, it would seem perfectly natural that they could also point the way for us when we are wrong.

The patriarchal family was the vehicle for the creation and preservation of many of the ideals which have formed our civilization. Honor, modesty, wisdom, and justice, all on the level of personal responsibility, were always reflected through the agency of the family. As belief in the individual and belief in a standard of morality waned among the Greeks, it naturally brought a decline to the family, representing as it did the very values that the new spirit of the age had set out to destroy.

As the life ebbed from the institutions and values that for a moment had made Greece great in the full flower of her creative genius, the individual human dignity which had been protected by those institutions and by a fixed moral code declined as well until the Greek citizen was both rootless and defenseless. Without standards, without a moral guide, without the ability either to create or to stand firm against adversity, the Greek now found his sole satisfaction in the exercise of his unlimited political power. That he destroyed Athens through the exercise of that political power should not be surprising.

As Greek society declined around him, Socrates chose to stand firm in defense of the principles and attitudes to which he had devoted his life. Perhaps he understood the idea that Ralph Waldo Emerson was to phrase twenty-four hundred years later: "God offers to everyone his choice between truth and repose. Take which you please—you can never have both." Socrates chose truth.

To a society which had come to recognize coercion and absolutely unlimited political power as the final arbiter of all matters, Socrates' insistence on principle was anathema. He was tried and sentenced to death. Even at that moment, the serenity that comes to a man when he senses the truth and knows that he does, came to Socrates. To those who had just condemned him to death, he responded, "Be of good cheer and know of a certainty that no evil can happen to a good man either in life or after death. I see clearly that the time has come when it is better for me to die, and my accusers have done me no harm. Still, they did not mean to do me good—and for this I may gently blame them. And now we go our ways, you to live and I to die. Which is better, God only knows."[18]

Socrates did go on to die, in one of the most moving death scenes recorded in literature. To the end he maintained that good and truth did exist and that man could move toward an understanding of that good and that truth by an increased realization of the potentiality of his mind and spirit.

The name and ideas of Socrates come to us as a hallowed part of the tradition of Western man. The petty politicians, who destroyed a man whom they could not coerce, perished in their own time. Thus ended an early round in Western man's struggle to understand himself and his universe and, in the process, to free his soul.

3

Plato and Aristotle

❧❧❧❧❧❧❧❧❧❧❧❧❧❧❧❧❧❧❧❧❧❧❧❧❧❧❧❧❧❧❧❧❧❧❧❧

ATHENIAN DEMOCRACY COLLAPSED AND DIED OF ITS OWN EX-
cesses, and the so-called Golden Age of Greece died with it. Yet
the tragedy of Athenian collapse and the execution of Socrates
were destined to bring forth a new burst of original thinking. Ideas
are hard to keep down.

Disillusioned by the execution of Socrates and the collapse of
the social order around him, a young student named Plato decided
to devote his life to the pursuit of philosophic inquiry. Using the
methods and ideas of Socrates, Plato carried them further along
the road to knowledge and erected the first comprehensive philosophic system in the history of Western man.

Plato's search for answers to the age-old questions that lie
behind man's existence brought students and followers to him for
enlightenment. One of these was Aristotle. In time, Aristotle was
destined to advance the political and ethical thinking of his master, as Plato had done with the ideas of Socrates.

In these two men, Greek philosophy was to reach its greatest
height, and Western man was to receive a vast addition to the
storehouse of his knowledge and his understanding of human existence.

PLATO'S POLITICAL THEORY

Any discussion of the political theories of Plato and Aristotle should make clear in the beginning certain peculiarities of time and place that permeated their thinking (as such peculiarities permeate the thinking of all men in their own particular time and place). Although the days of competent, informed, individual Greek citizenship in the polis had passed, both Plato and Aristotle, as products of that system, tended to see themselves and their ideas couched in the framework of the polis. Thus some of their political ideas are best understood against the background of the small and highly individualistic societies that existed when Greek civilization was at its height.

In the same vein, *Demokratia,* our word democracy, meant more than merely the "rule of the people." To Plato and Aristotle, drawing on the experience of the immediate Greek past, democracy had the connotation of "government by the poor" and thus was often condemned by these philosophers as being only an inverted form of tyranny, with the dictatorship coming from the bottom of society rather than from the top. Whether absolute control was lodged at the top or bottom of society, it was viewed as equally reprehensible by Plato and Aristotle if such government was inspired by self-interest. The ideal toward which Plato and Aristotle worked in their political thinking was "Polity," that is, government by general consent, without reference to class, and motivated by the self-interest of no single member of society. The Greeks thought that power wrongfully exercised was reprehensible, no matter what segment of society might be exercising that power.

Thus Plato and Aristotle drew their values from the polis, a society in which government was not conducted in terms of the self-interest of any element or segment of that society, and in which citizenship was viewed as a responsibility requiring the highest level of interest and confidence. If we understand Plato and Aristotle in the light of this highly motivated, individualistic view of politics, we can more fully appreciate the value of their thinking for our time.

To Plato, who had seen the decline and collapse of Athenian

democracy in an atmosphere of war and revolution capped by the death of his beloved teacher, Socrates, the restoration of order and justice became the primary goal of political life. Sensing that some basic human failing lay at the base of the disasters he had experienced in his lifetime, Plato wondered how society might be planned so that man might come to enjoy order and justice. His founding of the school which he called the Academy was for the training of philosophers who would one day govern Athens. In *The Republic*, written in the early years of the Academy, Plato set forth his ideal of government, with the governing power to be limited to those qualified. This "qualification" necessary for governing was a disinterested pursuit of truth. Thus, only a philosopher in the broadest sense of the term would be qualified to govern in Plato's ideal state. This "philosopher-king" was to be sufficiently wise to perceive and implement each person's place in society so that all might best serve themselves and their society in this totally planned state.

We are immediately repelled by the rigid classes present in Plato's ideal republic. But we might understand that these rigid classes were in large part a revulsion of the young Plato against the excesses and failures of Athenian democracy he had witnessed. Plato had given up on democracy and decided that only the "philosopher-king" could solve the human dilemma. He even twice visited Sicily in the hope of making some such "philosopher-king" out of the young ruler of Syracuse, Dionysius.

However wrong we think Plato's solution to the problem, we can learn something from his political theories as they developed, if we are willing to understand the basis of the thinking whereby he reached his conclusions. The aim of Socrates, and of Plato after him, was to make virtue not a mere unexamined opinion, but a subject of which man might have precise knowledge. But if a man were to have such knowledge, he would then quite naturally be something like Plato's "philosopher-king." Because if virtue is to be the basis by which we judge the goodness of society, and if some chosen few have a superior knowledge of how that virtue is to be defined and attained, the highly individualistic government of the polis must ultimately be set aside in favor of the planned society within which this virtue can be attained. Plato viewed this society as achieving a balance by implementing the best that is in all men and therefore operating with their consent and without coercion.

Thus, while Plato advocated a "planned society," he did not wish to implement an authoritarian regime. As one observer has remarked: "Plato suggested that the real authoritarian is the real slave; that he is obliged to practice adulation, servility, and flattery. His desires are impossible of satisfaction, and thus he is truly poor. He grows worse from having power; for power necessarily promotes jealousy, faithlessness, injustice, unfriendliness, and impiety. Not only is he miserable himself, but he also makes others equally as miserable. The authoritarian attempts to be the master of others when, obviously, he is not even master of himself. Plato likens the authoritarian to the man who passes his life, not in the building of his inner self, but in fighting and combating other men. Need we do more than to look about us to confirm the rightness of Plato's observations?"[21]

Though Plato did not intend the totalitarian state of our time when he talked about a planned society, and though the excesses and failings of Athenian democracy offer an excuse for some of the conclusions which Plato reached, his system of politics outlined in *The Republic* is not defensible. In practice, it seems that "philosopher-kings" are difficult to find. The record of the planned society, whether in ancient Sparta or modern Russia, makes clear that everybody can be put to work at some task. However, it is not equally clear that those who rule are necessarily "the wise," nor is it clear that their rule is in the interest of the people. Historically, the planned society simply has not worked.

Yet, in defense of Plato it should be pointed out that his political thinking extended beyond what he had written in *The Republic* as a bitter young man. In middle age he wrote *Politicus (The Statesman),* suggesting that his "philosopher-king" had obligations to those whom he was governing and therefore was limited in the exercise of his power. As an old man looking back on the thoughts and experience of a lifetime, Plato wrote *The Laws,* progressing even further toward limited government and now insisting that the "philosopher-king" be limited by a constitution which gave him only certain specifically delegated powers.

Thus we are confronted by the interesting fact that as Plato grew in wisdom and maturity and saw in practice how some of his political theories worked out, he departed further and further from the ideas of the planned society and the all-powerful "philosopher-king," and came instead to favor increasingly limited governmental authority.

ARISTOTLE'S POLITICAL THEORY

There is considerable evidence to suggest that when Aristotle came to Plato as a young student, he immediately objected to the idea of a planned society as set forth in Plato's earlier *The Republic.* We have the interesting question, which must remain forever only a question, as to whether Plato's gradual departure from the idea of the planned society was the product of his own growth in understanding, or whether it came from the prodding of the young Aristotle. As is so often the case, we are unable to distinguish the influence of the master on the pupil from the influence of the pupil on the master. The one central fact of which we may be sure is that both Plato and Aristotle came to insist more and more upon the necessity of limited government.

Aristotle himself, of course, was indebted to Plato as a source for many of his ideas, just as Plato had been indebted to Socrates. Yet, while *The Republic* is a discussion of what a state *ought* to be, Aristotle's *Politics* is a discussion of the state *as it actually exists.* Aristotle examined the constitutions of some one hundred fifty-eight city-states, reaching the conclusion that different forms of government might work best in different situations. Looking back upon the ruins of the Athenian experiment, he questioned the efficacy of direct democracy and favored instead a constitutional system in which the exercise of political power by *any* agency within the society was strictly limited.

This idea of limiting the exercise of political power, even the exercise of political power by "the people," is unpalatable to our democratic age, because we frequently tend to confuse ends and means, making democracy an "end" in politics, when it actually is only a means to an end. Perhaps one of the greatest political blunders of our time in the Western world has been our assumption that democracy will work anywhere, under any circumstances, as well as it works in the United States.

If Aristotle were alive today, applying his empirical, commonsense, approach to the problem, and checking such an assumption by the result, he could surely point out to modern man that primitive peoples are ill-suited to practice "democracy," since they lack the essential civilization and tradition and understanding of citizenship. Only a body of tradition and experience, such as came to us through our English heritage, can prepare a people to achieve the *self-discipline* necessary for successful democracy. Again and again, our Latin American neighbors have copied our Constitution and political forms in great detail, only to gyrate between dictatorship and revolution through a long and sad experience, precisely because they have lacked the necessary tradition and citizenship and self-responsibility. These qualities may be developed eventually, but undue haste in the meantime will have wrought much havoc in the name of democracy.

The ideal of constitutionalism, Aristotle's insistence that government must be limited, has had wide application throughout the Western world. Constitutionalism, of course, often has appeared in conjunction with democracy, but is not identical to it. Aristotle's concept of "government by law," of limiting the state in the exercise of its political power, has lain dormant for long periods of time since it was conceived. Yet, for brief eras, most notably in our American experiment, the idea has enjoyed resurgence and lies at the base of much of our traditional American political fabric as established by the Founding Fathers.

"Man is a political animal." This is Aristotle's famous statement, but it would be equally in character if said by Socrates or Plato. As men of the polis, they also felt that all of man's interests, intellectual and social as well as political, were of importance for good citizenship, because a good citizen ultimately was an *interested* and *capable* citizen. If we wonder why our "rule of the people" doesn't seem to operate too well at times, we might compare this Greek definition of citizenship with our own present demonstration of citizenship, in which large proportions of potential voters never bother to vote, and in which many of those who do vote seem to concern themselves more with voting in terms of what they will get from the decision they make, rather than what they will give to it. We seem to have confused the Greek ideal of *interested* citizenship with the feeling the Greeks abhorred most, that of *self-interested* citizenship. When voting comes to be equated with looting, such details as who casts the ballots cease to be a guarantee of a sound political life.

Like the other Greeks before him, Aristotle also condemned extremes, whether in the excessive exercise of the power of a ruler or in the irresponsible action of a mob. This is the basis of the famous "golden mean," which insists that ethics and politics are one, and that any attempt to divorce political life from ethical considerations is a sure guarantee of disaster. Thus Aristotle came to advance his concept of "natural justice." He insisted that the definition of justice enforced by the state was a definition which bound the state as well as the citizen, pointing out that ". . . the essential ingredient of the justice which is enforced by the state is not of the state's own contrivance; it is a discovery from nature and a transcript of its constancy."[22]

A list of the contrasts in political thought between Plato and Aristotle can easily be compiled, especially if "Plato's political thought" is felt to be expressed only in *The Republic.* Many people overlook Plato's later work in *The Statesman* and *The Laws*, and point with satisfaction to Plato's urging of the planned society, in which no room was left for the family or for private property or for other guarantees of the individual's dignity against the coercions of his planned society. Yet, as we have seen, in *The Statesman* and *The Laws* a rather major shift occurred in Plato's thinking as he moved further and further from the planned society and insisted more and more upon the necessity of limiting the exercise of political power. This coincided with Aristotle's own growth and development in which he opposed the planned society and insisted that society was stronger when founded upon the individual and upon the roots from which the individual derives his strength: tradition, private property, and the family.

Thus the direction of both Plato and Aristotle, if we look at the entire picture, is toward limited government, toward the importance of individual, responsible, self-reliant citizenship, and especially toward a great concern for the moral and ethical foundations underlying meaningful politics. To understand completely the political thought of Plato and Aristotle, it is necessary that we also consider their ethical and metaphysical thinking, because the Greeks knew well what the modern world seems to have forgotten: politics and morality, like all other human endeavors, can only be effectively understood as a part of the *total picture of human nature.*

THE ETHICS AND METAPHYSICS OF PLATO

Following the lead of Socrates, Plato and Aristotle came to understand that politics, like all other human concerns, is ultimately a matter of morality; and the Greeks faced the same age-old questions with which man is forever confronted. What is the nature of man? What is the nature of man's moral choice? What is the source of the framework within which man makes this moral choice? The problems of God and man, and right and wrong, came to confront the Greeks, as it ultimately confronts any man who thinks far enough beneath the surface of events.

The Greeks approached this problem through several questions: What is reality? What can man know of that reality? Is reality only sensory phenomena? Or is there a higher reality than mere material things?

Furthering the thought of Socrates, Plato and Aristotle insisted that men must attempt to understand themselves by understanding the moral intelligence which governs the universe. Within the complexities of Plato's "Theory of Ideas" is the claim of an *immaterial reality* not susceptible to complete understanding by man, a reality in tune with man's ethical need for a level of knowledge far beyond that gained by mere sense perception.

To understand Plato's metaphysics, and the ethical and religious conclusions he drew from them, we must begin where he did, with an examination of the objects that we see around us in our everyday sensory experience. At first glance, we tend to imagine that these objects are solid and durable, and therefore the stuff of which reality is made. Yet what we regard as the fixed qualities of some particular object are really only relative to the circumstances around it. Whether a rock or a house or a cow is heavy or light, large or small, hard or soft, beautiful or ugly, is, if we will but stop to consider for a moment, relative to what we are comparing those qualities with at the time.

"Ah," you may well object, "whether the rock we are examining is heavy or light, large or small, hot or cold, may depend on the conditions around it, but the *substance* of the rock itself is there; we can touch it, and we know that it exists." But can our mind perceive substance, without attaching descriptive qualities to that substance? Let's try, and see what happens. Let us take a large, heavy, smooth, round, gray stone, and remove those relative qualities from it. If we begin with something that is large, heavy, smooth, round, and gray and then begin to subtract these relative qualities, what have we left? If we subtract the relative quality of largeness, we have a heavy, smooth, round, gray object. If we next subtract the relative quality of weight, we now have a smooth, round, gray object. If we subtract ths quality of smoothness, we now have something round and gray. If we subtract the quality of roundness, we now have something gray. If we subtract the quality of grayness, we now have . . . What *do* we have?[14]

Substance is thus revealed as something that has no meaning apart from its qualities. And the qualities of a substance, as perceived by our senses, are relative to the objects of comparison which we have available to us at the time. Thus the "real" world around us, the object of sensory experience, is totally relative to the situation and has no existence at all apart from our perception of these relative, constantly shifting qualities.[14]

If we thus can never come to know the world of our sensory experience, is definite knowledge impossible for man? Even modern science suggests that the material world is in a constant state of flux, that is, a state of *becoming*, rather than *being*, and therefore never *is* anything at all. Yet, man does know some things. We know that good is preferable to bad, that justice is better than injustice, that honesty is preferable to dishonesty. Yet we have also seen that man can only know what exists. And, to exist, anything must have some unchanging and identifiable quality which can be known.. Plato decided that if the world of sensory perception contains no such definition of reality, then the world of mind and ethics, of a higher order than mere sensory perception, must contain the sort of reality that man can know.[14]

Even in Plato's time, some Greeks, Heraclitus, for example, had pointed out that all material things in the universe are in a constant state of flux. For example, it is impossible to step into the same river twice, for the very simple reason that on the second step, the river is no longer the same river. Plato was thus driven to find reality beyond the world of mere sensory experience. He understood that it is the union of mind and spirit which makes man something quite apart from the rest of the animal world, since man alone can come to know the truth or feel so strongly that he has come to know it sufficiently well to be willing to die for it. Thus, while Plato realized that the world of sensory experience is formless, a conclusion finally also arrived at by modern science, he also sensed that man had the dim perception of a higher reality which gave form to the formless.

Plato's idea that reality exists as a system of nonmaterial forms or ideas makes the important point that when man searches for reality, he comes closest to finding it in his examination of what the modern world calls "values." Such values as justice, beauty, and truth are typical examples of what Plato regarded as those nonmaterial forms which constitute genuine reality. The assumption that such forms or values constitute reality is the halfway point to arriving with the theologians at the assumption that such values are only the manifestations available to man of a yet more ultimate reality, the means by which an infinite personality, whom we call God, reveals himself to mankind.[14]

Thus it was through Plato that an understanding of two worlds—the world of constantly changing appearance and the world of timeless reality—was given to Western man. It was in the eternal forms, not limited by sensory perception, that Plato discovered, ". . . the very Being with which true knowledge is concerned, the colorless, formless, intangible essence, visible only to the mind, the pilot of the soul," *(Phaedrus)*". . . a nature which is everlasting, not growing or decaying or waxing or waning, but Beauty only, absolute, separate, simple, and everlasting, which, without diminution and without increase or any change in itself, is imparted to the ever-growing and perishing beauties of all other things." *(Symposium)*.

Together with Socrates, Plato had insisted that the proper

field of study for mankind was man and the system of right and wrong within which man must live. Like Socrates, he also believed that virtue was knowledge, and that a man who understood virtue would necessarily practice it, since virtue, being good, was necessarily preferable to evil. It would seem at first glance that Socrates' and Plato's assumption that man would always choose the good was hopelessly Utopian; we all know from personal experience how often man chooses the worse over the better. But what makes Plato's view understandable and defensible is the meaning which he gave to the word "knowledge." He meant far more by the word than modern man understands.

Knowledge to Plato was not merely what a man had seen, or heard, or had been taught in school. Rather, knowledge to Plato was what man had achieved in *understanding* by long and painstaking examination. What man had thus learned must be of permanent, not temporary material; that is, the objects of our sensory experience, which, as we have seen, are always in the act of becoming something else, would not be suitable material for Plato's "knowledge." Only what he regarded as forms or ideas, and what we call values, would be suitable material for "knowledge." Thus, although Plato reached the point by a very different road, he arrived at a position almost identical to that of the Psalmist in the assertion that, "The knowledge of God is the beginning of wisdom."

Thus Plato's sort of knowledge, limited not to mere sensory experience, but devoted instead to the contemplation of genuine reality, is a function of mind, a striving toward the higher reality, or idea, or form, the highest of which is the concept of good. Plato never completely made the final step to identifying this ultimate reality of good with the specific idea of God, yet he defined good in such divine terms as to make the concept almost identical with what we call God.

Thus a knowledge of good was the sort of knowledge which to Plato would not allow a man to do wrong. Obviously, such knowledge is far deeper than the definition usually accorded the word by modern man, since Plato's concept included moral as well as intellectual assumptions.

In the field of ethics, the study of right and wrong, Plato thus took an important step toward explaining the difference between "what is" and "what ought to be." For, if man were to assume, as much of the ancient world and much of the modern world in fact has assumed, that no higher reality exists to guide man than that which he can perceive within the sensory order, how is man to explain that insistent urging within his breast to do as he *ought* to do? Plato, of course, offers an answer to this problem when he points out that goodness is a form and an idea and an expression of reality not limited to the sensory order, a fixed and unchanging reality which expresses a Divine Will not subject to the whims of man's animal nature.

Plato's assumption of a world of reality higher than mere sensory experience led him both to the concept of an infinite goodness and the doctrine of immortality for man, because his ideas forced upon him the necessity of distinguishing sharply between the human body and the human soul. Thus it was Greek philosophy, especially Plato's conception of an absolute, eternal, and fixed good, which prepared the world for the reception of a universal religion. The Platonic influence upon Christianity was extremely large and played an important role in the development of Western religious ideals. Both the Christian Church and Plato insisted that man is at once of a higher and lower order, the lower order deriving from the world of sensory experience and the higher order the result of influences eternal and timeless, influences far beyond man's powers of initiation or control. Thus, Western man was moving toward a definition of man's growth and goodness based upon the existence of eternal truths that extend through and beyond the material universe around us.

THE ETHICS AND METAPHYSICS OF ARISTOTLE

Like Plato, Aristotle rejected the view that morals are relative and insisted that man could arrive at values true for all times and places. Aristotle built upon the assumptions of Socrates and Plato that a moral intelligence controlled the universe. Yet Aristotle also insisted that matter as well as form made up reality. He did not deny that perfect concepts and ideas were a vital part of reality, but he did insist that individual copies of these perfect forms also contained a part, albeit an imperfect part, of that reality. Thus Aristotle insisted that man had to live in this world even while he contemplated a higher reality to govern that life.

Working from this assumption that the material world also constituted reality, he insisted that such reality had form, and that such form had to be imposed upon matter by a First Cause, a Prime Mover, by what we would call God.

Aristotle insisted that man's progress from his imperfect material forms to his perfect idealistic forms was the purposeful intent originally set forth by the Prime Mover. Reasoning from the material world around him, Aristotle speculated that the purpose of any species was toward the production of a perfect specimen of that particular vegetable or tree or animal. Thus in the case of man, the only resident of the world of sensory perception who could aspire to a higher reality, the only resident of the material universe capable of rational thought, the realization of this ideal concept was the good to be achieved by the development of the human mind. He felt that man was imperfect and would remain imperfect until he realized his fullest development through the achievement of his highest possible reality, that provided for it in the forms and ideas of the Prime Mover.

Aristotle demonstrated in his *Ethics* that the achievement of excellence in anything is to be found in the performance of the function for which it was originally designed. Thus, if the function of an ear is to hear, the virtue of an ear is to hear well. Since man alone of the animal kingdom possessed reason, and since it is the function of reason to guide toward intelligent action and purposeful existence, man alone could lay down goals and ends and work toward their achievement; thus man achieved his fulfillment only by working toward a higher order.[14] Reasoning from the natural order, Aristotle arrived at the same conclusions as to the nature and destiny of man, that Plato reached, reasoning from the non-material bases of human existence. Thus Aristotle's pattern of nobility was the "high-minded man" or the "man of great soul."

It was Aristotle who first separated philosophy in the broader Greek sense of the word into the component parts used by modern man, that is, science on the one hand and ethics and metaphysics on the other. Yet, he remained deeply rooted in the doctrine of ideas and metaphysical reality developed by Socrates and Plato. Still, in many ways he remained a practical man of affairs, recognizing the presence of reality in this life as well as in the next and insisting that life existed not only in *being*, but also in *becoming*. He pointed out that matter (the merely potential) could be moved without itself moving anything, while God (the solely actual) could move without Himself being moved. Between matter and God stood man, living in the material world around him and yet striving to attain a unity with the higher reality of God. Thus man evolved toward God by the development of his "active reason" and by the development of the spark of divine self-consciousness within his breast. In the ethics and metaphysics of Plato and Aristotle, the foundations were laid for the development of Christianity.

THE MEANING OF PLATO AND ARISTOTLE FOR MODERN MAN

All of us would agree, I think, that the highest elements within human personality are distinctively man's, elements not shared by the animals and plants of the natural universe. These higher reaches of the human personality seem to be attained by the pursuit and cultivation of the ends which we call goodness, beauty, truth, and happiness. Why are these things so valuable in themselves? Things which are ultimately valuable are self-evidently so, and no really satisfactory answer can be given to the question of *why* they are valuable. We can only say that mankind has again and again throughout his existence pronounced them to be ultimately valuable. The really important truths are self-evident. For example, despite the innumerable varieties of moral codes and religious creeds that exist in modern society, we can agree with C. E. M. Joad in his assumption that: "(1.) We can most of us recognize a good man when we see one; and (2.) The affirmations of all the world's great religions, however they may differ in their more primitive stages, tend, as the religions develop, to coincide in regard to the nature of moral good. The good man, all the religions have held, is merciful, not self-centered, kindly, compassionate, tolerant, just."[14]

If we look to those who have contributed most to mankind, we find men who have with success pursued the true, the beautiful and the good. We look to men who have excelled within themselves by recognizing what is distinctive in man: his ability to think and his spirit which senses a reality beyond mere physical things. Only here does man excel.

> Fighting, feeding, making love, acquiring, possessing, hoarding, developing his body in the virtues of the body such as toughness and endurance, cultivating the qualities which have survival value, such as fortitude, fleetness, fertility or guile, man is doing those things which the animals do as well if not better than he. Loyalty, discipline, uniformity? Ants run the corporate state better than any Fascist. Strength and ferocity? The lion beats us every time. Patience, grace and fleetness? In patience the tortoise, in grace and fleetness, the deer, are our undeniable superior; Nightingales are more musical, rabbits more fertile, sheep more gentle. If we value ourselves by any of these criteria, we cannot but hold that we are inferior to many of the animals. By what, then, are we distinguished from them; the answer is by virtue of our reasons and our spirits, and it is, therefore, to those who have led us in our evolutionary journey through the vast epoch of man's past in thinking, in appreciating beauty and in achieving goodness, that we owe the advance of our species beyond the animals. They are the true leaders of mankind, and it was their vision and pursuit of what is pure, good and beautiful which distinguish their lives and place posterity in their debt.[14]

Over the past two thousand years, Western man has largely agreed with this view of the higher side of reality and of human nature, and has measured his progress by his ability to move in the direction of that higher reality. Such principles, however, are under attack in our time, the claim being that the individual has no such higher side and that the rights of "collective humanity" empower the state to say that man exists for the state, rather than the state for man. The political goal of providing order, law, and justice, within which the individual can pursue his everyday material life and the development of the higher side of his human personality, has now been set aside for the much more exciting goal of remaking man in a new political image, in which the development of his higher reality is to be achieved on this earth, measured by the standards of the strictly sensory order.

Socrates, Plato, and Aristotle are important to us in an attempt to regain our bearings and once again place politics in their proper, limited perspective. With Socrates, man began to suspect the existence of absolute values of a higher reality. With Plato these absolute values and the existence of such a reality were made far more distinct. Plato, however, made the mistake as a young man of believing that such values could best be implemented by the state. He realized his error as he grew older and paved the way for his student, Aristotle, to reaffirm the existence and the importance of those absolute values as the source of human dignity, creativity, and growth. Aristotle made clear that such values could not be achieved by the state, but, on the contrary, could only be achieved by protecting the individual from the coercive power of the state. The Greek heritage to Western man is two-fold: (1) Man has a higher side and a higher dignity; (2) That dignity must not be interfered with through the exercise of coercive political power.

4

The Stoics

❧❧❧❧❧❧❧❧❧❧❧❧❧❧❧❧❧❧❧❧❧❧❧❧❧❧❧❧❧❧❧❧❧❧

As GREECE CONTINUED ITS DECLINE, THE SNUG AND SECURE world of the Greek polis was swept away in the Hellenistic world of Alexander. As the Hellenistic empire spread thoughout the then-civilized world surrounding the Mediterranean, much of Greek culture spread with it. From this matrix was destined to rise the next major power: Rome. The Greek decline, the age of Hellenistic culture, and the rise of Rome together form the transitional period from the first to the second great civilization of Western antiquity. In this transitional period the ideas were formed which gave rise to Roman civilization and the next chapters in Western man's search for identity.

As the older Greek society collapsed, and individual existence was increasingly threatened by that collapse, the search for an ideal society and for abstract truth that had characterized the thinking of Plato and Aristotle was set aside so that men might search instead for a world view and an ethical system designed to help the individual when all around him appeared to be crashing to ruin.

The founder of the school of Stoicism was Zeno, who came to Athens as a young man, arriving shortly after the death of Aristotle. Building on the views of some of the other philosophies popular at the time of Greek decline, Zeno contributed substantially to the field of ethics. In its original form, Stoicism, like its principal rival, Epicureanism, was a response to the enlargement of the world that had taken place through the victories of Alexander the Great. The limited framework of the small city-state had been destroyed, and the individual Greek now found himself faced with an enormously enlarged environment. Stoicism, then, was one of the many attempts to redress the balance between tiny man and gigantic world, by arming tiny man with self-sufficiency, or what the Greek called *autarky.*

Directed toward individual salvation, Stoicism never developed a thoroughly consistent moral philosophy. But this was of little concern to the Stoics, who were primarily searching for a way of life.

The Stoics, of course, were not alone in this search. As the individual came to feel increasingly exposed to the blows of circumstances, the Cyrenaics assured him that the road to happiness was through sensual pleasure. The Cynics promised happiness through virtue, virtue being defined as the renunciation of all such encumbrances as money, family, reputation, or anything else whose loss involved pain.

The Skeptics went one better than their rival philosophies, and, under the direction of their principal leader, Pyrrho, told men to give up their search for truth since "knowledge is impossible." It is instructive to consider how the Skeptics arrived at this intellectual shrugging of the shoulders, since it tells us so much about some of the thinking taking place in our modern world. Pyrrho began by demonstrating, as it has always been easily demonstrable, that previous philosophers had never agreed about the problems of mankind and their solution. Thus everything must be governed by personal belief. If so, how can man have any knowledge outside the field of the physical senses? Yet the senses do not agree either . . .Any married couple knows that the temperature in a bedroom is usually too hot or too cold for someone, whether the windows are open or closed; in fact, it is often too cold for one and too hot for the other at the same time. Since man's physical senses do not convey consistently accurate information to him, who is to say what is the truth? Pyrrho's answer was that a wise man must hold no opinion and limit himself to the customs of the area where he lives. This is what the mid-twentieth century calls cultural relativism, and is therefore not quite as new an idea as our modern "social scientists" would lead us to believe.

This philosophy, when considered from the point of view of the state, rather than the individual, leads to serious results. When the individual says that truth is relative, varying with circumstances, time and place, he is paving the way for the agreement of the state that truth indeed has no absolute basis. If this idea is carried far enough, the time comes when the state defines "truth," as for example in totalitarian Russia and in George Orwell's *1984* or *Animal Farm*.

A Greek philosopher named Epicurus held out a bit more promise to the beleaguered Greek of his time. Epicureanism also favored a maximization of pleasure for one's mind and body, but felt that this was best achieved by lessening one's dependence on creature comforts, lest the withdrawal of those creature comforts might give pain. Instead, the Epicurean adjustment to the fortunes of life was to take place in the mind. Happiness was to be derived from intellectual pursuits since these were less likely to come to a sad end than physical pleasures. The Epicurean believed in no higher standards or goals in life, but at least taught a measure of self-discipline. Only later did all this become debased into the old Oriental proverb of, "Eat, drink, and be merry, for tomorrow we die."

If man is to be given self-sufficiency, *autarky*, in a world which threatens to overpower him, either the world must be made less important or man more important. The Epicureans attempted the first approach; the Stoics, the second. Ultimately, the Epicureans rested their ethics upon the exclusion of all but material considerations. They offered man only the hope of ignoring these material satisfactions so that their loss would not upset him. So, to the Epicurean, the world and everything in it was composed only of an endless array of atoms moving in absolute emptiness. All phenomena, whether the tiniest sense perception or the mightiest tidal wave, were to be explained by the motion of atoms and nothing else. According to the Epicureans, man had no spiritual goal for his aspirations. Death was to be merely the dispersion of atoms and the extinction of personality. Thus, though the Epicureans had taken a substantial step above the Cyrenaics, the Cynics, and the Skeptics, philosophy seemed to offer little hope to the Greeks in the era of their decline.

Though the Stoics tried to free the individual from dependence upon temporary fortune, thought happiness must be attained by each individual for himself, and rejected sensual pleasure, choosing instead intellectual satisfaction, and thus paralleling the Epicureans in many ways, it was in Stoicism that the one real hope of Hellenistic philosophy shone forth. The difference was primarily one of method: The Epicurean saw a world without design, while the Stoic saw a universe of law ruled by a guiding Providence.

The Stoic universe was as systematic and well ordered as the Epicurean universe was anarchic. The guiding principle for the Stoic was Nature, but the concept of Nature as used by the Stoic was interchangeable with the idea of Zeus, Providence, or Cosmos. One of the most familiar of Stoic phrases is, "Life according to nature," that is, life moving toward a consummation. That consummation was to be the achievement of the potentiality present within the nature of man, distinct from the rest of creation, since man alone possessed reason, and man alone within nature could move toward higher concepts. Unlike the Epicurean, the Stoic achieved his self-sufficiency not by rejecting the Divine but by finding his place within the Divine.

The Stoics, then, developing their philosophy in a time of transition, more nearly combined the Greek past with the Roman and Christian future than any other Hellenistic philosophy. They kept the Greek belief in the existence of universal principles and the Greek faith in human capacity to live in accord with such principles. Yet at the same time they shared with their Hellenistic age a loss of faith in their power to change the world through political institutions. Instead, they placed their faith in the individual achieving his own goals and fulfillment without help from society. Stoicism was therefore hard and severe, but it completely surpassed all competing forms of Hellenistic thinking and was a major influence, not only on Roman thought but on later Christian thought as well. Through Christian thought, Stoicism had a major impact upon the subsequent history of Western man. Thus while

Aristotle had thought of "natural justice" as primarily a guide for the legislator, the *Jus Naturale* conceived by the Stoics was a way of happiness to be achieved by all men. The concepts stressed by Stoicism were those of a moral order within which man, through his God-given capacity to reason, achieved an ethical completeness far more important than mere political or legal concepts. Plato and Aristotle had hoped, as men of the polis, that human happiness could be achieved by political means. The failure of those attempts, no matter how well intended, had forced the Stoics to create a new ethical framework more individualistic than that understood by the earlier Greeks.

ROMAN STOICISM

As in most cultural matters Roman philosophy was heavily dependent upon Greek example. Yet, usually when the Romans copied something from the Greeks, they placed a high premium upon "practicality," "usefulness," and "utility." So the grand problems of the nature of the universe and of human knowledge lacked the appeal for the practical Roman mind that they had held for the speculative Greeks. Plato and Aristotle thus tended to be passed over and the later, more individualistic, Greek philosophers, especially the Stoics, came to be principally emphasized. When we discuss the world view of Rome, we are therefore in large part investigating the impact of Stoicism.

Though the Stoics were unwilling to deal in abstraction, and constantly attempted to turn to the problems of the real world within which man lived, they invariably concluded that genuine wisdom for man lay in understanding causes and moral codes beyond the merely material universe. To the Stoic it was the principle of rationality which pervaded the cosmos and enabled man to comprehend the world and thus direct his own affairs. The Greek word for this wisdom was *logos*, meaning not only "the word," but "reason." Coming to understand this *logos* through the exercise of human reason was for the Stoic to come to understand and practice a universal morality. To the Stoic, the world was controlled by this perfect and universal morality, or reason. Since men thus lived in a morally planned universe, and since they contained within themselves the divine spark called reason, Stoics conceived the human task as living in accordance with this guiding principle of universal morality. For all the vaunted differences between the "idealism" of Plato and Aristotle and the "realism" of the Stoics, it is obvious that, by whatever route, a similar direction in thought made the Stoics far more a continuation of Plato and Aristotle than they themselves realized.

To the Stoic, evil existed in this world. Yet, if an all-powerful and completely virtuous reason directed the world, how could evil exist? The Stoic insisted that the plan of moral perfection given the world by Universal Reason, Cosmos, God, the Word, or whatever other name might be applied to the idea of an all-guiding intelligence, could only be meaningful if men were given freedom of choice, since only by the exercise of such freedom could moral *choice* be achieved. If men were to *choose* the virtuous life, they also had to be *free to choose* the temporal satisfactions of wealth, prestige, or sensual pleasure instead. The Stoics insisted that if man did choose such temporal pretensions, his choice was error and error is evil. Yet the Stoics maintained that genuine goodness was not possible for man *unless he retained his freedom to choose.* Thus, by an ethical rather than a political route, the Stoics arrived at Aristotle's assumption that human freedom was a prime requirement.

In Rome, Stoicism became the "religion" of the educated classes. It provided the moral framework within which Rome became great. Pre-supposing the existence of a system of order in nature, the Stoics insisted that the truly important values were a *Natural Law* more perfect than any man-made law governing human affairs. Since virtue consisted in living in accordance with this universal law, and since observance of duty made one virtuous, the Stoic insisted that human law not in accord with divine law was therefore an imposition upon the right of the individual human to choose virtue. At a time when the entire world sought freedom from fear, the Stoics found that freedom by having faith in Divine Providence and in the individual's human capacity to strive toward attainment of the moral perfection offered by living in harmony with what that Providence directed. The Stoics thus came to advocate that man alone can reject his environment, thus once again anticipating the capacity for self-transcendence that Christianity would make explicit.

In a very real way, the Stoics were the most practical of the Roman philosophers. They concerned themselves not with the fact that man was going to die, which of course they took for granted, but rather with the manner in which the individual man would choose to live; that is, with or without standards and values. Feeling that the individual man had a higher side and that he must be free to choose, the Stoics insisted that value in life must be determined by the individual, since no one else apprehends the truth *as seen by that individual.*

This ideal of human self-discipline has cropped up at many times and many places, as, for example, in Buddha's famous aphorism, "Though one should in battle conquer a thousand men a thousand times, he who conquers himself has the more glorious victory." Yet in few places is this concept of individual self-discipline more strongly stated than in the Stoic insistence upon individuality, self-help, strength, and morality. The key to an understanding of Stoicism is the insistence that self-discipline is to be achieved according to a plan and a law that directed the entire universe. This emphasis upon duty, upon individual morality, upon a higher law than man, and upon a necessity for man's freedom to live in accordance with that law, would have the utmost importance for the growth of the Roman citizenship which built the Roman Republic.

CICERO AND NATURAL LAW

To understand fully the Stoic impact upon Rome, we must turn to an examination of a few of the principal Stoic thinkers and the ideas which they advanced. Probably no more important Stoic thinker than Cicero, and no more important Stoic concept than Natural Law could be suggested. Strictly speaking, Cicero was not a Stoic. In most textbooks he is called an Eclectic; that is, a sampler of numerous viewpoints. A lawyer of the highest reputation, he became Roman Consul in 63 B.C., a time when the Roman Republic was in its last stages and when various contests for total power were being waged within the Republic in a series of bloody wars. In the midst of this coercive struggle to gain power, Cicero spoke up for the old order, and against the new type of one-man rule. He spent the last twenty years of his life in an effort to turn Rome from the downward path of political coercion on which it had embarked. In 43 B.C., he was assassinated under orders from Marc Antony, who was contending for power following the death of Julius Caesar.

Cicero gave ideal expression to the dominant traditions of the man of classical antiquity. His oratory, his letters, and his philosophy are pervaded by the highest sense of public interest. Cicero consistently urged *humanitas*—the mental and moral qualities making for a civilized man. More of Cicero's writings are extant than of any other author of classical antiquity. Molding his thinking on the Greeks, he brings forward to us much of the best of the ancient world, and has long exercised a great influence in the thinking of Western man.

To understand properly Cicero in his historical setting, it is necessary to differentiate between the short run and the long run. His attempted restoration of the values of an older, limited, moral, political framework was a total failure and apparently was already an anachronism in his own time. Cicero's importance in political thinking lies rather in the fact that he propounded the Stoic doctrine of Natural Law in a form which preserved that concept from his own time until the nineteenth century. From Cicero, the concept passed to the Roman lawyers, to the early Fathers of the Christian Church, and in fact to the entire Medieval period of Western man.

The brilliance of Cicero's espousal of Natural Law was especially important in its timing, bringing as it did the Stoic conception of Natural Law into contact with Roman law at a time when the Roman Empire was to spread Roman Law, and with it the Stoic concept of Natural Law, throughout the Western civilized world.

What was this *Jus Naturale* espoused by Cicero? Even as he failed to re-institute an ethical framework of political life in Rome; he continued to insist on the Stoic idea that, ". . .the Chief Good consists in applying to the conduct of life a knowledge of the working of natural causes, choosing what is in accordance with nature and rejecting what is contrary to it; in other words, the

Chief Good is to live in agreement and in harmony with nature."
In *De Finibus (Concerning The Ends of Life)* Cicero went on to
define moral worth as,

> . . .that which is of such a nature that though devoid of all utility,
> it can justly be commended in and for itself apart from any profit
> or reward. . .Good men do a great many things from which they
> anticipate no advantage, solely from the motive of propriety, moral-
> ity, and right. For among the many points of difference between
> man and the lower animals, the greatest difference is that Nature
> has bestowed on man the gift of Reason. . .It is reason moreover
> that has inspired man with a relish for his kind. . .Nature has also
> engendered in mankind the desire for contemplating truth. . .This
> primary instinct leads us on to love all truth as such, that is all that
> is trustworthy, simple and consistent, and to hate things insincere,
> false, and deceptive, such as cheating, perjury, malice, and injustice.

Surely, this is a statement of political goals higher than most!

How could man achieve such political heights? In *De Legibus
(Concerning Law)* Cicero went on to explain, "That animal which
we call man. . .has been given a certain distinctive status by the
Supreme God who created him; for he is the only one among so
many different kinds and varieties of living things who has a share
in reason and thought, while all the rest are deprived of it. . ."
Writing to his son, Marcus, in pursuit of the voluminous correspondence which he constantly carried on, Cicero insisted that no
phase of life, whether public or private, whether in business or in
the home, can be without its moral duty; and in the final analysis
the proper discharge of that duty is the means whereby man
achieves moral right, while the neglect of that duty brings failure,
with resultant collapse into moral wrong. He warned, "Death is to
be chosen before slavery and base deeds," and "Nature and Reason command nothing unseemly, nothing effeminate, nothing las-
civious be done or thought." Urging his son, as indeed he urged
all Romans, to the observance of the "four cardinal virtues: Wisdom, Justice, Courage, and Temperance," Cicero in reality spoke
to all men in all times:

> These virtues are nothing but an attempt to fit our lives and our
> relations with others into that eternal order which serves as a model
> for us while it imposes an obligation on us. We have to distinguish

between justice which is a product of government and justice which is natural. It follows that although man-made laws vary, God's law is the same for all men. True law is right reason in agreement with nature. It is of universal application, unchanging and everlasting; it summons to duty by its commands, and averts from wrongdoing by its prohibitions. . .We cannot be freed from its obligations by senate or people, and we need not look outside ourselves for an expounder or interpreter of it. And there will not be different laws at Rome and at Athens, or different laws now and in the future, but one eternal and unchangeable law which will be valid for all nations and all times, and there will be one Master and Ruler and that is God over us all, for He is the author of this law, its promulgator and its enforcing judge. Whoever is disobedient is fleeing from himself and denying his human nature, and by reason of this very fact he will suffer the worst penalties, even if he escapes what is commonly considered punishment. . .

Thus Cicero spoke to Rome the words which she would not heed.

SENECA AND CHRISTIANITY

Several generations after the death of Cicero, a new Stoic thinker of importance came on the scene. This Roman playwright and jurist, Seneca, was regarded with especially high favor by the leaders of the early Christian Church and came very near to both the concept of monotheism and the doctrine of immortality.

In describing the Supreme Power which shapes the universe, Seneca even came close to describing the Trinity: "This Power we sometimes call the All-Ruling God, sometimes the incorporeal Wisdom, sometimes the Holy Spirit, sometimes Destiny." Thus the Christian Trinity of Father, Word and Spirit was set forth under different Stoic names for Divine Unity.

Many of the precepts of Seneca closely parallel passages in the New Testament and are on the same high moral plane. Indeed, authors have often presented side by side passages from the New Testament and from Seneca, demonstrating the close kinship in sentiment and style. For example, it was Seneca who remarked, "Let us so give as we should wish to receive."

More famous in his own time as a playwright, Seneca's subsequent fame has rested upon this close connection with the Christian faith. The Church Fathers knew full well that he was no Christian, yet highly respected his moral doctrines. This remained true of Christian philosophers until the age of the Renaissance.

Thus, long over a thousand years after Seneca's own time, the spark of his teachings which had been kept alive by the Christian Church penetrated the minds of Montaigne, Rabelais, Bacon, Shakespeare, Ben Jonson, and Milton, to exercise a profound influence upon Western civilization. As late as the nineteenth century, English poets such as Wordsworth and American philosophers such as Emerson were especially attracted to the teachings of Seneca.

EPICTETUS AND INDIVIDUAL MORALITY

The next Stoic of significance was a slave and cripple who was active in Rome at the time of the death of Seneca or shortly thereafter. This man, Epictetus, taught entirely in the oral tradition. He wrote nothing, and the little we know of this man— perhaps the most important of the Stoics—comes through Arrian, the biographer of Alexander the Great, who recorded some of the work of Epictetus, especially the *Manual* and the *Discourses.* Epictetus taught during the reign of Nero and obviously was out of step with his times, since, as in the case of Seneca and most of the other Stoics, a strong parallel exists between the teachings of Epictetus and Christian morality.

As is often the case with important thinkers, men whose clarity and depth of thought shine through in their every word, Epictetus is his own best expositor. From the *Discourses,* then, let Epictetus state his case: "The road leading to freedom, the only release from slavery, is to be able to say cheerfully,

> Lead me on, O Zeus and Destiny,
> Where I was once assigned by Thy decree."

"I must die, but must I die groaning? I must be imprisoned, but must I whine as well? I must suffer exile. Can anyone then hinder me from going with a smile and good courage, and at peace?"

"Tell the secret!"

"I refuse to tell, for this is my power."

"But I will chain you, what say you, fellow?"

"Chain me? My leg you will chain, yes, but my will, no. Not even Zeus can conquer that."

"I will imprison you."

"My bit of a body you mean."

"I will behead you."

"Why, when did I ever tell you that I was the only man in the world who could not be beheaded? It is yours to kill, mine to die without quailing."

Thus Epictetus saw that he who is miserable is the man who has compromised his spirit so completely that he is incapable of giving up this life, including the body itself, while he who is happy is the man who is free in spirit because he has complete control of his will. "Of one thing beware, O man; see what is the price at which you will sell your will. If you do nothing else, do not sell your will cheap."

Epictetus knew that happiness in the sensory order was not man's lot. He fully understood the Biblical meaning of "ashes to ashes, dust to dust." But he also understood that man could transcend this merely material order through an act of his will and mind. "Difficulties are what show men's character. Therefore when a difficult crisis meets you, remember that you are the raw youth with whom God, the Trainer, is wrestling."

Epictetus understood that no man is ever really alone, since his higher side is in constant communion with a force far above material concerns. "When you have shut your doors, and darkened your room, remember never to say that you are alone, for you are not alone; but God is within, and your genius is within,—and what need have they of light to see what you are doing?. . .Make up your mind at last to please your true self, make up your mind to appear noble to God; set your desires on becoming pure in the presence of your pure self and God."

Epictetus believed men would be better if only they grasped the fact that a Divine Providence rules the world.

Has the world no governor? And how is it possible that a city or a family cannot continue to exist, not even the shortest time without an administrator or guardian; and that so great and beautiful a system should be administered with such order and yet without a purpose and by chance? . . . .There is a God and. . . He provides for all things; also. . .It is not possible to conceal from Him our acts or even our intentions and thoughts. . .God has need of irrational animals to make use of appearances, but of us to understand the use of appearances. It is therefore enough for them to eat and drink, and to sleep and to copulate, and to do all the other things which they severally do. But for us, to whom He has given also the intellectual faculty, these things are not sufficient; for unless we act in a proper and orderly manner, and conformably to the nature and constitution of each thing, we shall never attain our true end. For where the constitutions of living things are different, there also the acts and the ends are different. . . .It is shameful for man to begin and to end where irrational animals do; but rather they ought to begin where they begin, and to end where nature ends in us; and nature ends in contemplation and understanding, and in a way of life conformable to nature. . .

Small wonder that such men as Epictetus served as a bridge between the idealism of Socrates, Plato, and Aristotle, in the pagan world, and the idealism of the Christian Church in the new era about to begin.

MARCUS AURELIUS AND RESPONSIBILITY

The last of the great Stoic philosophers was the Roman Emperor, Marcus Aurelius. Adopted by the childless emperor, Hadrian, Aurelius had been given the best possible upbringing and education, and had been deeply influenced by Stoic philosophy. By the time he had become Emperor, barbarian pressures at the frontier had become so great that, though Aurelius was a peace-loving man, he spent the largest portion of his time as Emperor waging war in protection of the Roman Empire. The principal work of Aurelius is his *Meditations*, which, unlike the *Discourses* of Epictetus, was not intended for the instruction of others. The *Meditations*, rather, is a personal journal of this great Stoic philosopher, describing his innermost thoughts, and his most deeply felt philosophy, written at random moments stolen from his heavy duties as Emperor and warrior. Shining through the *Meditations* is Aurelius' belief that man may possess divinity in the practice of wisdom, justice, fortitude, and moderation.

Like the *Manual* and *Discourses* of Epictetus, the *Meditations* of Marcus Aurelius deserve being read in their entirety. Yet we can catch something of the flavor of this work:

"This being of mine, whatever it really is, consists of a little flesh, a little breath and a part which governs." What Aurelius called "a part which governs" was, of course, the conscience and the soul of man, that spiritual essence not bounded by the merely material. He felt that this spiritual essence was responsible for man's dignity and insisted that, "A man should *be* upright, not be *kept* upright."

Thus man had a vocation to fill in this life. "What is thy vocation? To be a good man. But how be successful in this save by assured conceptions on the one hand of the Universal Nature and on the other of the special constitution of man?"

This "Universal Nature" and "special constitution of man" were defined as the basis of what Marcus Aurelius called the "Natural Life." "That it consists for every creature in a strict conformity with the essential principle of that creature's constitution. In the case of man, this essential principle is his reason, which is a part of the universal Reason. In so far, therefore, as he follows this rational law of his being, he approaches happiness; in so far as he departs from it, he falls short of happiness. The Natural Life, in fact, is the life controlled by reason; and such a life is briefly described as 'virtue.' It is this meaning of virtue which explains the Stoic dogma that, 'virtue is the only good, and happiness consists exclusively in virtue.' "

The meaning of philosophy to Marcus Aurelius was identical with what religion has since come to mean for Western man. In a very real way the *Meditations* is as much a manual of personal devotion as is the *Imitation of Christ*, written centuries later by the German mystic, Thomas á Kempis. Indeed a close comparison exists between these pagan *Meditations* and their Christian counterpart.

THE IMPACT OF THE STOICS

No less a student of liberty than Lord Acton credits the Stoics with bridging the gap between the ancient and the Christian state, on the way to leading men from despotic rule to freedom. He finds the key to this Stoic championship of freedom in their insistence that there is a will superior to the collective will of men, a will that governments as well as men must obey.[19]

The Stoic impact upon Rome was even more immediate and basic, building as it did the Roman virtues, and paving the way directly to Christianity. In its emphasis upon self-control, self-discipline, the will, and imperviousness to the pain and confusion of the world, Stoicism was clearly pointing toward the ideal of individual salvation which became explicit in Christianity. The Stoics believed that the universe behaved in accordance with a system of laws fathomable by the human mind. Since they grasped that man's life as a rational animal involved the use of reason and the establishment of order, they insisted that a similar order must exist in the universe as well, necessitating intelligence on a large enough scale to guide such a process. Thus the Stoics came to the idea of one God, monotheism.

The theology of the Christian Church owes a large debt to Stoicism in a number of other ways as well. The New Testament had emphasized moral and spiritual elements almost exclusively, but as the message had spread throughout the civilized pagan world, thoughtful men asked for a reasonable definition of those moral and spiritual elements. The groundwork had already been laid by the idealist philosophy of Plato and Aristotle in their espousal of absolute values and their insistence upon the necessity for a *logos*, a Guiding Intelligence in the universe. It is this concept that Stoicism furthered. In fact the Christian concept of "Divine Spirit" is Stoic in its origin. Other such examples of the affinity between Stoicism and Christianity could be suggested. It was a Stoic idea that men are the offspring of God and partake of His divine nature. It was a Stoic ideal of nonconcern for the merely material and temporal that led to the Christian idea of asceticism.

So, though Roman philosophy originated little, drawing as it did upon the Greeks, it did more fully explain the Christianity to come and serve as the bridge between the pagan and Christian world. It was a work of Cicero that was responsible for the conversion of St. Augustine. Cicero's *On Duty*, adapted by St. Ambrose, served as the basis for the Christian priesthood. A thousand years later, St. Thomas Aquinas borrowed from the Stoics, and especially Cicero, to develop his ideas of Natural Law.

Some nonreligious thoughts of the modern world owe their origins to the Stoics as well. The great international lawyer, Hugo

Grotius, developed the principles of International Law from the Stoics. Our own Founding Fathers here in the United States drew heavily upon Cicero in their framing of the Constitution. But above all, the abiding Stoic principle of Natural Law was absorbed into Christianity and reinterpreted as the demand of the Christian God, surviving through the Middle Ages and into our modern world. Despite all the assaults that have been made upon these ideas of Natural Law, a definite right and wrong, and an Eternal Creator, such doctrines have survived into our own day. Even now when we condemn an act, for example, Nazi genocide, as "immoral" or "unjust," we are speaking in essentially Stoic terms.

When we compare the views of the Stoics with the materialism and relativism of the other philosophers of their time, the Cynics, the Cyrenaics, the Skeptics, and the Epicureans, we find the same basic difference in world view that still confronts us in our own time. When men debated whether or not there was a plan for the universe, they were really in effect debating the question, "Is there a God?" They were arguing the question, "Are there absolute values or are all things relative?" They were debating, "Can man best rise through individual self-reliance and strength, or by conforming to the pattern of his society?" They were pondering, "Is man primarily an animal, best satisfied with creature comforts, or can he rise toward the image of a Creator, through self-discipline and pursuit of a divine plan?" They were wondering, "Who knows best about such values, men as individuals, or men in a planned society in which each has an assigned role?"

These same questions, argued by Socrates and the Sophists, discussed by Plato and Aristotle, restated by the Stoics and implicit in the struggle over Christianity, are still very much alive in our modern world.

5

Rome

🌷🌷🌷🌷🌷🌷🌷🌷🌷🌷🌷🌷🌷🌷🌷🌷🌷🌷🌷🌷🌷🌷🌷🌷🌷🌷🌷🌷🌷🌷🌷🌷

IF WE VIEW WESTERN CIVILIZATION AS A STREAM OF EVENTS, ideas, and institutions moving toward us, and if we trace this stream back toward its source, we find that it originates in a number of small watersheds in Africa and Asia Minor, notably Egypt and the Tigris-Euphrates River Valley. These admittedly small, comparatively minor contributions to Western civilization are then absorbed into one of the two major tributaries producing the Western world: the Hebraic tradition and the Greek tradition. To the Hebrew we turn for such concepts as monotheism, ethics, a personal God, and the faith of the Old Testament. From the Greek we acquire such concepts as a basic faith in the use of man's mind, the beginnings of science, and numerous contributions in literature, government, and, above all, philosophy.

There is a point at which these two streams combine to form the one mighty body of tradition which we call Western civilization. That point is Rome. Rome borrowed and built upon the best of the ancient world and preserved and spread that civilization across most of the European continent. Even when Rome itself declined and passed from the scene, the legacy it left was so rich and so deeply rooted that it formed many of the patterns of the subsequent Middle Ages and even played its part in the formation of modern Western civilization. Rome, that meeting place of an-

cient and modern, that civilizing agent to which we owe the preservation of so many classical values and the origin of so many
modern concepts, is a vital link in the chain of ideas, institutions,
and values which stand ready to serve us for the asking.

As a way-station for the previous heritage of Western man,
Rome was especially dependent on the Greeks, using Greek mod-
els for its literature, Greek teachers for its students, and Greek
culture for its ideal. The Roman contribution was largely of a
practical nature, not only in the sense that it was limited to the
practical application of these ideals, but also in the very important
sense that it was Roman law and order which gave the necessary
stability to the ancient world to allow the development and
maintenance of all that had gone before.

To the Roman, ideas were always viewed as valuable to the
extent that they could be applied in everyday life. Even in the best
of the Roman philosophers, this trait is evident. Cicero discussed
the same topics as Plato, but when he discussed jurisprudence or
government he always limited himself to a treatment of the law
and government then in practice, consistently emphasizing the
real rather than the ideal. This practicality tended to tie the Romans to the present and often made them blind to the future. The
Roman poet, Horace, living shortly before the time of Christ,
showed this down-to-earth quality at its best. Yet, even here, the
limited nature of the concept is readily apparent.

> Happy the man—and happy he alone—
> He, who can call today his own;
> He who, secure within, can say
> Tomorrow do thy worst, for I have lived today;
> Be fair, or foul, or rain, or shine,
> The joys I have possessed, in spite of Fate, are mine
> Not heaven itself upon the Past has power,
> But what has been, has been, and I have had my hour.

Such an attitude in many ways makes an admirable philosophy of
life, yet it falls far short of the speculations of the Greeks.

It is, perhaps, unfair to saddle the Romans exclusively with
the burden of worldliness. The entire emphasis of the ancient
Greco-Roman community was oriented to the affairs of this world.
The later Judeo-Christian influence was not yet so great, since, for

a long while after the birth of Christ, Christianity remained a minor strain. Yet, even though the emphasis upon a higher order than worldly concerns had not yet reached its peak, it is still true, as we have seen, that such idealism and insistence upon a definite right and wrong were already present in Greco-Roman antiquity in the work of Socrates, Plato, Aristotle, and the Stoics.

Neither can the direct contribution of the Romans, considered apart from their preservative function, be neglected in an attempt to discover the roots of Western civilization. Latin was destined to become the language of the medieval Church, and Latin and Greek were long the languages of all educated men of the West. The rhetoric and classical stance of the Roman order is evident throughout the papers of our own American Founding Fathers, just as Latin roots and grammar are evident throughout all the languages of the Western world. Rome also made her share of contributions in art, architecture, science, and literature, but her best efforts were consistently devoted to law and government. It is thus in the Roman concepts of law and politics, and in the moral ideals underlying those concepts, that modern man can find those teachings and examples most useful for today's world.

THE OLD ROMAN CHARACTER

Some of the Greeks, feeling somewhat superior to their practical Roman brethren, attributed the Roman success story less to merit than to good luck. In actual fact, Rome's greatness rested upon very deep foundations. That greatness rested upon moral principles deeply ingrained within the individual Roman citizen. In a very real sense, the Republic rested upon virtue and honor.

Civilization, after all, is an accumulation of what men think and do, together with the values which underlie their thoughts and actions. Though these values ultimately determine man's use of material things, the merely material aspect of civilization is only a pale reflection of the true civilization, that which exists in the minds of men. As the Roman historian, Tacitus, once suggested, only the ignorant think that elaborate buildings and patterns of life make up civilization. The Romans at their best knew that true civilization, what they called *humanitas*, demanded an inborn sense of the dignity of one's self and a recognition of the dignity of the individual personalities of others, a quality requiring self-restraint and high moral courage.

The Romans knew, as few other people have known, that a man must first subordinate his own will to a higher order if he wishes to be able to direct his own affairs intelligently. As the Romans had been told on more than one occasion, "Because you bear yourself as less than the gods, you rule the world."[23]

The Romans had two words for "man." A mere human creature was *homo;* but a true man was *vir.* The self-discipline and moral restraint reflecting genuine manhood was contained in the Roman expression *virtus.* No precise English translation of *virtus* can be made, but an examination of the legends and traditions making up the Roman heritage gives a strong example of the qualities important to the Romans. Romans were raised on the stories of Horatius at the bridge, standing alone against insuperable odds to defend Rome from the Etruscans. All Romans knew of Brutus, an early consul, who had faced the duty of decreeing the death of both his sons because they had plotted against the state. Surely, what we call "patriotism" was one element of the old Roman character. Roman leadership and citizenship were both closely identified with "duty, honor, country." Great amounts of responsibility and integrity were expected from the self-reliant individual.[23] This is one point at which the Stoic philosophy stood the Roman in good stead.

The quality of good citizenship for the Roman was carried out in miniature in the Roman attitude toward the family. In no other society has the family played a more important role. To the Roman, *familia* was a larger concept than our family, including as it did not only the father and mother and children, but also all those who worked on the land of the highly individualistic yeoman-farmer. All members of the family were subject to the control of the oldest man of the household. The Roman attitude toward the head of the family and the training given to the children consistently reflected a high moral tone, bound by ties of natural affection and service. No law could have been more binding on the Roman than that of service to family. The result of such upbringing was a stability of Roman character which was reflected in Roman society and government and which pointed toward the role Rome was destined to play in the civilized world.

Taken as a whole, the pattern of life and the character expected of the individual Roman closely paralleled the *mores majorum,* that is, the manner of life of one's ancestors. These traditions reflected the political and legal framework of Roman society. Taken together with the unwritten rules and precedents of duty and behavior which formed the non-public framework of Roman life, a massive tradition of principle and usage bound the Roman to duty, honor, and self-restraint. Whether in political life or in the standards of morality and taste, the Roman orator, poet, soldier, and statesman invariably turned to such standards for the pattern of his existence.

If *virtus* was one prime Roman virtue, *gravitas* and *pietas* were of nearly equal importance. *Gravitas* to the Roman meant the highly important quality of dignity. *Pietas* implied performance of one's duties in all the relationships of life, within the family, as a citizen, as a friend, as a human being. Individual responsibility was thus the key to understanding of the Roman character.[23]

The Roman respected eternal values and an objective standard of right and wrong, coupling this with a basic faith in human personality, whether concerned with family or state. This respect for the personality of each individual was the basis for the insistence upon the maintenance of his freedom of choice *(libertas).* Respect for tradition, stemming from a faith that the accumulated wisdom of the past was greater than any one moment or any one man could supply, coupled with the Roman respect for the pledged word *(fides),* combined to make the Roman value his integrity, and the integrity of his society, above all else.

These were some of the qualities most admired by the Romans. Without exception, these qualities were moral in nature. As one scholar has described them: "The qualities which served the Roman in his early struggles with Nature and with neighbors remained for him the virtues above all others. To them he owed it that his city-state had risen superior to the older civilization which surrounded it—a civilization which appeared to him to be limp and nerveless unless stiffened by the very virtues which he himself had painfully cultivated. Perhaps they can be summed up under *severitas*, which means being stern with oneself."[23]

The Roman was thus trained in the home, in public life, in life itself, to pursue integrity, individual responsibility and constancy of purpose. This "old Roman character," reflected in Rome's statesmen and in the simple yeoman-farmers composing its legions and its citizenry, produced a moral vitality making Rome great.

ROMAN LAW AND GOVERNMENT

Considering the Roman character, it is not surprising that the chief Roman contribution to Western civilization was the concept of law and order. The stability produced by this law and order not only allowed Rome to act as a repository and conveyor of previous Western culture, but it also gave the Western world its own unique contribution of law and government. "Because you bear yourself as less than the gods, you rule the world." The Romans had learned that through obedience comes power. Through that Roman obedience developed the ideals of Roman law. Oriented to tradition, responsibility, and integrity, the Romans enshrined those ideals in a legal system which they broadened and applied to the entire Western world. This capacity for legal and political organization is reflected not only in the legal systems of the Western nations, but is also readily apparent in the legal frameworks of the Moslems, of International Law, and of the canon law of the medieval Church.

Though Roman practicality had limited the Roman capacity for philosophical speculation, that very down-to-earth quality had allowed them to devise a legal framework by drawing principles of conduct from the experiences of their everyday world. The result was a combination of written and unwritten laws and customs which accumulated for hundreds of years until they were summarized and edited in a process of codification attempted by Justinian, a codification laying the legal basis for subsequent Western civilization. Most of continental Europe derives its law directly from the Roman model. Even the two notable exceptions to this, England and the United States, using English common law, derive many of their principles and terms from this Roman heritage. It is more than coincidence that our legal textbooks and our court systems abound in Latin words and phrases.

What is this heritage that has had such a wide influence upon our Western world? Based on Stoic philosophy, Roman law produced a concept of justice that was larger than mere human law. The concept of *jus naturale* has been a vital influence upon Western man. This is the source, for example, of our eighteenth-century Declaration of Independence: All men have certain inalienable rights. The Roman ideal of a concept of Natural Law and fixed right and wrong, applicable to all men at all times, has led in turn to most of the outstanding political thinking that has taken place since that time in the Western world. The idea that the ruler as well as the ruled is bound by a higher law has led to such concepts as the separation of powers into the legislative, executive, and judicial branches and has produced the concept of rule of law in government. If modern man believes that a suspect must be presumed innocent until proven guilty, or that all free men are equal before the law, or that the letter of the law must sometimes recognize motive and circumstance to be truly equitable, he should recognize that the source of such thinking is the Roman concept of Natural Law.

In the first century B.C., Cicero outlined the concept of Natural Law which he defined as "what a man of good taste and common sense would do." Other Romans had referred to the concept as "that which constitutes the natural, rational method for all people," or "that which is naturally fair and just." And it is here that the genius of Roman government begins to be understandable. It is a Roman idea that a fixed concept of Natural Law, a higher law, is *above* the laws of any community. The Greeks had granted that their citizens should be equal before the law, but it was the Romans who extended the rights of citizenship to all. A Greek had no legal rights outside his own city-state, but a Roman could appeal to a standard of law binding all men. In the days of the Roman Empire, Paul of Tarsus, a member of a minor religious sect known as the Christians, could stand before a Roman governor in the provinces and insist, "I am a Roman citizen." When he made an appeal to Caesar, he received the answer from the provincial governor that was the secret of Roman success in government, "Thou hast appealed unto Caesar; unto Caesar shalt thou go."

This capacity for good law and good government, consonant with a higher law, was the basis of the law and order, as well as the cultural and economic success, of Rome. In our own era, filled with war and the threat of war, it seems almost miraculous that there was a period of uninterrupted peace in the civilized world for well over two hundred years. The *Pax Romana* was indeed a great accomplishment.

In this era of peace and prosperity, the Romans pioneered in the development of the laws of property, the basis for the individual framework which is the precondition for lasting economic prosperity. The Romans consistently pursued a hands-off policy which left local affairs within the Empire to as large an extent as possible in the hands of the provinces concerned. Our own concept of dual citizenship, by which each of us in this country is at once a citizen of the United States and a citizen of his home state, is a direct offshoot of Roman government. This system of decentralization, coupled with a high concept of justice and implemented by a population whose watchword was integrity and self-restraint, produced an era with an immense volume of trade and a great prosperity. If the luxury of the period was equal to anything the world has seen since, there also was a solid and prosperous middle class. Roman currency was valid anywhere; such concepts as checks, letters of credit, banking, and many of the other tools of credit capitalism, were surprisingly well advanced. Quite literally the Empire was a paradise for businessmen. The world was the Roman businessman's oyster: "In foreign traffic, traders found their way to Denmark or up the old amber route from the Danube to the Baltic and across it to Sweden. Furs and slaves poured through the Brenner Pass into Italy. In the Near East Greek merchantmen worked their way to Somaliland and beyond and Roman traders pushed by land into Abyssinia."[24]

This, then, was the tremendous achievement of the Roman Empire. The stability and prosperity of the *Pax Romana* gathered and preserved the heritage of the ancient world and erected a civilization through which this heritage could pass to medieval and modern Europe.

THE DECLINE OF ROME

The Roman historian, Livy, saw clearly what had made for Roman success, and saw equally clearly that grave dangers were involved should the Romans ever depart from the virtues that had made them great. He spoke to the Romans of his time in an earnest attempt to convey what he saw so clearly:

> I hope my passion for Rome's past does not impair my judgment for I honestly believe that no country has ever been greater or purer than ours, or richer in good citizens and noble deed. None has ever been free for so many generations from the vices of avarice and luxury; nowhere has thrift and plain living for so long been held in esteem. Indeed, poverty with us went hand-in-hand with contentment. Of late years, wealth has made us greedy, and self-indulgence has brought us through every form of sensual excess, to be, if I may so put it, in love with death, both individual and collective.

> But the study of history is the best medicine for a sick mind; for in history you have a record of the infinite variety of human experience plainly set out for all to see; and in that record you can find for yourself and your country both examples and warnings: fine things to take as models, base things rotten through and through to avoid.

Livy was beginning to worry about the possibility that Rome was falling upon dark days. But such things are harder to see at the time they are happening than they are to see in historical perspective. As quoted earlier, Albert Jay Nock once mused, "Someday I should like to write an essay on the subject, 'How can one tell one is living in a dark age?'"

No doubt, distinguishing such things, at least distinguishing them in time, is a difficult task. Yet, such dark ages do occur. Arnold Toynbee lists some twenty-six civilizations in world history, sixteen of which are long-gone and nine of the remaining ten of which are dead or dying. In fact, the only one of these identifiable *prior* civilizations which he views as still being reasonably healthy is our own! Toynbee demonstrates that the collapse of these civilizations has been due to the inability of the people within those civilizations to respond to the challenges with which they were faced. In other words, civilizations seem to reach a point of darkness at which the individual citizens must decide whether to turn the lights back on or slip into a darkness in which no lights remain to be turned on. If Toynbee's analysis of history is accurate, there would seem to be a great deal of evidence to suggest that men never pay their moral electric bills in time, and only recognize the error of their ways after the service has been cut off and the power company has gone out of business. At that point, it is no longer difficult to tell that one is living in a dark age. Edward Gibbon, in his *Decline and Fall of the Roman Empire*, has expressed the opinion that if a man were called upon to pick the point in the history of the world when the condition of the human race was most happy and prosperous, that point would surely be between the first and second century A.D. Yet, as another historian describes it, ". . . in the next century the Roman Empire crumbled. There were civil wars between A.D. 180 and 285. Of twenty-seven Emperors or would-be Emperors, all but two met violent deaths. Meanwhile, the Persians raided to Antioch in the East, and in Europe the barbarians broke through the frontiers. Huge tracts of country were devastated. The middle class was squeezed out of existence. Farmers and laborers were transformed into serfs. When in A.D. 285 Diocletian pulled the Empire together again, there was but little left of the prosperity of the *Pax Romana.*"[24]

What had happened to the splendid society of law, order, and individual integrity?

> The loss of freedom under a dictatorship brought inevitable spiritual and political repercussions. The growth of a top-heavy bureaucracy and of a benevolent paternalism went unnoticed. Most of the inhabitants of the Empire did not care. The extension of Roman citizenship, the leveling influence of a world-wide trade and prosperity, and the excellent government of the provinces under the imperial administration, left them contented so long as they could make money. There was slavery, but slavery was an accepted fact. There was an idle and unemployed proletariat which had to be kept quiet by doses of "bread and games," but the Empire was an Eden for the banker, the capitalist, the ordinary businessman. Consequently, only a comparatively few cried warnings of the dangers to come. The first two centuries of our era were, in fact, as materialistic an age as any until the present . . . The world of the Roman Empire in the first two centuries is almost frighteningly similar to modern North America in its excesses and its wealth and, above all, in its devotion to materialistic success at the expense of the spiritual and the intellectual. Yet it retained a hard core of solid,

down-to-earth virtues, and a prosperous middle class. It was when that middle class was squeezed out of existence by high taxes, paternalistic legislation, and an ever-increasing bureaucratic control that the abyss between wealth and poverty was, at last, nakedly evident[24]

When the eighteenth-century historian Gibbon completed his *Decline and Fall of the Roman Empire*, he looked around the Western society of his time and expressed relief and satisfaction that no barbarians appeared ready to overrun civilization. Yet, today, we seem a good deal less assured about the state of health within our society, and a good deal more interested in answering the question, "Why did Rome fall?"

POLITICAL DISASTER

Why did Rome fall? To learn the sources of Rome's weakness, we must first learn the source of Rome's strength. Rome, like America, began as a small agrarian republic which placed a high premium upon integrity and citizenship. Rome, like America, grew tremendously in size and power until its influence reached over a vast area. Eventually the burden of government began to dwarf the simple republican machinery designed to bear it. At that point, the Caesars entered the picture and offered dictatorship and centralization as the solution to the problem.

Rome, like America, had never *really* intended to follow such a course. Each step from the simple republican virtues and the limited vision of power was taken with great hesitation. But some good reason always seemed to demand a further extension of Roman influence. The argument was always advanced that such extensions of power were necessary for self-defense. And who would complain if such a necessary step as self-defense brought with it wealth, power, and prestige? Besides, Rome felt an obligation to bring the "benefits of civilization" to those territories beyond the pale, just as America feels a great enthusiasm for bringing the benefits of "democracy" to all the under-developed regions of the earth.

Such a quest for safety, wealth, power, and prestige, especially when coupled with a sense of "mission," is heady business and hard to resist. Unfortunately, such adventures are also expensive. How were these expenses met?

Silver was the primary medium of exchange in the Roman Republic. The Roman *denarius* was originally worth about twenty cents and was over 90 per cent pure silver. But as the tremendous expenses of empire, coupled with the expenses of welfarism at home, placed increasing financial strain upon the Roman system, the Roman Senate took a fatal step and began to meet financial pressures through inflation. The *denarius* was time and again diluted with base metals, finally reaching the point at which it contained almost no silver and possessed a value of less than one-half cent. Rome, like America, assured its population that the coins were worth as much as ever, "since the value of the coins is not *really* in the silver anyway, but rests instead in the good faith and credit of the government issuing the currency."

Nevertheless, people worried about the *denarius* and what it was worth, and by 87 B.C., the Roman Senate was without resources. When fiscal responsibility was gone, the end of the republican form of government was destined soon to follow.

A government and a society suffering the effects of a severe inflation tend to disintegrate rapidly. The old republican virtues no longer contained their certainty for the Roman statesman and citizen. Some of the strongest figures of the age, including Cicero, warned of the dangers which lay ahead in the abandonment of integrity, insisting that in the ways of government as well as in the ways of personal life, a return to a standard of moral superiority and integrity was the only course which could save the Republic.

For a time, the Senate, despite its corruption, managed to represent the ancient and established order. Time and again, would-be dictators, attempting to make political capital out of the sad days on which the Republic had fallen, were stopped short of success by the Senate. But finally, the man on horseback could not be denied. Julius Caesar, supported by an army fresh from the exciting conquest of Gaul, and welcomed by the economically distressed masses to whom he promised relief, became dictator of Rome.

The constitution of Rome, like that of America, had developed in opposition to the idea of kingship, and centered around a system of checks and balances. In the late days of the Republic, the Romans felt that, at times, extraordinary powers had to be vested in a single man. (Such powers were only for a temporary emergency, of course, the Romans assured themselves.) A situation soon developed, however, in which one conspiracy after another grew up in an effort to control who should be the one man in whom these "temporary" dictatorial powers should reside. When two conspirators entered the field at the same time, civil war resulted. This endless round of conspiracies and civil wars, coupled with the disastrous inflation, made it clear that the Republic could not long survive. It was relief from this desperate situation that Julius Caesar promised. Caesar won the final civil war between his forces and those of Pompey, and went on to become Dictator, Pontifex Maximus, and Commander-in-Chief of the Army. The Roman word for military commander-in-chief was *imperator* . . . the source of our word "emperor."

Caesar's assumption of dictatorial power did not solve matters, however. He was assassinated by a group of conspirators, touching off another period of chaos. Finally, Octavius, Caesar's nephew, defeated the last remaining rival, Marc Antony. But Octavius was a smarter dictator than some of his predecessors. He restored the forms of the Republic! The Senate, the Consuls, and all the trappings of limited, representative government, were reinstated. The people were told that the best of the old system had returned, but would now be directed through the efforts of a man so wise, so well-intended, and so powerful, that Rome would once again be on the way to order and prosperity. Octavius was careful to govern through a number of offices. He was Consul (re-elected every year by an understood agreement), he was Governor of all the provinces, he was Imperator, and he also was given two new titles by the subservient Senate: Princeps, that is, "First Citizen of the Republic," and Augustus, that is, a combination of "His Majesty" and "His Holiness."

Romans had been given what they wanted. As one of the foremost students of antiquity has commented:

The result foreshadowed by the condition in Cicero's day came to pass: the citizen body could not cope with its own corruption; the frightful evils that followed had to be terminated; hence a dictator with all the responsibility and all power to regulate everything in the state. And the many brilliant and able men of the great Augustan age drew deep breaths of relief at seeing themselves freed from trouble and concern about public matters to devote themselves to their own business. They had been angrily impatient of the dishonesty and stupidity and inefficiency of the Republic's officials. They were sick to death of the wars and the mismanagement of home affairs, foreign affairs, and miscarriages of justice. That was ended now. A strong and sagacious man was Emperor, whose will was the only law that counted, and Romans rejoiced. What lay before their country in the future, the most irresponsible despotism the Western World had ever seen, they could not know; nor were they interested to build for the future. That kind of disinterested patriotism was dead in Rome and would not rise again except here and there in a few men, so few they never mattered at all.[25]

The all-powerful executive, whether he be called Caesar or given some other title, seems to arise in a framework of limited government when an overextension of the appetite for power breeds an internal and external situation with so many problems that men are willing to abdicate their responsibility to an all-powerful figure who promises much. The dictator gives the appearance of great achievement by the creation of new methods and solutions, thus completing the work of destroying the old methods and standards which have already become corrupted within that society. Octavius, now the Emperor Augustus, realized the value of propaganda and soon centralized and systematized all the means of influencing public opinion. It was carefully explained to the population how all would profit in the "new order" and how Rome would be "regenerated" in the process.

When the Republic thus became the Empire shortly before the time of Christ, the full effects of inflation and social decay were apparent everywhere. Rome was filled with unemployed mobs who had to be pacified at whatever cost. The new Emperor immediately put a quarter of a million Roman citizens on a dole of free corn, and promised the rest of the population that they could buy it below cost. Later, bread and bacon were added to the dole, to the tune of millions of pounds a year. Magnificent circuses, staged at public expense, were also provided to keep the welfare recipients properly entertained.

Yet, as we have seen, Augustus was always scrupulously careful to mask his performance behind a facade using the old names and traditions of Republican Rome. In the *Decline and Fall of the Roman Empire*, Gibbon describes how successful this technique proved to be:

> Augustus was sensible that mankind is governed by names; nor was he deceived in his expectation that the Senate and people would submit to slavery provided they were respectfully assured that they still enjoyed their ancient freedom.

Step by step, Caesar Augustus accomplished the gravitation of more and more power into fewer and fewer hands, always assuring the citizens that such power was to be exercised in the role of "watchdog of the people's interests."

As this despotism grew, another element further aggravated the situation. The territory of Egypt had never been annexed by the Republic, and only became a part of the personal dominion of the Emperor at the time of Augustus. The Roman Emperor thus stepped into the tradition of the pharaohs and found himself in charge of a society embodying the most total system of state socialism that the ancient world had known. This virus of total control was destined to prove especially harmful to Rome. Unlike the open economic life of Greece and Italy, the entire Egyptian economic organization was premised upon centralization and governmental control, including nationalization of all agricultural and industrial life. Nothing was left to the individual. Everything became the province of the state. It has been suggested that nowhere else in the history of mankind have so many and such total restrictions been applied to the concept of private property as in ancient Egypt. In the time of Augustus these ideas for the first time came in direct contact with the administration of Roman government. The Empire thus became increasingly socialized at home and imperialistic abroad. Thus Rome, like America, was governed in an increasingly centralized framework which leaned on radical elements and pressure groups at home to maintain power on the domestic front and become more and more aggressive abroad at the same time, since "national defense" served as the other prop of the regime. As one modern observer phrases it:

Thus evolves the deal: popular demands are satisfied, the poor and the proletariat are cared for by free grain and circuses; but the military budget is also approved, the foreign bases and allies are well supplied, the foreign potentates are flattered and kept in power, the legions and divisions splendidly equipped. The price is ever-climbing budgets, higher taxes, and built-in inflation.[26]

The successors of Augustus were faced with a situation in which they had become absolute master of the civilized world. These men had limitless power to indulge every wish, to allow nothing to stand in the way of any desire, to be "above" any individual, law, or religion in the entire world. The record of the Roman emperors then increasingly came to be the story of men made mad by such awful power. Their actions in office are living proof that, once coercion becomes the key to the operation of society, the lowest elements within that society will ultimately run the program, to the destruction of themselves and the rest of society. A more appropriate example could hardly be selected than the later emperors of the Roman Empire as a demonstration of what Friedrich Hayek has described in *The Road to Serfdom:* that is, "Why the Worst Get on Top" in a socialized, centralized framework.

It has been said that "an arch-dissembler was succeeded by a madman, and a fool by a monster"—Tiberius, Augustus' stepson, by Caligula, and Claudius by Nero. The excesses in which these men indulged defy description. The steady concentration of all power in the hands of one man continued. Soon, no criticism of the system was allowed. Tiberius, for example, made it a practice to seek out and punish all makers of literary allusions to himself, *real or supposed,* thus evidencing the tendency that all centralized regimes since then have made abundantly clear.

Nero's excesses finally provoked revolt, and a series of emperors came to the throne maintained by the stark, open power of the army. No longer could anyone continue to believe in even the polite fiction that the Republic still existed. Meanwhile, the Empire sunk lower and lower toward disaster. The key to power became "enrich the soldiers and scorn the rest." Rome became a complete military despotism. The legions made and unmade the emperors at their pleasure, while the civilized world was destroyed with civil war and barbarian invasions.

Late in the day for the Roman Empire, another dictator came on the scene promising "reform." We have a first-hand account by Lactantius of the civil service and secret staffs and heavy taxes of this "reformer," Diocletian:

> . . . the receivers of taxes began to be more in number than the payers, so that by reason of consumption of husbandmen's goods and by the excess of land taxes, the farms were left waste until the lands turned into forest . . . many presidents and sundry companies of officials lay heavy on every territory, and indeed almost on every city; there were many receivers besides, and secretaries and deputies of the prefect. All these very seldom had civil cases before them, only condemnations and continual confiscations and requisitions . . . of every kind of property.

When the government begins to play that large a role in the lives of its citizens, economic dislocations begin to occur. But when those dislocations occur, the centralizing, coercionist mentality always has the answer to the problem, *more coercion*. Listen again to Lactantius:

> . . . when by various evil deeds he caused a prodigious scarcity, he essayed by law to fix the prices of goods in the market. Then much blood was shed for trifling in faulty wares, and through fear nothing appeared in the market so that the scarcity was made much worse. Till after the law had ruined multitudes, it was of sheer necessity abolished.

Of course, when things aren't going altogether properly in the private sector, public works is another time-honored "remedy." Again, Lactantius discussing the reign of Diocletian:

> In addition to this, he had an unlimited taste for building, and levied of the provincials unlimited exactions for the wages of workmen and artifices, and the supplying of wagons and everything else that was wanted for the work in hand. There were public offices, there a circus, here a mint, there a factory of arms, here a palace for his wife, and there one for his daughter. On a sudden a large part of the city is turned out-of-doors: they all had to remove with wives and children, as if the city had been taken by enemies.

This, then, is the program: confiscatory taxation, vast numbers of government officials, seizures of private property, price fixing and the resultant scarcities induced by it, public works, and even, apparently, a bit of urban renewal.

The cost of the welfare programs, including public entertainment, became so high as to be almost totally insupportable. If the Roman dole, the Roman games, and the Roman excesses are not attractive to us, we might remember that such a fate awaits any society which comes to value material possessions over the achievements of mind and spirit.

As welfare costs mounted, the cost of the army continued to swell at an alarming rate as well. All these expenditures had ultimately to be recovered from the taxpayer, in one way or another. By the time Rome was so far gone economically, an adverse balance of trade had naturally also developed. Thus the Roman Empire, like the Roman Republic before it, was forced to turn to inflation to support its constant excesses. The Roman *denarius* went on another sleighride. At the time of Augustus, the *denarius* had a value of approximately twenty cents. It had fallen to ten per cent of its former value by the time of Diocletian. It is sobering to recall, looking about us, that Rome was not the only nation in the history of the world which has suffered from inflation and gold drain and debased currency and the crushing burden of a rising number of welfare recipients. But such facts are difficult to see when one is living through such a period. (Or perhaps it is just that they are too unpleasant to see.) The Romans, for example, did not seem to grasp the fact that inflation and rising taxation were driving the middle class to the wall. The comforts of the highly materialistic age of latter-day Rome thus served to disguise the fact that the society was living on borrowed time.

Under the pressures of welfare and war, taxation and inflation led to such a disastrous rise in prices and loss of economic stability that the normal means of financing were no longer adequate. Forced levies of men and material thus came to be the rule, quite literally making the Romans a slave population. Once the devaluation had deprived the *denarius* of ninety-eight per cent of its original value, Diocletian issued an edict fixing maximum prices for all wages and goods. As laws, directives, edicts and more and more coercion proved steadily less successful in remedying the situation, the coercionists, as always, turned to the one solution they seem to have for all problems: *more coercion.* As taxation and inflation stripped the middle classes to the point where they were no longer able to pay, "voluntary loans" were exacted from any citizen who had been able to escape with any remaining holdings. Local municipalities fell into economic disaster and representatives of the Emperor were put in direct charge as the cities lost their independence. As one historian has remarked, "The people did not seem to mind. As often happens today, they were quite willing to resign their control of affairs and to let the government take care of them . . . Naturally too, as benevolent paternalism and bureaucracy took over, personal freedom tended to disappear. By the third century, to quote the historian, Trevor, 'the relentless system of taxation, requisition, and compulsory labor was administered by an army of military bureaucrats . . . Everywhere . . . were the ubiquitous personal agents of the emperors to spy out any remotest case of attempted strikes for evasion of taxes . . .' "[24]

Death became the penalty for violation of the endless edicts and laws. Yet prices continued to rise and taxes became so uncollectible that the local senatorial classes throughout Italy, the last representatives of the middle-class Roman world, were now given the responsibility of raising the taxes in their area. If they failed to collect from their fellow citizens, they were expected to make up the difference from their own holdings. When these unwilling taxpayers attempted to enlist in the army or move away to avoid this situation, they were returned to their position by force. Thus the Roman citizen was no longer able to move about freely or to dispose of his own property. Eventually the Roman middle class, the backbone of Roman political and economic prosperity, ceased to exist.

A modern historian has described the situation: "The same principle of regimentation was imposed on farmers and on free labor. Farmers were tied to the soil, and, by law, the son of a farmer had to become a farmer. Similarly the son of a baker or of a metal worker or of a dock worker, each had to follow the profession of his father. Furthermore, all artisans, traders, ship owners, and the like had to furnish each year to their city and to the state a specified number of their products at a price fixed by the state.

"There was no escape from this relentless regimentation, for regimentation was the end-result of the abdication of political freedom and of the pursuit of materialism. The welfare state had become a despotism."[24]

SOCIAL DISASTER

Any discussion of Roman decline that fails to include the question of morality neglects half of the picture. Closely inter-related with the political and economic collapse of Rome was the moral disaster which occurred in the life of the individual Roman citizen.

Polybius, the historian of the early Roman Republic, describes the people and government of Rome as simple and hardy, and thoroughly devoted to patriotism for their nation and integrity for themselves. Yet, less than a hundred years later, as the Republic fell on evil days, we find that a great change had begun to take place with the individual Roman citizen as well. Fifty years before the time of Caesar, a wealthy foreign prince visited Rome, consummated his business, and as he left described the Eternal City as "The city in which everything is for sale." It is this "city in which everything is for sale" that was the Rome of Cicero's time, the Rome in which he and others like him vainly urged the population to return to the simple virtues and integrity of an earlier day. As we have seen in following the political history of Rome, these warnings were not heeded, and the Republic soon came to an end.

It should not surprise us that Cicero was unsuccessful, human nature being what it is. Edith Hamilton describes the scene in Rome:

> Wealth was pouring into the city from conquered countries; easy money had become possible for a great many and the ideal for most. To have three able men take the responsibility of looking after Rome's wide interest, saved a vast deal of trouble for others. The old Republic had exacted a great deal from her citizens and left them poor. Now people wanted politics at a profit; they were out for a share in the riches they saw around them.

> Politics have seldom offered a better field for that purpose than they did then. Rome had in truth become the city where everything was for sale. Cicero's letters make it possible to see the inwardness of the political situation clearly as in hardly any other period in history. Bribery here, there, and everywhere, he writes over and over again, not an official exempt, not even the highest. Politics have

become a money-making business; votes are bought and sold, so are judges.[25]

As the wealth of the Near East flooded into Italy, the old Roman character began to dissolve. Business was good at the time, so why worry? Self-indulgence thus became the rule.

Meanwhile, the great flood of wealth was changing Rome to a money economy. It thus became more profitable for the proprietors of the *latifundia* to drive their free tenants from the land and buy up the land of the independent yeoman-farmers. The vast estates thus created could then be operated with slave labor. Because of this the city of Rome became a city of landless men, cut off from the means of their sustenance and their dignity. Rome had become a haven for speculators, better suited to engaging in the slave and corn trade than in producing anything themselves.

The now-landless Roman member of the middle class, the man who had served as the backbone of the Roman legions and of the Roman political framework, had become a member of a mob which could be manipulated one way and another by men on horseback as they conspired to seize political power. The conspiracies, civil wars, slave wars, and political and financial corruption that resulted spelled the end of the Roman Republic.

> . . . it was literally Rome that killed Rome. The great cosmopolitan city of gold and marble, the successor of Alexandria and Antioch, had nothing in common with the old capital of the rural Latin state. It served no social function, it was an end in itself, and its population drawn from every nation under heaven existed mainly to draw their government doles, and to attend the free spectacles with which the government provided them. It was a vast useless burden on the back of the Empire which broke at last under the increasing strain.[13]

Once a civilization is no longer understood by the people and citizens who are to support it, it cannot long be maintained. If integrity and virtue and citizenship and patriotism and responsibility and self-restraint no longer have meaning to the individual citizen, then such values, and the society founded upon them, cannot long endure.

The Stoic impulse, lying at the heart of the old Roman character, was essentially religious in nature, in consonance with a higher law. When Rome became the incarnation of all that was anti-spiritual, it lost the vitality of its moral life and became increasingly evil. For proof of this, we might well consider the rise of asceticism that occurred at what appeared to be the very height of Roman success. An increasing number of monks and ascetics came to believe that only through a total departure from the corrupt society of Rome could they retain their individual spirituality. These ascetics seemed to sense that Rome had become so rich in culture and material prosperity that society was no longer able to restrain a feverish struggle for the gratification of any appetite. As we have seen, government paternalism, bureaucracy, inflation, the destruction of the middle class, and the brutal spectacle of the Roman amphitheater were pointing the way toward a political decline which actually had its origins in the moral realm. Increasingly Rome's political history tended to become that of a gang of criminals quarreling over how the loot should be divided. Though the Roman Empire was to last for several hundred years more, the old Roman character had departed.

What Rome wanted was not restraint, but spectacle. Satisfaction for the mind or the spirit was now forced to give way before satisfaction of endless physical appetite. Roman society gloried in size and wealth and power. The individual Roman citizen gloried in an abundance of material things. "Enrich yourselves" became the order of the day, and never before in history had such opportunities for material enrichment been present. Romans now found it easier to let slaves do the work; and, as this slavery-oriented society moved more and more slowly, desperate attempts to stop the economic decline were made by the emperors, as they bound free Romans in their economic and social positions. Thus a new serfdom was created which combined with the increasing use of slavery within the Roman world to produce a more and more totally subject population.

In such circumstances the old Roman character became vile and degenerate. As society became more brilliant, it also became more corrupt. Edith Hamilton has described the bitter comments of the satirist, Juvenal, upon the Roman society of his time:

It is a nightmare city where men must "dread poison when wine sparkles in a golden cup," and wives "learned in the arch-poisoner's arts carry to burial their husband's blackened corpses," and every day in the year you meet a man who "has given aconite to a half-dozen relatives." Where "no one can sleep for thinking of a money-loving daughter-in-law seduced, of brides that have lost their virtue, of adulterers not out of their teens, where "every street is thronged with gloomy-faced debauchees," and banquets celebrate unnatural and incestuous vice; where spies abound "whose gentle whisper cuts men's throats"; where no woman is decent and no man to be trusted and all wealth dishonestly got and all position attained by abominable means: "The way to be somebody today is to dare some crime."[25]

Surely the "old Roman character" which had built Rome was by then gone forever.

WHAT HAPPENED TO ROME?

If Roman law and government were indeed one of the great contributions to the Western world, then why and how did such a highly successful system fail? A great variety of reasons have been advanced to explain the collapse of Rome. At times the fall of Rome has been alleged to have been due to a "failure of nerve" or an "excessive prosperity." Yet, such psychological arguments, even if true, beg the question, since they tell us nothing of why the Romans lost their nerve.

Others have suggested that the decline of Rome was primarily economic in its origin. They point to the fact that the small yeoman-farmer class of Roman society disappeared as the *latifundia* (absentee-owner slave plantations) grew. It is also true that a crushing taxation and runaway inflation destroyed the productive Roman middle class. Roman society was also plagued with the fantastic inefficiency and corruption of a gigantic bureaucracy. Thus the endless round of big government, bureaucracy, taxation, arbitrary governmental decision, interference in private lives, and destruction of the small operator, produced the situation in which the Roman world no longer enjoyed economic health. Agriculture and trade were drawing to a standstill. Yet, throughout Roman history, economic crises had been overcome before, so the economic argument, like the psychological, still fails to explain what caused the decline, even though it demonstrates that decline in action.

Some observers argue that the decline of Rome was primarily

political in its origins. It is true that ultimately political authority did become totally corrupt and inefficient in Rome. Crises, when they occurred, were no longer handled with that highly touted Roman "practicality." The situation in Rome repeatedly degenerated into anarchy, for which the Romans now only had one answer: despotism. Even this despotism was so corrupt and so inept that it soon degenerated again into anarchy. Roman skill in goverment had long been something of a speciality. Rome had survived numerous other political crises; why was she unable to survive this time? Again with political affairs, we find the troubles of Rome to be more a symptom of the Roman decline than its cause.

Others, among them the historian Edward Gibbon, blame at least a portion of the collapse of Rome upon the rise of a new religion, Christianity. They point to the largely negative attitude that the early Church adopted toward pagan learning, insisting that such attitudes were divisive of Roman society. It is true that Christianity was at least potentially divisive to a pagan state which practiced emperor worship. The Christians obviously could not participate in such ceremonies and therefore could not be "good citizens" by the Roman definition of the word. Yet the Roman emperors eventually converted the Empire to Christianity. Since other states have been prosperous under Christianity, why not Rome? Further, wasn't it the particular Roman genius to be able to assimilate numerous sub-cultures and make them a thriving part of a prosperous empire? If Rome failed to do this with Christianity, does not that suggest that Rome had lost its vitality, rather than that Christianity in itself was necessarily an enemy of the state? Here again we find more symptoms of Roman illness, evidences that Rome had lost its vitality and powers of assimilation and recuperation. We must look further still to identify the disease which produced those symptoms.

It is more accurate to view Roman civilization as an entity, separating cause from effect and symptom from illness. If all of the psychological, economic, political, and religious failures of Rome discussed above were truly only symptoms, what was the disease which brought on Roman decline? The basic cause for Roman collapse was moral and ethical, since in the last analysis all political and economic problems are of a moral nature. The core of the civilized world rests in the moral and ethical values held by its citizens. Roman leadership and Roman citizenship had long espoused standards of family honor, self-reliance, responsibility, and patriotism. These standards and the sturdy middle-class, yeoman-farmer citizen were the elements upon which Rome's military and political strength had been built, in the Roman legions and in the Roman concept of citizenship. Yet prosperity and excess power for Rome's leaders destroyed this responsibility and courage, smothering it beneath an endlessly self-perpetuating bureaucracy. These sturdy yeoman-farmers, the middle-class individuals, the self-reliant, responsible, patriotic backbone of the Roman state, had been destroyed through absentee land ownership, big government, paternalism, and moral decline. As the power of that middle class vanished, the moral values that had built Rome also vanished. Rome was then headed for decline. The Roman family, which had served as the matrix for the Roman virtues, declined to the point of nonexistence. Conditions of life in the Roman Empire came to favor a man without a family who could better devote his entire energies to the duties and pleasures of public life.

> Late marriages and small families became the rule and men satisfied their sexual instincts by homosexuality or by relations with slaves and prostitutes . . . The same factors were equally powerful in the society of the Empire, where the citizen-class even in the provinces was extraordinarily sterile and was recruited not by natural increase, but by the constant introduction of alien elements, above all from the servile class. Thus the ancient world lost its roots alike in the family and in the land and became prematurely withered.[13]

How did these basic Roman qualities and values change as Roman society grew older? The leaders of society began to falter and to find power and prosperity more engaging. Thus Roman leadership ceased to express the wishes of the people and ceased to reflect personal responsibility, causing the whole structure to decline. Such a collapse in leadership and values is often not clear to the people who are living through it:

> . . . other civilizations have neglected the roots in their life in a premature concentration on power or wealth, so that their tempo-

rary conquest of the world is paid for by the degeneration and perhaps the destruction of their own social organs. The most striking instance of this morbid and catastrophic decline—and that which most closely resembles our own condition—is that of ancient Rome . . . Here there was no question of senescence. Society came near to dissolution while at the very height of its cultural activity, when its human types were more vigorous than ever before. The danger to civilization came not from the decline of vitality, but from a sudden change of conditions—a material revolution, which broke down the organic constitution of the society.[13]

Roman leadership should not be blamed entirely for the decline. The Roman body politic was also declining rapidly. The mass of Romans had sunk into a coarse lethargy, and devoted themselves only to seeking escape in sensuous and material pursuits that only aggravated the condition. As economic freedom died out for the small farmer, as the rolls of the unemployed grew, as initiative for the common man disappeared, and as bigness in government, bigness in land ownership, and bigness in all Roman affairs were killing the citizen's will and opportunity to handle his own affairs, the average Roman became a commoner without employment, a man without a stake in the system, a creature without dignity.

Rome was being barbarized from within through the decline of its values and standards. Yet this "internal barbarization" was hastened by an external barbarization as well. Long surrounded by barbarian hordes, Rome had admitted large numbers of these into the Empire over the centuries. While many were of good stock, most were of a much lower cultural level. Rome proved unable to assimilate such a large number of these people, thus producing a cultural indigestion. As the Roman character declined, more and more of these barbarians were used to replace gaps in the Roman legions, gaps which the Roman citizens themselves no longer were willing to fill. Thus, the quality of Roman legions tended to decline steadily, as did the intelligence and discipline that had made those legions great.

Rome was thus assaulted by the effect of the half-civilized man on society. She was barbarized by the half-civilized men pouring over her borders even while she was barbarized from within by the destruction of her own character. Caught in a flood of barbarians both within and without, Rome sunk to destruction.

This decline took time. Just as Rome had not been built in a day, neither would she decline in a day. But as the sum of all these problems mounted higher and higher, the Roman leader and the Roman citizen were progressively less able to meet problems which had been met and successfully overcome many times before. Rome has much to teach the world if we will but listen: "He who knows no history is doomed to repeat it."

A LESSON FOR MODERN MAN

Whether speaking of Rome, or of the United States of America, it does little good to talk about the "good old days." But it might pay to recall that Rome before her decline, like America, had a number of definite rules, governing property, manners, and, above all, individual conduct. Rome had definite rules describing and prohibiting dishonor, misconduct, and any act involving loss of integrity. Of course, Rome or any other society, even at its best, never perfectly obeyed all these rules, yet the rules were acknowledged and understood, and their violation brought punishment.

Pondering the American scene, John Steinbeck tells a story:

> Once Adlai Stevenson, speaking of a politician of particularly rancid practices, said, "If he were a bad man, I wouldn't be so afraid of him. But this man has no principles. He doesn't know the difference." Could this be our difficulty, that gradually we are losing our ability to tell the difference? The rules fall away in chunks, and in the vacant place we have a generality: "It's all right because everybody does it." This is balanced with another cry of cowardice. In the face of inequity, dishonesty in government, or downright plundering, the word is, "Go fight City Hall!" The implication is, of course, that you can't win. And yet in other times we did fight City Hall and often we won . . . Over the millennia most of us have learned to obey the rules or suffer punishment for breaking them. But most important even the rule-breaker knew he was wrong and the other right; the rules were understood and accepted by everyone. At intervals in our history, through unperceived changes usually economic, the rules and the enforcing agents have come a cropper. Inevitably the result has been a wild and terrible self-destructive binge, a drunken horror of the spirit giving rise to the unspeakable antics of crazy children. And this dark mass-mania has continued until rules were reapplied, rewritten, or re-enforced.[27]

The strong points of particular cultures are far more than dead ends. The "old Roman character" was the means by which the Romans approached and apprehended a system of right and wrong larger than their own understanding and power. A way of life, when it is genuinely successful, is a way of serving God. If it is anything else, ultimately it becomes a way of death. This is what happened in Rome. We all know the end of the story. "Caesar reaches for absolute power, and absolute power corrupts Caesar first, the public and its morality next. Priests or television screens divinize his Image. Eager, famished enemies appear at the gate ..."[26]

Thus ended another important lesson which Western civilization has to teach us.

6

Early Christianity and
St. Augustine

❧❧❧❧❧❧❧❧❧❧❧❧❧❧❧❧❧❧❧❧❧❧❧❧❧❧❧❧❧❧❧❧❧

ORIGINS OF CHRISTIANITY

THE MORAL CHAOS OF LATTER-DAY ROME WAS WELL REFLECTED
in the satires of Juvenal, in which he described the bored, sex-
crazy, selfish city of his times. To those unable longer to tolerate
their society, Juvenal spun dreams offering excape into a golden
Roman past. But while Juvenal could offer only escape into the
past, a new agency offered far more: Christianity promised a new
way of life.

In any society, when the old forms have lost their religious
vitality and have become purely social institutions, the spiritual
elements always present within society inevitably turn from the
old forms to some new source of spiritual values offering redemption. The decline and social collapse of the later Roman Empire
afforded such a moment, when people in their insecurity turned
more to philosophy and religious activity as a source of salvation.
At that time, Christianity was ready with a largely developed
doctrinal and institutional framework, thus meeting the needs of
Rome.

Christianity had been born in another time of crisis several
centuries earlier. The civil wars leading to the establishment of the

Roman Empire had been responsible for the death of a large number of Jewish young men. Rebellion against this state of affairs had produced widespread crucifixions. At such a troubled time in the middle eastern portion of the Roman Empire, Caesar Augustus issued his famous decree that a census should be taken of the entire Roman world as the basis for new taxation. It was during that census that Joseph and Mary journeyed to Bethlehem. The Biblical story tells us little of the events of the next thirty years. But a noted scholar of Christianity, Roland Bainton, writing in his *Early Christianity*, tells us the end of the tale:

> We know only that he set His face to go up to Jerusalem. That there He drove the money-changers from the Temple. He did not then proceed to challenge the Romans by organizing an insurrection. He simply sat in the Temple and taught, witnessing to God's truth. That was His role. All else was committed to the hands of God. The opposition quickly consolidated. The high priest could not tolerate His interference with racketeering in the Temple courts. The Zealots could not forgive a leader who would only teach and not fight. The Pharisees considered Him an apostate because in their eyes He broke the law. But none of these considerations would condemn Him with the Romans who alone had the power to inflict His execution. They would act only if He were a political menace. The charge must therefore center on His Messianic pretensions; and He who said, "Resist not evil" was crucified through the fear that He was the focus of a rebellion.

The infinitely more important portion of the story of Christ is not, of course, the story of the political events leading to His crucifixion, but is instead the religious and ethical impact of His life, teachings, and death. As the Old Testament was the story of the Hebrews, including the ethical teachings of the Ten Commandments, the story of God's creation of earth, and the promise of a Messiah, the New Testament is a description of the arrival of the Messiah, the promise of salvation which He brought, and the teachings of the Son of God, incorporated in the same ethical framework which permeates the Bible as a whole. In this way, many of the principal teachings of Judaism were to become those of Christianity. Both espoused a faith in a single, personal God and both demanded employment of man's life on earth in pursuit of the Divine Will. Thus the promise of the Old Testament had been fulfilled in the New.

After the death of Christ, the Church began, slowly at first, to develop power and organization from its humble beginnings. St. Paul of Tarsus was the prime mover in this effort. He and others spread Christianity until it became, despite all the persecutions leveled against it, the dominant religion of the Roman Empire, thus laying the basis for the Christian Europe of the Middle Ages, where the Church dominated society and thought for centuries to come. In the first years of Christianity, freedom was enjoyed by the Christians, less because it was formally granted than because Christianity was not distinguished from Judaism either by the Roman government or by the people themselves. Early conversions were almost exclusively from the Jewish population. The New Testament book of Acts tells us that the Church grew rapidly from 500 to 5,000 members. To the bulk of the Jewish population, the growth of this new Church was unpalatable, and Christian leaders were soon driven from Jerusalem to Samaria and Syria. It was decided that in the future the Gospel was to be preached to Gentiles as well as Jews. While the New Testament is primarily an account of the teachings, death, and resurrection of Christ, it also is a record of the efforts and tribulations of the early missionaries of the new Christian faith. Paul, himself, never knew Christ. In fact, while still an Orthodox Jew, Saul of Tarsus had participated in persecution of the original small group of Jewish Christians. The story of the change of heart which Paul experienced on the road to Damascus remains a classic instance of one means whereby Christ has called those who are destined to do His work. Paul was by birth a citizen of Rome. He spoke more than one language, but relied primarily upon Greek in his epistles. As a former Jew, Paul always made his attempt at conversion first through the synagogues, though when rejected he continued his work among the Gentiles. Thus, Christianity became increasingly a non-Jewish religion.

As an administrator, Paul was extremely effective. He maintained tight control over the small groups scattered throughout the Roman world. Making first contact on the basis of his great eloquence and strong personal appeal, he maintained contact with his groups of converts through a series of letters addressed to those congregations. These are the epistles of the New Testament. At the same time, Paul was more than an administrator. He was an effective theologian who directed his efforts to universalizing the new Church in the idiom of the Gentiles. He was the originator of the Christian doctrine of "Justification by Faith," that is, faith in the idea that Christ died to atone for the sins of mankind, and set forth the idea that Christ was literally the Son of God.

Perhaps Paul's greatest contribution to the spread of Christianity was his ability to bridge the gap between the original Jewish concepts of the Church and a broader Christian universalism. The material with which Paul built this bridge was largely composed of Greek philosophy, and he was particularly familiar with Greek philosophic and religious ideas. He was at once the practical man and the mystic, desiring to free men from worldly entanglements and yet recognizing that men must live in a real world, pursuing "Faith, Hope, and Charity." As a member of that real world, Paul performed with great missionary zeal. He spent his life teaching and preaching, constantly on the move to cover more territory, and writing to areas where he could not go. He was repeatedly imprisoned, persecuted, and mobbed almost to death. In Jerusalem the high priest of the Jews charged him with being "a pestilent fellow, a mover of sedition among all the Jews throughout the world; a ringleader of the sect of the Nazarenes, who hath also gone about to profane the Temple." Paul might never have survived these accusations and could easily have been killed at the time, but since he was a Roman citizen, he appealed for a trial in Rome. Finally, after shipwreck and imprisonment, he was tried and executed in the early sixties of the Christian era.

Others met the same fate. Stephen, perhaps the first Christian martyr, was stoned to death in Jerusalem. Such persecution seemed only to drive the Apostles on to greater activity. Some were administrators, some were orators, some, like John, were theologians, deeply withdrawn from the world. Together they spread the doctrines of Christianity far and wide.

The institutional organization of the Church closely paralleled the political organization of the Roman Empire. A system of hierarchy quickly developed, producing a chain of authority running all the way up to the bishop, a word deriving from the Greek word, *episcopos*, meaning "overseer."[33] If the early Church profited from copying the organizational methods of the Roman

Empire in its breakdown of geography and personnel, it also profited from the Roman idea of tolerance. In the Roman world, local religion was viewed as local custom. Persecution by the central government began only after the Christians were suspected of disloyalty. Thus the early Church had to face persecution only within the Jewish community. Later, however, the idea of Christian disloyalty developed because the observance of the Roman state religion was regarded as a part of Roman citizenship. While these duties of state religion were not rigidly enforced, the Christians refused to pay any attention to them at all, ultimately forcing the Roman authorities either to persecute the Christians or abandon all civil order. Yet intolerance was never the problem. The great tolerance exhibited by the Roman Empire in the first two hundred years of Christianity played a major part in the religion's development and expansion.

Christianity seemed to be destined to grow under any circumstances. Just as it prospered in the relative tolerance of the first two hundred years of its existence, it seemed to prosper even more in the face of the persecution which was finally leveled against it. In fact, the idea of Christian martyrdom spread the faith ever wider within the Empire.

The network of individual cells or churches which composed the early Christian organization survived internal and external crises of all sorts. Another reason for Christian success might well have been that the nature of the Roman world itself also aided Christianity and its spread, especially since ancient civilization tended to be concentrated in cities. Just as Roman civilization had spread from city to city throughout the civilized world, so did Christianity. The internal unity of the Roman Empire overcame barriers of race or nationality just as it removed barriers to travel. This internal communication, transportation, and tolerance opened the door to Christian universality.

Although primitive Christianity developed among the poor, it quickly spread to the highest levels of the Roman intellectual community. The outstanding Christian writers and thinkers were the product of Greco-Roman civilization, and the very means of thought and expression which the Christian leadership exercised stemmed from that civilization. The Church came finally to achieve great influence within the Empire. Yet in much of its intellectual content and in much of its organizational growth, the debt of Christianity to Greco-Roman civilization was large. The ties of the ancient, pagan world and the Christian world remained closer than we sometimes realize.

THE VICTORY OF CHRISTIANITY

Christianity spread to the intellectual community because it offered elements available in no other philosophy. The members of the contemporary Greek intellectual community wished, however, to base their new faith on reason in an effort to make a rational whole of the new Christian teachings. Thus the fourth and fifth centuries after the death of Christ saw the crystallization of the creed in an attempt to reduce the doctrines to a coherent system. Such an attempt was necessary because no earlier formulation had taken place at the time of Jesus or immediately after his death. Jesus had not erected a system of philosophy but had issued a set of principles. These principles exercised a tremendous influence, but tended to stand as a series of separate pronouncements. Besides, the meaning of "Man must be born again" or "The meek shall inherit the earth" is not self-evident to all men. Thus, in a very real sense, the great rash of heresies which troubled Christianity in the third century after the death of Christ marked the doctrinal coming-of-age within the Christian Church. Such heresies were natural while questions remained concerning definitions of right and wrong and of the ways of God to man. Yet these heresies could not be allowed to continue, since the basic organizational goal of Christianity was the development of unity.

The formulation of Church doctrine was accomplished by three separate agencies: The pronouncements of the "Church Fathers," the positions adopted by the Church Councils, and the teachings of the head of the Church. Based upon the Old and the New Testament, the doctrinal decisions emanating from these sources became an integral part of Christian doctrine.

As the early missionary work of the Apostles grew to a close, the age of the Fathers, sometimes known as the Patristic Age, carried on the work. Most of the best known Church Fathers were

Roman, and, without exception, all were closely connected with classical learning and were especially close to Greek thought.

The leadership of the Church Fathers often took the form of offering protection to the interests of the common man in Roman society. Increasingly the bishops of the Church, not the magistrates of the empire, came to exercise a role of leadership in society. Often popular acclaim forced the role of bishop upon outstanding men in the community. The Bishop of Milan, St. Ambrose, was not yet a baptized Christian at the time he assumed the role of a Church Father. The correspondence of the Church Fathers and bishops of the early Church show them acting as arbiters of official disputes while guarding the people in the problems faced in their everyday lives. While offering resistance to any official tyranny from the state, these men increasingly became the prime movers in the alleviation of distress, providing schools, orphanages, and charity activity of all kinds.

Most of these early Church Fathers were not particularly original thinkers. For their theology, they were heavily dependent on the Greeks. And yet, even while they were heirs of the older Western tradition, they also displayed a tremendous moral strength and discipline which gave new purpose to that older tradition. In their writings, these Church Fathers came to be key figures in the exposition of Christian doctrine, and were usually venerated as saints and martyrs.

Prominent among the Church Fathers was St. Ambrose, the Bishop of Milan, who lived from A.D. 340 to 397. Preaching in a time of rapid social decay, he warned men that their troubles stemmed from sin so great that only the Grace of Heaven could save them from disaster. Another Church Father, St. Jerome, became the leader of a protest movement against the secular world. Leaving Rome, he spent the remainder of his days in a monastery near Bethlehem. Devoting his life to study and writing, he not only helped introduce the monastic concept, but also provided the first Latin translation of the Bible, the *Vulgate*. These men, and many others like them, most notably St. Augustine, provided a large measure of the leadership for the early Church. But neither the translation of the Scriptures nor the positions taken by the early Church Fathers, provided in themselves a suffi-

cient doctrinal source. For this reason a number of Church Councils, meetings of outstanding Christians, were called to settle ques-
tionable points. Here again the Church attempts at unity were
patterned after the goal of unity achieved in the ancient Roman
world. By the time the Emperor Constantine had called the Council of Nicaea in A.D. 325, Christianity had arrived as the dominant
force of the Greco-Roman world. The future of Christianity was
assured as the religion of the Western world.[34] The total body of
doctrine developed from these sources laid the basis for the canon
law of the Church which was to remain dominant throughout the
Middle Ages.

MONASTICISM

Monasticism is one area of early Christian thought in which
the life of the spirit was especially highly valued, and tells us a
great deal about the world view of the coming Middle Ages.

The Christian movement had initially been a revolt against
the prevailing values of the world. To become a Christian was to
renounce worldliness. It is just such a renunciation of worldliness,
often even of life itself, that the early missionaries and martyrs
achieved. But, like most movements that prosper over an extended
period of time, Christianity seemed to lose much of this fierce
dedication. While it had been dangerous to join the early Church,
several centuries later it had become "the thing to do." If faith had
been the early basis of Christianity, it had now become corrupted
through a strong emphasis upon the luxuries of this world. Yet
even during this long period of secularization, the Church's sense
of spiritual mission had not failed. At the very moment when the
basis was being laid for the great temporal power and worldly
achievement of the Christian Church, a conscious and determined
effort was being made to return to the original Christian other-
worldliness. Monasticism, the withdrawal from the world in pursuit of a solitary life, provided the sanctuary and privacy which
many felt necessary for their communion with God. More and
more devout Christians were turning from the corruptions of classical pagan culture, and from the urban framework of the Roman
Empire, to pursue an ascetic ideal of Christian piety.

In monasticism, as in so many other aspects of Western culture, much of the organization and sanity present in the idea and its application came from the pre-eminent practicality which distinguished the Romans. St. Benedict (A.D. 480-543) was a Roman noble who turned from the world to found the most famous monastery in the history of the world, Monte Cassino. The order which he founded, the Benedictines, insisted upon strict vows of poverty, chastity, and obedience. Yet they did not turn from the world, insisting upon labor, the duty of reading, and the collection and preservation of all available books and manuscripts. Thus the monasteries became at once spiritual and cultural centers, preserving the heritage of classical antiquity through the dark days of Roman decline and barbarian invasion that lay ahead. These monasteries, devoted to God, were a typical medieval agency which tell us a great deal about medieval Christian man, a man who worked and lived in the world even while subordinated to God and the Christian Church.

THE PRESERVATION OF CULTURE

All too many of us today still tend to view the "Middle Ages" as a thousand-year period of decline separating the two great eras of success, the ancient world and the modern world. We usually refer to the first five hundred years of that period, roughly the time from A.D. 500 to 1000 as "the Dark Ages." Modern man, in his tremendous capacity for self-congratulation, is thus able to dismiss this entire era of human history as little more than a blot on the record. As a matter of fact, there can be no such neat separation of periods. There is no instant at which the Roman Empire declines and the Dark Ages begin. Nothing makes this modern view appear more ridiculous than the realization that the Empire left behind it a great inheritor and preserver, the Christian Church. Through that agency, more than any other, the glowing coals of ancient civilization were kept alive.

Those who have witnessed the tragedies and barbarities of our "enlightened" twentieth century should no longer conceal from themselves the paper-thin nature of the barrier that separates civilization from barbarism. We cannot delude ourselves that such

brutalities can occur only in some long-past stage in our development. In fact, such terror awaits any society which loses touch
with its own controlling moral authority. Viewed in this light, the
last stages of the Roman Empire should acquire a new significance
for us. As the Romans struggled desperately to maintain their
civilization against the constant assault of war and barbarian invasion, they were fighting a losing battle. All appeared lost. And yet,
such was not to be the case. The reason? The Christian Church.
In the bishops' houses and the schools, in the charitable activities
of the Church, and especially in the monasteries, the best of the
ancient world was destined to live on.

At first, ancient civilization seemed so disintegrated and so
destroyed, so completely at the mercy of the barbarian horde, that
the qualities of mind and understanding which had characterized
the ancient world could not possibly survive. But what the Roman
state could no longer do, what Greek philosophy could not accom-
plish, religion achieved. The Germanic hordes sensed a grandeur
and power in the preaching of the Gospel which laid hold of their
deepest feelings.

In the virtual absence of organized government, the Church
stepped in not only to convert the barbarians to Christianity, but
in the process to educate and civilize them as well. Thus Christianity at once preserved cultural life and created new spiritual life.

> In that age, religion was the only power that remained unaffected
> by the collapse of civilization, by the loss of faith in social institu-
> tions and cultural traditions, and by the loss of hope in life. Wher-
> ever genuine religion exists it must always possess this quality,
> since it is of the essence of religion to bring man into relation with
> transcendent and eternal realities. Therefore it is natural that the
> Dark Ages of history —the hour of human failure and impotence
> —should also be the hour when the power of eternity is manifes-
> ted.[28]

It is this situation which Arnold Toynbee described when he suggested that the fall of the Roman Empire could best be viewed as
the emergence of a religious community from the wreckage of a
totally politicalized and legalized civilization. The collapse of the
Roman political organization had left a void which the barbarians
themselves could not fill in their attempt to continue some form

of orderly existence. Thus the Church was not only the spiritual guide for the barbarians, but was the teacher and law-giver as well. It was through the Church Fathers and the spiritual community of Christendom that a common Western culture was achieved. With the advantage of historical perspective, the success of the civilizing mission of the Christian Church can be readily seen. But at the time, the despair and the sense of impotence produced by the collapse of civilization could only have been overcome, as it was overcome, by men of tremendous dedication and spirituality. This was the gift of the Church Fathers to Western man:

> . . . of St. Augustine, who saw the vanity and futility of the cult of human power; of St. Benedict, who created a nucleus of peace and spiritual order amidst the disasters of the Gothic Wars; of St. Gregory, who carried the cares of the whole world on his shoulders while civilization was falling in ruins around him; of St. Boniface, who in spite of profound discouragement and disillusion gave his life for the increase of the Christian people.[29]

"The nucleus of peace and spiritual order amidst the disasters of the Gothic Wars," founded by St. Benedict in an age of insecurity and disorder, made the monastery an oasis of peace in a time of total war. Often the forces of barbarism were too strong even for the Benedictines. Monte Cassino was destroyed by the Lombards in A.D. 581. But the courage of the Benedictines and the rest of the early Christian leaders was so strong that they returned to the fray again and again, ultimately accomplishing the civilizing task which preserved the best of classical culture and which founded Western civilization as we know it. The monumental size of this endeavor is perhaps clearer to us if we understand that during the period of the barbarian invasions, Europe remained almost literally in a state of siege until well after the year A.D. 1000.

Much rebuilding had to be done. Although the Dark Ages did not see the total destruction of all the ties that bind us to our heritage, tremendous damage had been inflicted. In this trying time, the Christian Church was the single European institution that functioned effectively. In this age, towns in Europe were little more than centers for local commerce. Trade was rare, travel almost impossible. The Roman roads were abandoned, and few men indeed were hardy enough to venture far from their home. In the face of such disorder, we should not be surprised that institutions declined and culture failed, but rather should be surprised that anything survived. The civilizing effect of Christianity persevered through every hardship. In *The Medieval Church*, Roland Bainton writes, "The Vikings, whose beaked prows in the ninth century invested a moonlit night with terror, by the end of the tenth were pruning apple orchards in Normandy."

Thus no one in the Western world can totally avoid the influence of Christianity. What we know of classical antiquity is due primarily to the preservative function of the Christian Church. What civilization, law and order, and culture persisted are due to Christianity; and Christianity also has molded the thoughts and emotions of seventy-five subsequent generations of Western men.

ST. AUGUSTINE

In any era there are certain great personalities who seem to be playing a role not merely for their own time, but for the entire history of the human race. Such men invariably influence the lives and thoughts of their contemporaries, yet also have an influence not interred with their bones. One such man, a bishop of the Christian Church in North Africa, has been dead more than 1,500 years, yet exerts an influence upon Western civilization and upon man's spiritual values that remains fresh and alive. St. Augustine, the greatest of the Church Fathers, was born near Carthage and was given the best education his pagan father could provide. He was a college professor, first at Carthage, later at Rome, and finally at Milan. In A.D. 387 he became a Christian. Within a few years he was made Bishop of Hippo, and his personality and writings made him what St. Jerome described as "The Second Founder of the Ancient Faith." As a young man Augustine had led an extremely worldly life, and he came to understand that man's salvation could not be accomplished exclusively through his own efforts. In his autobiography, entitled *Confessions*, Augustine traced the route by which he had come to that understanding. In *The City of God*, he set forth the doctrines which have exerted an influence on Christian thought to our own day.

Most of the Church Fathers of the fourth century were the products of Greco-Roman, pagan civilization. Many of them, especially St. Augustine, sought a common ground between the new moral and spiritual direction of Christianity and the older classical heritage. Thus in many ways the thought of St. Augustine drew on the past as well as the present to produce a vision of the future which few men had both the genius and the faith to see.

Augustine worked in an age of ruin and distress. As Roman civilization collapsed all about him, he continued to concern himself with the refutation of heresy and the conduct of everyday Church affairs. To those of less faith, the endeavors of Augustine at such a time must have seemed totally futile. "He looked beyond the aimless and bloody chaos of history to the world of eternal realities from which the world of sense derives all the significance which it possesses. His thoughts were fixed, not on the fate of the city of Rome or the city of Hippo, nor on the struggle of Roman and barbarian, but on those other cities which have their foundations in Heaven and in Hell, and on the warfare between 'the world-rulers of the dark aeon and the princes of light.' "[30]

By some observers Augustine has been viewed as the first medieval man. For others he is the last representative of antiquity. Actually he is neither; or, perhaps he is both. In reality, Augustine is a man of his own age, of one of the most trying moments in the history of the world. Rome, the controlling force of the world for over five hundred years, was collapsing, carrying with it the tremendous heritage of the classical world. Yet at that very moment, the foundations of a new heritage were being laid. In the preservation of the old and the creation of the new, St. Augustine was in the front rank, fighting to bridge the gap at a perilous moment in world civilization.

Augustine is clearly one of the major thinkers of the Western world, in the select company of such as Plato and Aristotle. Thanks to our lucky possession of his *Confessions* and his *The City of God*, we know more of Augustine and of his personality than of almost any other figure of antiquity. In his work, a deep emotional current is clearly present, a current which somehow suggests the almost miraculous ability of Augustine to be one with the spirit of God. Augustine was an intense man. His acceptance or rejection of ideas and values was always accomplished at a fever pitch. He was once asked, "What was God doing before he created Heaven and Earth?" Augustine roared, "Creating Hell for people who ask questions such as that!" Yet, for all this passion, Augustine had a fine mind and he used it. He invariably selected the harder course, the line of greatest duty, especially for himself.

Augustine understood that it was not necessary for him to turn from his classical, philosophical culture in order for him to embrace Christianity. He continued to acknowledge the part played in his thinking by Plato and Cicero. Instead of turning from these great tutors, he borrowed from them all possible learning to strengthen the foundations of his new belief. Thus, in Augustine, as in so many other Church Fathers, Platonic thought had a strong influence on Christian ideas. Stoic ethics had also been well-represented in early Christianity. The task of weaving these elements together with the new Christian faith was superbly achieved by St. Augustine. As St. Thomas Aquinas was later to observe, St. Augustine had reconsidered, from the Christian viewpoint, the essential elements of Platonism, bringing his intuitive genius to the task.

Augustine was not content with the mere intellectualism of the Greek philosophers. However, he credited Plato with sensing that the truth existed, fixed and stable. But he recognized that the Platonists had only sensed that truth from afar. Within Christianity, Augustine believed he had found a means to the *possession* of the truth. In the emotional experience produced by his own conversion, he had come to realize that what the intellect could perceive, the heart could possess. Augustine remained a Greek in his insistence on the existence of a rational order, but he was both Western and Christian in his insistence upon the moral preoccupations of that rational order, necessitated by the Christian doctrine of man's free will. Thus the philosophy of Augustine is both intellectual and spiritual, the source of both Western mysticism and Western ethics. In this sense, the world of our time is shaped more by Augustine than by Plato. In fact, the Judeo-Christian view of history and of Western civilization was originally set in motion by St. Augustine.

THE CITY OF GOD

The City of God was written with a definitely controversial aim. Augustine labored for fourteen years upon it, only to find the original controversial pamphlet growing into a gigantic world view embracing the history of man and the meaning of time and eternity. More than any other work of Christian antiquity, *The City of God* examines the relationship of Christian principles to human society and civilization.

Augustine, both in his own life and in his role as a thinker, was engaged in the search for God:

> And what is this? I asked the earth and it answered me, "I am not He;" and whatsoever are in it confessed the same. I asked the sea and the deeps and the living, creeping things, and they answered: "We are not God, seek above us" . . . I asked the sun, moon, stars. "Nor (say they) are we the God whom thou seekest." And I replied to all things that encompass the door of my flesh: "Ye have told me of my God that ye are not He; tell me something of Him" And they cried with a loud voice: "He made us" . . . I asked the whole frame of the world about my God: and it answered me: "I am not He, but He made me." *(Confessions)*

By insisting that the very nature of creation implied a Creator, Augustine was moving beyond the classical Greek concept of virtue and Natural Law. He was insisting that, while human perfection was a suitable goal of Natural Law for the Stoics, the mere concept of "goodness for its own sake in this life" was too small a concept for a Natural Law which had its source in a Creator. Thus the Natural Law theory of the Stoics, which had hovered on the edge of a God-given Natural Law without quite taking that final step, was now made into an infinitely larger concept, the Christian vision of existence and reality. Natural Law thus became that part of the Divine Law which God had apportioned to men. Classical philosophy became merged with Christian theology.

Augustine knew that a great gap existed between the human and the Divine. Despite the use of man's intellect, faith was also required to comprehend God. "For although, unless he understands somewhat, no man can believe in God, nevertheless by the very faith whereby he believes, he is helped to the understand-

ing of greater things. For there are some things which we do not believe unless we understand them; and there are other things which we do not understand unless we believe them."
(Sermons)

Thus, even though man's powers point to God as a Creator of such powers, those powers in themselves are insufficient to comprehend that Creator. To make too much of man's powers can become a dangerous sin for man: "Insofar as concerns the nature of man there is in him nothing better than the mind or reason. But he who would live blessedly ought not to live according to them; for then he would live according to man, whereas he ought to live according to God . . . We are speaking of God. Is it any wonder that thou dost not comprehend? For if thou dost comprehend, he is not God . . . To reach God by the mind in any measure is a great blessedness, but to comprehend Him is altogether impossible."
(The City of God)

Still, Augustine saw that the very quality of man which could be most abused was also the quality of man most like unto the Creator:

> For not in the body but in the mind was man made in the image of God. In his own similitude let us seek God; in His own Image recognize the Creator . . . It is in the soul of man, that is, in his rational or intellectual soul, that we must find that image of the Creator which is immortally implanted in its immortality . . . Although reason or intellect be at one time dormant within it, at another appears to be small and at another great, yet the human soul is never anything but rational and intellectual. Hence if it is made after the image of God in respect to this, that it is able to use reason for the understanding and beholding of God, then from the very moment when that nature so marvelous and so great began to be, whether this image be so worn down as to be almost none at all, whether it be obscure and defaced or bright and beautiful, assuredly it always is. *(The City of God)*

Thus while man may be a poor copy, still he is a copy of his Creator.

What relation then exists between this Creator and His creation, man?

The true God from Whom is all being, beauty, form and number, weight and measure; He from Whom all nature, mean and excellent, all seeds of forms, all forms of seeds, all motions both of forms and seeds, derive and have being; . . . He (I say) having left neither heaven nor earth, nor angel nor man, no, nor the most base and contemptible creature, neither the bird's feather nor the herb's flower, nor the tree's leaf, without the true harmony of their parts, and peaceful concord of composition; it is in no way creditable that He would leave the kingdoms of men and their bondage and freedoms loose and uncomprised in the laws of His eternal providence. *(The City of God)*

If God thus concerns himself with man and his actions, how does evil enter the world? Augustine defines sin: "What could begin this evil will but pride, that is the beginning of all sin? And what is pride but a perverse desire of height, in forsaking Him to whom the soul ought solely to cleave, as the beginning thereof, to make the self seem the beginning. This is when it likes itself too well . . . What is pride but undue exaltation? And this is undue exaltation, when the soul abandons Him to whom it ought to cleave as its end and becomes a kind of end in itself." *(The City of God)*

Thus Augustine interpreted the course of universal history as an endless conflict between two dynamic principles, the city of man and the City of God, Babylon and Jerusalem. Both exist in this world, yet a gigantic spiritual gulf exists between them.

Thus St. Augustine sees history as the meeting point of time and eternity. History is a unity because the same Divine power which shows itself in the order of nature and from the stars down to the feathers of the bird and the leaves of the tree also governs the rise and fall of kingdoms and empires. But this Divine order is continually being deflected by the downward gravitation of human nature to its own selfish ends—a force which attempts to build its own world in those political structures that are the organized expression of human ambition and lust for power.[13]

The City of God was to Augustine a transcendent reality, a society of truth and love in eternal duration. It was the spiritual unity of the entire universe, produced by Divine Providence. Yet Augustine saw a need for the Earthly City as well. "Thou knowest how to make even that which is uneven and to order what is disordered, and unlovely things are lovely to Thee. Foreso Thou bringest together all things in one, the good with the bad, that there results from all, one reasonable order abiding forever." Thus Augustine gave the Earthly City its place within the universal order, recognizing the necessity for a soundly ordered social framework for the conduct of the affairs of this world.

Each man was, of course, a citizen of two cities at once, the city of his birth and the City of God. Man's nature was thus twofold; he was at once spirit and body, a citizen of this world and the next. Man was expected to live this life, but to live in accord with a system of Christian ethics that drew spiritual strength from the Heavenly City. Augustine's doctrine left little room for the claims of the state. At its worst, political power was viewed by Augustine as the very incarnation of man's self-will and injustice to man. At its best, Augustine viewed human government as legitimate and necessary, *so long as it was realized* that the power of government was limited to temporary and partial ends. Those limited ends terminated for Augustine at the point at which they began to interfere with the universal spiritual relationship that all men enjoyed with their Creator. In other words, Augustine believed that the state trespasses at the point at which it begins to interfere with God-given dignity and free choice of the individual, exceeding the minimum standards necessary for orderly operation of the Earthly City. Thus Augustine broke decisively with the classical tradition by depriving the state of its divinity, and seeking instead to order society through the exercise of the *individual* human will.

In this way, Augustine emphasized the ideal of a social order resting upon the exercise and development of the free, individual personality. The ideals of freedom and progress and justice so highly prized within Western society have their origins in the thinking of this man who himself cared nothing for secular progress since he looked instead "for a city that has foundations whose builder and maker is God."

Augustine saw the fall of Rome as just retribution for the ruthless pursuit of power in which Rome had so long been engaged. In his typical straightforward fashion, St. Augustine could ask, "What are great states without justice, if not robbery on a large scale?" Still, Augustine saw that there were other powers in the world besides human passion and greed. He deeply believed that God had not abandoned His creation and continued to insist that the spiritual power of God's love could transform man's nature. Just as man's self-love draws the world to destruction and disorder, God's love draws man back to purposeful and dignified existence. Augustine's conception of history was based on the struggle between these two forces. He insisted that the Earthly City could only prosper when it operated in conformity to the City of God, offering the individual the right to develop his own unique capabilities.

TIME AND MEMORY

And what role was man to play as an individual within this scheme of things? Here again Augustine saw a vision of a God-centered universe, a universe keyed to the realization of the potential dignity within the individual human personality. In his view of the human spirit, Augustine was a Christian mystic. He understood that the quality of the human spirit ranged from the deepest degradation to the most infinite elevation, depending upon the focus which the individual soul chose to adopt. He recognized that this focus, which individual man might decide for himself, involved far more than man's powers of thought.

Man alone in the universe is capable not only of transcending his world, but also capable of transcending himself. Because man's powers of thought allow him to stand not only outside of everything else, but outside of himself as well,[4] Augustine realized that man was the one creature in the universe who could find a home only in God. "If thou dost find that nature is mutable, rise above thyself. But when thou transcendest thyself, remember that thou raiseth thyself above the rational soul; strive therefore to reach the place where the very light of reason is lit." Augustine thus suggests that since the final answers are not present in an ever-changing natural order, man must use his rational powers to rise above that part of himself contained within the natural order; but when man uses his reason to rise above the natural order, he eventually rises above human reason itself, moving toward the source of that reason, God.

Man alone possesses memory as a tool to achieve these heights of self-transcendence. Augustine was endlessly fascinated with the human memory:

> When then I remember memory, memory itself is through itself, present with itself; but when I remember forgetfulness there are present both memory and forgetfulness . . . Great is the power of memory, a fearful thing, O my God, a deep and boundless mani-foldness; and this thing is the mind and this am I myself. What am I then, O my God? What nature am I? *(Confessions)*

In his thinking on the subject of memory, Augustine groped toward a concept of time far beyond the mere physical dimension which we modern men tend to give time. To Augustine, time was a psychological extension of consciousness. If man can store all of his experiences and his awarenesses and his perceptions in memory, he can reach the point at which his remembrance is not merely of the past, but also of the present and the future. Thus man's memory allows him to transcend time, transcending the material universe and the physical side of his own nature.

> When I enter there [the place of memory] I require what I will to be brought forth and something instantly comes; others must be longer sought after, which are fetched as it were out of some inner receptacle . . . nor yet do the things themselves enter in; only the images perceived are there in readiness for thought to recall . . . For even while I dwell in darkness and silence, in my memory I can produce colors if I will . . . Yea I discern the breath of lilies from violets, though smelling nothing . . . These things I do in the vast court of my memory . . . There also I meet with myself and recall myself and when and where and what I have done and under what feelings . . . Out of the same store do I myself with the past continually combine fresh likenesses of things, which I have experienced, have believed; and thence again infer future actions, events and hopes, and all these again I reflect on, as present. I will do this or that, say I to myself, in that great receptacle of my mind, stored with images of things so many and so great . . . Great is the force of memory, excessive great, O my God; a large and boundless chamber; whoever sounded the bottom thereof? Yet is this a power of mine and belongs to my nature; nor do I myself comprehend all that I am. Therefore is the mind too straight to contain itself. And where should that be which it containeth not of itself? Is it without it and not within? And how then does it not comprehend itself? A wonderful admiration surprises me, amazement seizes me upon this. *(Confessions)*

Thus, in Augustine's vision of human nature, memory, and time, the past is the soul's remembrance, the present is its attention, and the future is its expectation. Each moment in either the past or the future is of only a moment's duration, and neither the past nor the future has any existence except at the moment when each particular occurrence past or future is, for that moment, present. Thus a long future is really only a long expectation of the future, and a long past is actually only a long memory of the past. The mind alone among finite objects is therefore not bound by limitations of time or space.[13]

Human nature is thus free from natural processes and from time itself. It is from this freedom that Augustine derives the uniqueness of the human soul:

It is, then, in thee, my soul, that I measure time . . . The impression which things make upon me as they pass and which remains when they have passed away is what I measure. I measure this which is present, and not the things which have passed away that it might be. Therefore, this is time or else I must say that I do not measure time at all. *(Confessions)*

The conception of history which Augustine derived from his view of memory and time allowed him to break out of the classical concept that all of man's existence is a series of cyclical motions without purpose or direction. When Augustine gave significance to individual experience, he gave significance to history as a record of more than mere physical events.

Thanks to Augustine's conception of history, medieval thought bound time and eternity far more closely with each other than either the ancient world or modern man has ever done. To Augustine and to medieval man, human affairs, in what we modern men like to call the "real world," were a small part of an eternal panorama reaching at once backward and forward from this moment in time, a panorama with eternal values completely independent of the physical world. Augustine thus originated the concept of human history as an unfolding process in which divine purpose was to be realized. Because of the individual's ability to use memory and rational thought to stand outside himself and outside the process of history, Augustine saw the personality of the individual human being as the source and key of this process. Augustine's theory of memory freed man from being the creature of time, and made him the molder of history instead. History was to Augustine more than an endless cycle of experiences, but a part of a chain of growth moving toward a realization of God's will through the processes of human experience. To Augustine, progress was possible because society could grow through the individual's capacity for spiritual growth.

On August 28, 430, the Bishop of Hippo, old and weak, lay dying while the barbarians laid siege to his city and the last pretenses of the Roman state crumbled throughout the Western world. But surely a man of such great faith as St. Augustine, a man with such a vision of the human soul and of a God-centered universe, must have sensed, even at such a dark moment, that a new civilization was destined to arise from the ashes of the old. Augustine had devoted his life to "faith seeking understanding," and in his great faith had given great understanding and insight to Western man. Fifteen hundred years later, in many ways the Western world seems to be passing through another period of crisis. Materialistic scientism and coercive collectivism appear to threaten the older spiritual values of individual human dignity. At such a time, the message of St. Augustine is once again peculiarly applicable.

7

The Medieval World
and St. Thomas Aquinas

❦❦❦❦❦❦❦❦❦❦❦❦❦❦❦❦❦❦❦❦❦❦❦❦❦❦❦❦❦❦

THE MEDIEVAL MIND

THE UNITY OF THE MEDIEVAL WORLD CENTERED ON THE CHRIS-
tian church, the arbiter of religious, social, and political thought
until modern times. Theology thus tended to be the center of
knowledge for medieval man. When he spoke of theology, medieval man meant a world view which could only be mastered by an
understanding of *all* human knowledge. Thus medieval man
meant far more when he said "theology" than modern man means
when he says "religion." The theologian, like the philosopher, was
the man in the Middle Ages who concerned himself with the
functioning of the universe. With Augustine, he believed no man
could ever come to penetrate entirely the mystery of God. Yet
medieval man felt that great strides could be made toward an
improved understanding of the universe as God had ordered it.

The medieval mind accepted literally the teaching of the New
Testament that even though we are *in* the world, we are not
entirely *of* it. He thus understood that our attempt to understand
and control the world must remain forever incomplete, since the
workings of this world are not sufficient unto themselves. The new
Christian culture which had arisen from the ashes of the Roman

Empire had produced an internal change in the soul of Western man by fusing a new culture and a new religion to produce a new view of history and a new view of man. While the average man of the Middle Ages was not exclusively ascetic, he, far more than modern man, sensed values of great importance which were not exclusively of this world. Even while absorbed in the living of his life (and medieval man did lead a lusty and active life, notwithstanding the false image given us of the Middle Ages by its enemies) he derived his values from a view of the universe which sensed the significance of a life beyond. This spiritual unity of the Middle Ages was noted by the historian Henry Adams. He symbolized this unity by the Virgin and contrasted medieval unity with the multiplicity of modern times, symbolized by the dynamo. In the contrast between the Virgin and the dynamo, between unity and multiplicity, we can catch the essence of the difference between the medieval mind and the modern mind.

Medieval man was an organizer and a builder of systems. He led a turbulent life, but was extremely fond of order, system, and clearly stated purpose. As C. S. Lewis characterized the men of the Middle Ages, "Of all our modern inventions, I suspect they would have most admired the card index." Such a belief in order was not the modern totalitarian concept of order imposed upon a society from without, but was rather an order achieved through an equilibrium discoverable *within* society. Thus the medieval man viewed law and government as the unconscious internal creation of society, a reflection of the inner peace and self-discipline of its *individual* members. Medieval man took the classical concept of Natural Law, a principle of harmony and order within society and the universe, and added Augustine's conception of individual personality to that law. If classical Natural Law had provided a Law but no Lawgiver, medieval man made the Lawgiver the central fact of human existence and based the foundations of human society upon Divine Personality. This Divine Personality was not only the basis of human existence, but was an essence shared by each individual human personality. Medieval man, if properly understood, made more of the individual than even his classic forbears had done. Thus the Christian Church of the Middle Ages combined two views of human nature and morality, the classical Greco-Roman and the Biblical.

The Middle Ages had a strong belief in the concepts of Heaven and Hell. Their religion and their philosophy taught them to live the fullest possible life upon earth, but it also taught them that if earth were chosen in place of Heaven, in the process earthly life would become only a region of Hell; while if the hierarchy of values were put in its proper perspective and Heaven were valued above earth, earth itself could be a part of the heavenly process. Thus the problem centered upon man understanding and conforming to a proper system of value.

The medieval mind understood that the recognition of a duty was the perception of a truth. Such an idea had roots in antiquity. Socrates and Plato had understood that the bad action was ultimately the ignorant action. Both Aristotle and the Stoics had grasped that a man of "right reason" would understand unchanging values and standards of conduct which were binding upon him. It is this concept which the mind of the Middle Ages enlarged upon and perfected. Thus medieval man was not truly turning from struggle in this life; rather he was finding fixed values to serve as a basis for the human dignity necessary to face the struggle of this world. This was the medieval synthesis: the organization of their history and, above all, their theology into a single, functioning, harmonious universe in which all activities found their constructive place. In the erection of this model of the universe, medieval man's intense love of system found its perfect expression.

To understand the medieval model, it is necessary to return to the Augustinian concept of time, upon which medieval man built and embroidered. Human powers of reason in themselves cannot grasp the idea of a future being known except by reason itself. A future known in advance by reason would be predetermined, and therefore would involve determinism and the rejection of free will. But if we properly understand the Augustinian idea of time and the medieval concept of the universe, we can understand another sort of knowledge of the future, a knowledge which does not involve determinism and which thus retains the concept of free will. As C. S. Lewis has described it in his discussion of the medieval mentality:

Eternity is quite distinct from perpetuity, from mere endless con-
tinuance in time. Perpetuity is only the attainment of an endless
series of moments, each lost as soon as it is attained. Eternity is the
actual and timeless fruition of illimitable life. Time, even endless
time, is only an image, almost a parody of that plenitude; a hopeless
attempt to compensate for the transitoriness of its "presents" by
infinitely multiplying them. That is why Shakespeare's Lucrece
calls it "thou ceaseless lackey to eternity" (*Rape of Lucrece*). And
God is eternal, not perpetual. Strictly speaking, He never foresees;
He simply sees. Your "future" is only an area, and only for us a
special area, of His infinite Now. He sees (not remembers) your
yesterday's acts because it is still "there" for Him; He sees (not
foresees) your tomorrow's acts because he is already in tomorrow.
As a human spectator, by watching my present act, does not at all
infringe its freedom, so I am none the less free to act as I choose
in the future because God, in that future (His present) watches me
acting.[31]

In the medieval system God presided over the universe in all His
majesty and yet the individual retained his free will.

Thus medieval man saw himself ascending a stairway toward
the perfection of an all-understanding God. Modern man's view
of the universe is almost precisely the opposite. In present day
evolutionary thought, "Man stands at the top of a stair whose foot
is lost in obscurity; [in the medieval model] . . . he stands at the
bottom of a stair whose top is invisible with light . . . [the medieval
system] is vast in scale, but limited and intelligible. Its sublimity
is not the sort that depends on anything vague or obscure . . . Its
contents, however rich and various, are in harmony. We see how
everything links up with everything else; at one, not in flat equality, but in a hierarchical ladder."[31]

Medieval man was profoundly aware of his close ties with the
past. He consciously included in his system, or world view, the
tremendous cultural legacy which had been passed to him from
classical antiquity and reconciled with Christian revelation. Bernard of Chartres, in the twelfth century, understood far better than
modern man that:

We are like dwarfs seated on the shoulders of giants; we see more
things than the ancients and things more distant, but this is due
neither to the sharpness of our own sight, nor to the greatness of
our own stature, but because we are raised and borne aloft on that
giant mass.

Even the new chapter in Western history which began when man set out on the discovery of the new geographic and scientific world, the world of Columbus and Copernicus, did not truly depart from the spiritual ideals and religious motivations which had dominated medieval life. Western man continued to carry those ideals with him as he moved toward new fields for their realization. The tremendous enthusiasm which the modern world has come to feel for such medieval figures as the gentle St. Francis of Assisi is a case in point demonstrating that medieval values have not ceased to exist, but have only been buried in a welter of "modern" concepts, where even now they await modern man's rediscovery and reapplication. We should be less willing to criticize medieval man for what he did not know about economics or science, and instead be willing to learn from him, drawing on the tremendous reservoir of knowledge and understanding which he *did* possess.

MEDIEVAL POLITICS

Another strong reason for medieval man's penchant for order might well have been the terrible disorder of the early Middle Ages which followed the collapse of the Roman Empire. His answer to this disorder was the development of feudalism and manorialism, plus the institutional unity of the medieval Christian Church. Together, these institutions provided the necessary law and order for the preservation of civilization.

The system of local power and protection which characterized feudalism not only provided political stability, but also provided a measure of economic stability to overcome the economic chaos brought about by the collapse of the state-controlled economy of the Roman world. Feudalism was a complex mixture of both success and failure, but modern research is making it increasingly clear that, on balance, feudalism was principally a success. In the tenth century, even at its worst, it seems evident that the serf was in all probability living a better life than the commoner during the age of Augustus.

Since the feudal society was intensely local in character, feudal law and feudal land holding also stressed local rather than centralized administration. Feudalism thus linked the political structure and the economic structure in an intensely personal, noncentralized relationship. This personal quality of feudal society also deepened the sense of the obligation of contracts. Medieval society was a closely bound religious, political, and economic unit.

Some scholars attribute to this feudal organization, especially as it developed in England, much of the credit for the subsequent development of Western political liberties:

> In England these feudal tendencies set the stage for the background of developing liberty. Feudal localism was especially strong there. The Magna Charta of 1215 granted freedom to the Church of England, no taxation without representation of property owners, the rights of the City of London, constitution of a General Council of the Kingdom, trial by Peers, no forcible seizure without due process of law, liberty to leave and enter the kingdom . . . In sum, the king's absolutism was denied, and the king placed under feudal law. The principle of contract was strongly affirmed.[32]

The development of royal absolutism was thus a development of the modern state, rather than of medieval politics. The medieval king was restricted to acting through his council and through the feudal court which surrounded him. It is from this beginning that later constitutional ideas, such as representation, legislation by assemblies, control of expenditures, and control of taxation would subsequently emerge. In England, where the trend toward absolutism was turned aside, the right to legislate settled not in the king, but in parliament.

As we have seen, a faith in higher law pervaded the Middle Ages. This concept, built upon the Ciceronian conception of Natural Law, was viewed as being above the ruler and acted as a limit upon his exercise of power. One medieval theorist, John of Salisbury, drew the distinction between a "tyrant" ("one who oppresses the people by rulership based upon force") and a "prince" ("one who rules in accordance with the laws"). Later in the Middle Ages, St. Thomas could write on the same subject:

> A king who is unfaithful to his duty forfeits his claim to obedience. It is not rebellion to depose him, for he is himself a rebel whom the nation has a right to put down. But it is better to abridge his power, that he may be unable to abuse it. For this purpose, the whole

nation ought to have a share in governing itself; the Constitution ought to combine a limited and elected monarchy, with an aristocracy of merit, and such an admixture of democracy as shall admit all classes to office by popular election. No government has a right to levy taxes beyond the limit determined by the people. All political authority is derived from popular suffrage, and all laws must be made by the people or their representatives. There is no security for us as long as we depend on the will of another man. *(Summa Theologica)*

The majestic medieval conception of a higher law serving as the basis for the exercise of all political power limited the activities of Pope and Emperor, ruler and subject, alike. In the Middle Ages, when the precepts of higher law were matched against the claims of official authority, higher law almost invariably held sway. Even while the Middle Ages emphasized Natural Law, a considerable emphasis was also placed on natural rights. During the medieval period two of the most basic of modern legal institutions developed: contracts and private property. Quoting the German historian von Gierke, noted American constitutional scholar Edward S. Corwin has concluded:

Property had its roots . . . "in Law which flowed out of the pure Law of Nature without the aid of the State and in Law which was when as yet the State was not. Thence it followed that particular rights which had been acquired by virtue of this institution in no wise owed their existence exclusively to the state." Likewise, the binding force of contracts was traced from natural law, "so that the Sovereign, though he could not bind himself or his successors by statute, could bind himself and his successors by Contract." . . . The strong initial bias of American Constitutional Law in favor of rights of property and contract has, therefore, its background in speculations of the middle ages.[22]

Christianity itself had exerted a strong influence toward liberty, since the very beginning of the Middle Ages. The invading barbarians, possessors of little culture in their own right, had turned eagerly to the Church schools to draw on the heritage of the ancient and Christian world. To these barbarians, the Church had soon developed a far stronger and more basic appeal than the newly founded barbarian states. In fact, Christian teaching contained within it an element of anti-authoritarianism which carried the ideal of liberty far beyond that understood in the classical world. Socrates' method of resisting the state was to die for his convictions. The Stoics had taught that the wise man kept the Natural Law by leaving politics to others. But Christianity had opposed the absolutism of the Roman Empire, preaching, "render unto Caesar the things that are Caesar's, and unto God the things that are God's." For the first time in history, the limits of the state had been sharply defined, leaving the exercise of individual conscience outside the legitimate scope of such authority. The medieval idea of hierarchy, of appealing from lower to higher cosmic tribunals, thus incorporated into medieval society a limitation upon political power.

The rise of the new national sovereign states at the end of the Middle Ages tended to involve the Church in the struggle for civil authority, as for example, in the investiture controversy of the eleventh century. It is this political involvement of the Church which would ultimately lead to the undermining of the great medieval synthesis.

MEDIEVAL CULTURE

The darkness of the Dark Ages must never be exaggerated. In spiritual life, the Christian Church established a great unity, and, in political life, feudalism established a system of relative stability. The cultural and social life of medieval Europe was also probably never as bleak as historians have often intimated. Life did go on. The same monks who saved the manuscripts of antiquity also cleared the forests, drained the swamps, and introduced new methods of agriculture. Medieval man exercised an intensely practical attitude toward everyday life, displaying a willingness to experiment that led to all sorts of prosiac but practical advances in technology. Buttons, forks, and spectacles, all still in rather wide use in our modern world, are medieval ideas. It was during the period of the Middle Ages that the art of paper-making came to Europe. And how would modern man prosper without his clocks, another medieval invention? Still, for all this, it is easy to understand how the black view of the Dark Ages arose. The early Middle Ages were a period of economic stagnation; city life did tend to disappear; political organization and the legal framework did suffer. Yet at the very depths of the destruction stemming from the barbarian invasion, Western culture preserved a vital spiritual energy which pointed toward a general cultural renaissance, in fact, a series of cultural renaissances. In the so-called "Dark Ages," the institution of monasticism, with its quest for individual perfection and self-discipline, provided the first of the spiritual forces for the transmission and regeneration of culture. This tremendous energy and capacity for self-sacrifice was not exclusively a product of the monasteries, but radiated throughout Christian society as a whole. Later, the rise of such new religious orders as the Dominicans and Franciscans carried the spiritual renaissance and cultural renaissance still further.

As the Middle Ages advanced, this cultural development spread throughout all levels of society, producing a highly varied yet amazingly united cultural pattern throughout Western Christendom. Much of what is described as the Renaissance is actually the fruition of the freely communicated cultural aims and ideas of the Middle Ages which produced a common fellowship throughout Europe.

Similarly, it was this tremendous spiritual energy and moral prestige which produced the cultural phenomenon known as the High Middle Ages. Once the tremendous social upheaval produced by the collapse of Rome had been overcome in the early Middle Ages through the stabilizing influence of feudalism and the Christian Church, Western society was by the eleventh century beginning to move toward great cultural achievement. In economic life, social life, political organization, and arts and letters, as well as in philosophy, the High Middle Ages laid the foundations of the modern world by creating many of the institutions and concepts which the modern world has used to its advantage. The modern nation-state, the political institutions which compose it, the framework of classes which provide its hierarchy, and the cities which provide its way of life were all in process of development in the High Middle Ages. A respectable literature, art, and architecture grew apace. The High Middle Ages saw the attainment of a strong unity, thanks to the unifying effect of Christianity; yet tremendous diversity of thought and action were present throughout that unity. There have been few times in the history of Western man when life and thought were more active and varied than in the twelfth and thirteenth centuries of the Christian era.

Nowhere was this tremendous constructive and creative vigor more apparent than in the rise of a new institution destined for a great place in the Western world, the university. The way had already been paved within Western society for a system of education open to intelligent boys on all levels of society. Originally, the elementary schools had developed in conjunction with the monasteries, sometimes also developing as town schools. It has been said that the Middle Ages was a time in which almost everyone was constantly trying to advise or educate everyone else. Education was then viewed as an organic function of the social structure. As the High Middle Ages approached and the medieval city began its rise, the educational system, already evident on every hand in medieval society, was given a new capstone, the great universities. In huge centers like Oxford, Paris, and Bologna, doctors, lawyers, teachers, and especially theologians began to draw upon the rich heritage of antiquity, a heritage preserved, broadened, and deepened through a thousand years of contact with Christian theology.[33]

The High Middle Ages represented a basic moral equilibrium and practical social justice, based on a world view giving man great dignity as a creature of God. The cultural levels attained in this era equaled or excelled anything in classical antiquity and went hand in hand with a solid material and technological advancement. The Western world had indeed come into its own.

THE SCHOLASTICS

The highest and finest expression of medieval culture and the medieval world view can be seen in the philosophy of the Middle Ages. Throughout medieval times, the mind of Western man had been extremely active. The Nominalists and the Realists, for example, had engaged in extended discussion of Plato's and Aristotle's ideas, especially in an attempt to answer the old question, "What constitutes reality?"

The earlier Middle Ages, following St. Augustine, had tended to accept the direction of thought originally set forth by Plato. But by the later Middle Ages, Aristotle's work was receiving more and more attention throughout Europe. One of the first people to grasp the importance of Aristotle was St. Albert the Great. Born in A.D. 1193, Albert was extremely well educated, especially in classical literature. He understood that the philosophers of antiquity had been groping toward the same conclusions made explicit in Christianity:

> The sublimest wisdom of which the world could boast flourished in Greece. Even as the Jews knew God by the Scriptures, so the pagan philosophers knew Him by the natural wisdom of reason, and were debtors to Him for it by their homage . . . though shorn of the lights of the faith they have none the less spoken in a wonderful manner of the Creator and His creatures. Virtue and vice they knew, and a great number of truths which faith as well as reason announce from on high. (Commentary on the *Kyrie*)

Thanks to the renewed interest of St. Albert and others, much of Aristotle's work became accepted textbook matter in Western schools. Translations from Greek to Syrian to Arabic and finally to Latin brought Aristotle to Western man, adding a great deal to the curriculum of Western schools. The effect was revolutionary, since Aristotle's commonsense view of reality (consisting, as you recall, of *both* matter and form) was now contrasted with the Platonic concept of an ideal reality which Christianity had inherited through St. Augustine. Thus the traditional world view upon which Christianity was based was now suddenly confronted with another world view potentially revolutionary in its implications.

It was this challenge of Aristotelian thought to the medieval world view that gave rise to Scholastic philosophy. A group of scholars centering primarily at the University of Paris began the attempt of reconciling the traditional faith with the "new" reason of Aristotle. Greek reason had arrived to produce a headlong confrontation with medieval faith. In the *Sic et Non* of Peter Abelard and the *Sentences* of Peter Lombard, the challenge was taken up by the Scholastics. Abelard's *Sic et Non (Yes and No)* set forth a series of pronouncements of various Church Fathers concerning the nature of reality. Many of these statements appeared contradictory. To Abelard's ironic intelligence, it was clear that the problem rested more in a confusion in terms than in a fundamental contradiction of viewpoint. Unfortunately, however clear this was to Abelard, the subtle point did not come through to his readers. What the reader of Abelard's time saw in *Sic et Non* was an attack upon the credibility and consistency of the Church Fathers and the teachings of the Church. Many brilliant medieval men, especially St. Bernard of Clairvaux, were so oriented to faith as their sole guide to understanding that they reacted against the rationalism which seemed to dominate Abelard's work.

Sometimes this controversy between Abelard and Bernard is pictured as a struggle between the forces of light and the forces of darkness, those capable of learning (Abelard) and those desirous of staying in the dark ages (Bernard). When modern man thus interprets this medieval debate, he misses most of the point. Bernard of Clairvaux was himself a man of enormous intellectual power, gifted in expression, and devoted to the education of men. So, indeed, was Abelard. The point is that *both* men were representative of a respectable position. The controversy between them was not some dispute between the "modern" and the "medieval" world. Rather, it was an indication of the tremendous readjustments and rethinking which the High Middle Ages had to go through to complete the process of fully synthesizing the classical and the Christian world.

The work begun by Peter Abelard (1079–1142) was continued by Peter Lombard (1100–1164). As in ancient Greece, there was tremendous variety and activity in philosophical thought in the High Middle Ages. But, also as in Greece, this variety was working toward a point of understanding and unity. That unity in the Middle Ages was to be produced by Scholasticism. The Scholastics worked with the necessity of placing the real world in relation to the ideal world, thus producing a complete and balanced picture of reality. It is this process of the reconciliation of faith and reason, begun by Abelard, furthered by Lombard, and completed by St. Thomas Aquinas, which is the highest achievement of the medieval mind.

It would be misleading, however, to view this medieval unity, as so many modern men *do* view it, as some demonstration of what modern man slightingly calls a "closed mind." In actual fact, the

Scholastics engaged in active, aggressive, and genuine philosophic debate on and off the public platform, using reason honed to a razor-edge through dedication and intelligence, and demonstrating a level of thought far higher than much of what passes for "dialogue" in our own times. In the spirit of philosophic inquiry, the Middle Ages at their best were one of the freest and most effective of societies. As G. K. Chesterton has described it:

> In spite of all that was once said about superstition, the dark ages and the sterility of Scholasticism, it was in every sense a movement of enlargement, always moving toward greater light and even greater liberty . . . it was like the action of a plant which by its own force thrusts out its leaves into the sun . . .[34]

The man on whom fell the burden of producing the final medieval synthesis between faith and reason was St. Thomas Aquinas, a man of unparalleled power of mind, whose capacity for the clarification of ideas has seldom been surpassed in the history of human thought.

By the time St. Thomas had died in his forty-ninth year, he had produced a systematic and encyclopedic examination of all medieval philosophy and knowledge. His two principle works were the *Summa Contra Gentiles* and the massive *Summa Theologica*, running to twenty-two volumes. This brilliant scholar with such superb capacities of intellect maintained throughout the erection of the entire gigantic system his links with the real world of common sense. That world as seen by Aquinas was a world where man was intended to be, where he might find his home. That world was understandable to human reason but not wholly malleable to the human will. Thus both an understanding of and an adjustment to that real world, which was at once also an ideal world, was expected of the individual in the system of St. Thomas. The noted historian of the ideas of Western man, Crane Brinton, has described the system:

> Aquinas, who was very little of a mystic, nonetheless takes the concrete heritage of Christian mysticism, of Christian other-worldliness, with admirable ease, without struggling, as part of what was given him. He makes his peace with it, in a sense tames it. Aquinas is not the philosopher for the Christian anxious to storm heaven;

he is an admirable philosopher for the Christian seeking peace of mind, and a disturbing one for the peace of mind of the non-Christian.[33]

Thomas's intellectual capacity ranks with that of Plato, Aristotle, and Augustine. Like them, he advanced man's understanding of the major intellectual problems which he faced. Like them, he gave the answers to the "Big Questions," questions concerning the nature of man, of God, and of their relationship.

THE "DUMB OX"

St. Thomas Aquinas was born in 1225 at the castle of his nobleman father, located near the famous Benedictine Abbey of Monte Cassino. Educated at Monte Cassino and at the University of Naples, Aquinas decided to join the newly formed and energetic Dominican Order. Turning from the wealth and prestige of his family's position, he went on to continue his education at the Universities of Paris and Cologne. At the age of thirty-two he completed his degree, Doctor of Theology, and devoted his life to teaching and writing. He continued in the course he had set for himself although he was later offered both the Archbishopric of Naples and the Abbacy of Monte Cassino. In his relatively brief adult life of scholarship, Thomas completed sixty books.

Just as Augustine stands as a giant dominating the beginning of the Middle Ages, Thomas stands as a giant dominating their end. This often leads people into the error of contrasting Thomism and Augustinianism as though they were two systems. This tends to be dangerously misleading, since Augustine in fact was pointing the way toward what would become the completed system of St. Thomas, rather than erecting a finished system in his own right. In the words of Jacques Maritain, one of the best known of modern day Thomist authorities, "Thomism is the scientific state of Christian wisdom; in the case of the Fathers and St. Augustine, Christian wisdom is still a mere spring . . . The more one studies both of these Doctors, the better is Father Gardeil's statement verified: 'The positions on which they differ may be counted; it is impossible to number those in which they agreed . . . [Aquinas] . . . has devoured the whole spiritual substance of the eagle of Hippo . . .

He has made it, as much as Aristotle, the very substance of his own mind.' "[30]

Thomas was faced with a gigantic intellectual task in his reconciliation of faith and reason. His whole life was devoted to the single great task of reconciling the two, most simply characterized by "Aristotle" on the one hand and "the Bible" on the other. He was thus challenging the very dilemma which still serves as the basis for all the problems of intellectual definition and belief faced by modern man. In 1244, St. Thomas Aquinas, then nineteen years of age, became the student of St. Albertus Magnus. A powerful, beefy figure, so quiet as to be thought stupid by his classmates, Aquinas acquired the nickname of "the Dumb Ox." Yet Albertus saw in this large young man a spark of genius and dedication. One day, when other students chided Thomas for his silence in debate, St. Albert prophesied, "This Dumb Ox will fill the world with his bellowing." Thus it was to be.

FAITH AND REASON

To Aquinas, the world was a sensible place, a place created by God as a suitable home for man. Man himself had been created in the image of God, thus no such basic human activity as thought could be contrary to such a creation. True, man was to be faced with all the powers of evil in a constant struggle on this earth, but surely reason, properly understood, was the tool given to man by God to allow the individual to overcome the evil he saw around him and achieve the purpose which Creation had intended. Man's thinking, *if done properly*, could thus achieve the same results in the rational order that the revealed authority of faith provided in the spiritual order. Thus to Thomas the idea of the reality of the natural order, the sense-perceived world of physical things, was part of a single system which also included Divine Revelation and the reality of man's soul and man's God. The reason of man was akin to the reason of God, although operating on a lower level. Building on Aristotle's conception of God, Aquinas found no fault with that concept, only insisting that it did not go far enough. The Greeks had held that a superior power would be a being of pure intelligence whose perfection provided all meaning and rationality to the universe. But Thomas added to the metaphysical perfection which Aristotle reasoned must exist in God, drawing on Christian revelation to make God more than a mere metaphysical perfection but a loving Father and an exacting Ruler as well. Thus faith does not contradict reason. Rather, together faith and reason coalesce to produce an image of reality transcending what reason alone can provide.

In *Summa Contra Gentiles*, Aquinas distinguished between truth imparted by human rationality and truth imparted by Divine Revelation, insisting that both were necessary to man. Revelation to Thomas meant the Bible, the teachings of the Church Fathers, and the decisions of the Church hierarchy. But complementing this revelation was the sort of rationality which man could achieve through philosophy. Both types of truth, since they both came from God, complemented rather than contradicted one another. Thomas was willing to allow the single truth to be approached by two routes, simply because he was so sure that in fact only one truth existed. The faith in that one truth constituted the vitality of the Christian religion for Thomas. In his deeply held faith, Thomas understood that reason itself would never be sufficient to reveal the entire grand design to man. This was true because all things, everything in the universe except God, are the products of Creation and therefore partake of the meaning of that Creation without fully understanding it. Although every part of a watch is an integral, working piece of a functioning whole, only the watchmaker would possess the capacity for total understanding of the watch.

This is not to say that Thomas believed that God and the nature of things are unknowable. To him, the miracle of human reason, supplied by God, made all creation so utterly *knowable* that we could never come to the end of our attempts to know them. The inexhaustible content of the universe, supplied by an omnipotent and omniscient Creator, creates a situation in which no matter how much man knows, there is more, and more, and more which he may know. Thus the *Summa Theologica* is not a closed system. Thomas did not pretend to be erecting a system in which every question had an answer. Rather, he was proposing a system which gave man a chance to recognize how much there is to know about the universe, how much man can know about the universe, precisely because of the God-given nature of human intellect. The system which Thomas erected was independent of the data of faith, resting as it does upon experience and reason alone. Yet Thomas made clear that reason, properly understood, coincides, draws its strength from, and ultimately points toward the superior wisdom of theology. Thus, theology completed the system to which science and philosophy provided the beginning. Faith and reason together, without contradiction, built a temple of knowledge.

Thomas understood, far better than man ever had before, that truth is that which clarifies, not that which confuses, because truth is the true language of universality. It was that universality which Thomism offered to Western man.

HIERARCHY

In reading *Summa Theologica*, one is immediately struck by the systematic manner in which layer upon layer of the ideas unfold. Just as each portion of the *Summa* is a logically organized structure, the work as a whole builds a massive, structured hierarchy of matter and form, reproducing the very sort of hierarchical structure which Thomas held the universe itself to be. Thomas sensed in man's capacity for reason a quality at once less than God but more than other Creation. For him, man was the link between Creation and God. Man was viewed as rather like a tree, with its roots deep in the earth and its branches rising higher and higher toward the stars. In this system of hierarchy, of higher and lower, in which man found such an important place, all created matter, however lowly, had a station and obligations, and helped in its contribution toward the perfection of the entire system. All created things had a purpose, a subordination to an end. This universal synthesis, this harmony and conciliation of all created matter, offered in God and His Creation the almost endless diversity making up man's finite existence. Thus all human knowledge formed a single piece, yet contained its own hierarchy as well.[35]

On the lowest level, Thomas conceived this hierarchy of knowledge to be composed of the sciences, each with its special subject matter. The next higher level of knowledge was philosophy, a rational discipline designed to formulate universal principles from the specific findings of the specialized sciences. The capstone of the system and the highest level of knowledge, above both specific scientific knowledge and philosophy, was theology, based upon revelation and offering a consummation and explanation of the entire system. The important point in this hierarchy of knowledge offered by the system of St. Thomas is that these different levels of knowledge, although requiring different levels of perception, were in no way contrary to one another, since each formed a part in a functioning whole.[35]

This hierarchy of knowledge found its parallel in St. Thomas' hierarchy of nature. To him, the universe formed a single summit, reaching from God at the top to the lowest conceivable created being. Every member within that hierarchy operated in accord with its own nature, seeking the level of form and perfection natural to its kind and thus taking a place in the ascending order of things according to its own degree of perfection. Thomas saw the higher making use of the lower within the system as a part of that function, as, for example, in the idea that the soul rules over the body, or that God rules over the world. In this structure of nature, Aquinas reserved a special place for man, since he alone possessed not only a bodily nature but also a rational nature and a spiritual soul, making him directly akin to God. Since man alone is at once body and soul, Aquinas attributed special importance to the laws and institutions which men used in the direction of their life on earth. In this area of political thought, as in many other areas, Aristotle's concepts served as the basis for the Thomist system. It was from this source that Thomas derived his idea of the constitutional fabric of legally limited political power. Since Thomas was primarily a moral rather than a political philosopher, his thought in this area is not as developed as that of Aristotle, yet many of the basic moral presuppositions in Thomas serve as the basis of modern man's thinking on limited government. In Thomas' theory of politics, as in his theory of knowledge, he set up a hierarchy in which political authority in its various levels was limited by moral precepts.[35]

The idea of heirarchy, developed by Thomas in regard to

knowledge and in regard to political authority, was especially well developed in regard to law. It is here that much of Thomas' thought on politics merges with his thought on morality, producing a clear example of medieval man's view of how society should be ordered.

Like most medieval men, Thomas held a deep reverence for the tradition of the law, assuming its authority to be dependent not upon human origin, but instead derived from Divine Law. Thus man-made law was only a part, although an integral part, of a system which controlled everything on heaven and earth. This control Thomas saw as ultimately coming directly from the reason of God, the controlling force of the universe.

Thomas divided his hierarchy of law into four levels. Really, what Thomas called "law" consisted of four forms of reason, each manifesting itself at different levels of cosmic understanding: Eternal Law, Natural Law, Divine Law, and Human Law.[35]

Eternal Law, the highest level, was synonymous with the "reason of God." It amounted to the Divine Wisdom which provided the plan for all Creation. In Thomist philosophy, this level of law was viewed as being so far above the physical nature of man that it was not entirely comprehensible, though it was not contrary to human reason. Thus man participated in the wisdom and goodness of God without entirely probing the depths of understanding concerning that wisdom.

The next level of law was a reflection of Divine Reason in created things: Natural Law. Thus all things in nature attempt to preserve themselves and live the sort of life most suitable to their natural capacities. As the ancient Greeks had demonstrated, for mankind this attempt to live in terms of natural endowments was "the rational life," that is, the life in which man's rational capacities are most fully realized. As examples of this, Thomas offered the instincts which man displayed, such as tending to live in society, fighting to preserve life, seeking the truth, and the conception, care, and education of children. The implementation of these human inclinations was thus a demonstration of Natural Law at work.[35]

The next level of law beneath Eternal and Natural Law reached the borders of man's total understanding. This level was

Divine Law. What Thomas meant by Divine Law was what we would call Revelation, the code of law set forth in the Bible and defined by the Church Fathers. Comprehension of this level of law involved faith, and therefore was a gift to man rather than a discovery attained by the use of his reason. Here again, Thomas insisted that such revelation enhanced reason without contradicting it.

Human law completed the hierarchy of law set forth by St. Thomas. Such law was far more specific than the other categories, since it was directed toward the regulation of a single sort of creature, rather than the regulation of all creation. Yet all the principles demonstrated within this law, if they were correct, were entirely in consonance with the other, higher levels of law. Any exercise of coercion to enforce human law not consonant with this higher standard, was Thomas' definition of tyranny.[35]

Thomas understood that human law needed to be more precisely defined if it were to be effective in meeting the varieties of human life and the special circumstances arising in that life. Yet he also recognized that the fundamental principles guiding the formation of human law were unchanging. Government was thus viewed by St. Thomas as a series of changing patterns underlaid with one right, one law, and one justice behind them all. Life thus had a single end, but many means. Thomas saw a definite universe dominated by the definite values of a definite God, yet kept the Greek openness of mind toward means to attain those values in human existence.

BEING

Modern philosophy has erected such a high wall between the Thomistic system and the "modern world" that most of us are never able to see to the other side, and thus never have the chance to understand how much alike are the assumptions of St. Thomas Aquinas and the instincts of the average, middle-class, God-fearing American citizen of the mid-twentieth century.

The misunderstanding which modern philosophy has created hinges on a misinterpretation of the one basic concept which lies at the heart of the entire Thomistic system: The definition which

St. Thomas gave to the word "Being." Being, as defined by St. Thomas, covered everything that is and everything that possibly might ever be. Thomas understood what our common sense tells each of us: Things actually exist. Combining Plato's idea, passed through Augustine, that "ideas exist" with Aristotle's additional belief in concrete reality, Thomas grasped the concept of an entire universe in one magnificent hierarchy reaching from apples to eat and sunsets to see all the way up to vital truths to prove, experience, and understand.

St. Thomas erected a philosophy which is based on that uncommon quality called "common sense." Unlike the modern philosophers, unwilling or unable to grasp this simple idea that "things exist," Thomas saw through to the heart of the matter. As one of his biographers, G. K. Chesterton, describes it:

Against a number of modern philosophers stands the philosophy of St. Thomas founded on the universal common conviction that eggs are eggs. The Hegelian may say that an egg is really a hen, because it is a part of an endless process of Becoming; the Berkeleian may hold that poached eggs only exist as a dream exists, since it is quite as easy to call the dream the cause of the eggs as the eggs the cause of the dream; the Pragmatist may believe that we get the best out of scrambled eggs by forgetting that they ever were eggs and only remembering the scramble. But no pupil of St. Thomas needs to addle his brains in order adequately to addle his eggs; to put his head at any peculiar angle in looking at eggs, or squinting at eggs or winking the other eye in order to see a new simplification of eggs. The Thomist stands in the broad daylight of the brotherhood of men, in their common consciousness that eggs are not hens or dreams or mere practical assumptions; but things attested by the authority of the senses, which is from God. . . St. Thomas is arguing for common sense. He is arguing for a common sense which would even now commend itself to most of the common people. He is arguing for the popular proverbs that seeing is believing; that the proof of the pudding is in the eating; that a man cannot jump down his own throat or deny the fact of his own existence. He often maintains the view by the use of abstractions; but the abstractions are no more abstract than Energy or Evolution or Space-Time; and they do not land us, as the others often do, in hopeless contradictions about common life. The Pragmatist sets out to be practical, but his practicality turns out to be entirely theoretical. The Thomist begins by being theoretical, but his theory turns out to be entirely practical.[34]

It is modern philosophy that increasingly asks the question, "Does anything really exist?" St. Thomas answers, "Yes." He understands that any other answer would imply that no thinkers or no thoughts would exist as a bridge between mind and reality. Thomas is willing to take that first step, a commonsense step, a step most rationalists and materialist thinkers of our own time are unwilling to take. He can see the mind as a place lighted by the windows of the five senses. He thus uses this common sense as a first step to turn the light of those five senses upon the nature of the man within. Step by step, Thomas used this starting point to erect a mighty system reaching from the lowest level of sensory experience to the highest level of human intuition.

It is this *positive* quality about St. Thomas in which he differs so much from many modern philosophers. Despite its common-sense antecedents, St. Thomas' idea of "being" is admittedly difficult to grasp. Yet its importance demands that we make the attempt. The clearest and most simple example which conveys this idea originated with Gilbert Chesterton:

> When a child looks out of the nursery window and sees anything, say the green lawn of the garden, what does he actually know; or does he know anything? There are all sorts of nursery games of negative philosophy played around this question. A brilliant Victorian scientist delighted in declaring that the child does not see any grass at all; but only a sort of green mist reflected in a tiny mirror of the human eye. This piece of rationalism has always struck me as almost insanely irrational. If he is not sure of the existence of the grass, which he sees through the glass of a window, how on earth can he be sure of the existence of the retina, which he sees through the glass of a microscope? If sight deceives, why can it not go on deceiving? Men of another school answer that grass is a mere green impression on the mind; and that he can be sure of nothing except the mind. They declare that he can only be conscious of his own consciousness; which happens to be the one thing that we know the child is not conscious of at all. In that sense, it would be far truer to say that there is grass and no child than to say that there is a conscious child but no grass. . . It is a quaint and almost comic fact, that this chaotic negation especially attracts those who are always complaining of social chaos, and who propose to replace it by the most sweeping social regulations. It is the very men who say that nothing can be classified, who say that everything must be codified. Thus Mr. Bernard Shaw said that the only Golden Rule is that there is no Golden Rule. He prefers an Iron Rule; as

in Russia. . . St. Thomas Aquinas, suddenly intervening in this nursery quarrel, says emphatically that the child is aware of [being] . . . Long before he knows that grass is grass, or self is self, he knows that something is something. Perhaps it would be best to say very emphatically. . ., "There *is* an Is." That is as much monkish credulity as St. Thomas asks of us at the start. Very few unbelievers start by asking us to believe so little. And yet, upon this sharp pin-point of reality, he rears by long logical processes, that have never really been successfully overthrown, the whole cosmic system of Christendom.[34]

Once we overcome this first problem and decide that a thing that is really *is*, we immediately run into the next bugaboo advanced by many modern philosophers: The idea of change. If we look closely at these things which we now know exist, we find that they are almost constantly in a state of change, ceasing to be one thing and becoming another. It is this very problem of the changeability of matter which led Plato to believe that reality existed *only* in ideas, and not in physical matter. Many philosophers throughout history, reaching the point where they recognize this change, slide back to disbelief, back to insisting once again that nothing exists, i.e., nothing except change, nothing except flux. Thus they come once again to insist that nothing exists at all.

Aquinas is not so easily fooled. He holds firm to that first commonsense principle which we all share, "What is, *is*." Hot water may become cold water, and cold water may become ice, but it is never all three at once. This process of change does not make water unreal; it means that water can be only one thing at a time. No matter how fast this process of change is conducted, whatever matter is undergoing, it remains *something* at any given moment. Thus while many philosophers are trapped in an endless cycle of change, Aquinas builds upon the belief that, "What is, *is*," to reach the idea of an ultimate reality that is unchanging because it contains within itself all the other realities at once. As Chesterton phrases it:

"While they [the other philosophers] describe a change which is really a change in nothing, he [Aquinas] describes a changelessness which includes the changes of everything. Things change because they are not complete; but their reality can only be explained as part of something that is complete. It is God."[34]

If Thomas thus confounds the philosophers who would reduce all reality, man included, to a meaningless and directionless whirl of change, he deals an equally devastating blow to those who would turn inward upon the spirit and deny all external reality. The idea of renunciation of the world as a step toward perfect nothingness has been the goal of many since the time of Buddha, and still has its modern followers. But where one such as the Buddhist wishes to retreat from the world and the universe in an attempt to "uncreate" himself, the man of Western Christendom, together with St. Thomas, wishes to free himself from the world that he may expand into the universe. While Buddha would uncreate himself, Thomas would return to his Creator:

> Alone upon the earth, and lifted and liberated from all the wheels and whirlpools of the earth, stands up the faith of St. Thomas; weighted and balanced indeed with more than Oriental metaphysics and more than Pagan pomp and pageantry; but vitally and vividly alone in declaring that life is a living story, with a great beginning and a great close; rooted in the primeval joy of God and finding its fruition in the final happiness of humanity; opening with the colossal chorus in which the sons of God shouted for joy, and ending in that mystical comradeship, shown in a shadowy fashion in those ancient words that move like an archaic dance; "For His delight is with the sons of men."[34]

To St. Thomas it was clear that God had made man to be in contact with reality. Thus man should live and understand his life in terms of that reality. In this very real way, Thomas created a genuine working philosophy, one of the few philosophies which do actually work in practical terms. How could the philosophy of a skeptic or a fatalist work in practice if he did not assume what it is imposssible to believe? What materialist who thinks his brain is composed of racing atoms beyond his control has ever expressed any hesitation in stating his thoughts as though they had meaning? What skeptic who believes that no objective truth exists ever hesitated to state that belief as objective truth? St. Thomas, on the other hand, worked with the real world, with a practical, working philosophy capable of application. Finding reality, he began to build upon it.

Again, in the penetrating analysis of G. K. Chesterton:

It was a very special idea of St. Thomas that Man is to be studied in his whole manhood; that a man is not a man without his body, just as he is not a man without his soul. . . He emphasized a certain dignity in Man, which was sometimes rather swallowed up in the purely theistic generalizations about God. Nobody would say he wanted to divide Man from God; but he did want to distinguish Man from God. In this strong sense of human dignity and liberty there is much that can be and is appreciated now as ennobled humanistic liberality. But let us not forget that its upshot was that very Free Will, or moral responsibility of Man, which so many modern liberals would deny. Upon this sublime and perilous liberty hang heaven and hell, and all the mysterious drama of the soul . . . St. Thomas did, with a most solid and colossal conviction, believe in Life . . . It breathes somehow in his very first phrases about the reality of Being. If the morbid Renaissance intellectual is supposed to say, "To be or not to be—that is the question," then the massive medieval doctor does most certainly reply in a voice of thunder, "To be—that is the answer."[34]

The story is told of the great, beefy Aquinas, silent and withdrawn, though polite, who was ordered from his work in retirement to journey to the court of the King of France, St. Louis. Thomas usually declined any social invitations, including invitations from royalty, perferring to undertake his deep thinking in solitude. But, always obedient, he complied with the order from the Dominican authorities who wished him to accept the invitation of Louis IX. At a dinner party after his arrival, Aquinas was in the presence of the most brilliant imaginable collection of the highest French society. At such a witty and glittering event, the bulky, quiet Italian monk was soon forgotten. Suddenly the wine goblets danced in the air, and the great table shook the length of the room. As the astonished assemblage looked up, they realized that the huge priest had brought his fist down with a crash, as though to emphasize a point. Completely unaware of the company around him, Aquinas roared, "And that will settle the Manichees!" King Louis took no offense at the interruption. Turning to his secretaries, he asked them to hurry to the side of Aquinas, since apparently a good argument in opposition to a current heresy had occured to him and it should be written down before he forgot it. Something of that lusty and vital spirit of Thomas comes through in his work, in the flesh and blood belief that God has made this world for man to live in, as a real place rather than a figment of some philosopher's imagination. In a modern age which boasts of its freedom from values or restraints of any kind, the philosophy of St. Thomas offers a genuine freedom from the chains of materialism and rationalism in which we have bound ourselves. It was Thomas who taught that Reason could be trusted. It is modern man who has betrayed that trust.

8

Renaissance and Reformation

THE VIEW OF HISTORY TAUGHT TO MOST OF US IN SCHOOL describes the Renaissance and Reformation as part of a single movement designed to achieve freedom from the Middle Ages. So the story goes, the Renaissance achieved artistic freedom, while the Reformation achieved religious freedom, together pointing the way toward what we like to call "modern democracy." [33]

This division of history into the "good" and the "bad" has made a tremendous impact on the modern mind. It is difficult to imagine an adjective more negative in impact than the meaning which modern man gives to the word "medieval."

Renaissance, of course, means "rebirth," and is intended to convey the rise of new attitudes and new understandings which produced a level of civilization which the world had not seen since classical days. The implication is, of course, that the gap between classical civilization and Renaissance civilization is a moral and intellectual swamp not worthy of serious consideration. Like many generalizations, this will not bear close examination.

The term Renaissance has a very wide meaning. It is a handy catchall into which all the cultural achievements of continental Europe occurring between 1300 and 1600 may conveniently be placed. It is a term descriptive of the transitional period from the medieval world to the modern world. But it would be well to remember that such boundaries at best are highly artificial, describing modifications of the thoughts and attitudes of society which largely overlap. Much of the Renaissance draws heavily upon the medieval past, just as much of it points toward the modern future.

When did the medieval period end? Or, when did the Renaissance begin?

> Is your criterion the "revival of learning," a truer appreciation of pagan Latin culture? Charles H. Haskins in his *The Renaissance of the Twelfth Century* pushed this back well into medieval times. Is your criterion achievement in science and technology? Historians now hold that the last few centuries of the Middle Ages are centuries of marked scientific advancement. Indeed, as George Sarton liked to point out, the humanists proper of the Renaissance, the men of letters, theologians, moralists, were at least as contemptuous of grubbing natural science, at least as "deductive" and as respectful of written authority, as were the Schoolmen. It is even possible, though a bit extreme, to defend the thesis that the Renaissance proper means a *regression* in the growth of modern science. Is your criterion economic, the growth of a money economy, banking, extensive trade? Modern research pushes most of these back to the Crusades, to the high Middle Ages, and especially to the late medieval Italian city-states; Florence, Venice, Genoa, and the rest.[33]

Even the historian who originally applied the term Renaissance to the period of cultural change which marks the dawn of the modern world felt he was creating, rather than recording, an historical epoch. In Jacob Burckhardt's brilliant *The Civilization of the Renaissance in Italy,* he admitted as much. "My starting point has to be a vision [of] the first mighty surging of a new age." Burckhardt's "vision" of a new type of individual, featuring a many-sided personality, and a new culture devoted to the "discovery of the world and of man, was indeed an exciting creation, a creation which has so captivated the modern imagination that we now divide and describe our history in terms of that vision. The point to remember is that this vision was a highly idealized protrait of an age which tended to be populated by colorful personalities often somewhat larger than life. Our vision will be considerably clearer if we can appreciate the Renaissance for all its virtues, without going so far in that appreciation that we come to disparage the achievements and attitudes of the preceding ages.

The Renaissance is a colorful and exciting time. Whereas the thousand years of the Middle Ages appears to us as a process of slow and often painful growth, the Renaissance is a good deal more like a sudden eruption. In the century after 1450, the Pacific Ocean was discovered, the Western Hemisphere was discovered, man first circled the globe and came to understand its true dimensions, Copernicus revolutionized science with his concept of a heliocentric universe, the traditional Christian Church fragmented into many different versions of Christian truth, and the printing press replaced handwriting, pouring 20 million volumes into the waiting hands of the Western world. Even these few samples of growth and change should indicate the revolutionary and explosive nature of the Renaissance.

Still this should not disguise the fact that the Renaissance, like any other historical period, drew heavily upon the ages which had preceded it. The Renaissance looked backward to absorb many of the features of classical civilization. But it also looked forward to a new view of man whose power was both as yet undefined and unlimited.

This transitional period from the medieval world to the modern world, spanning roughly 1300 to 1600, included not only higher accomplishments in art, music, literature, and science, but also saw far-reaching changes in the economic bases of life and the structure of society, as well as pioneering in the new political theories which would give rise to the national state. A brief glance at each of these categories might suggest how sweeping these changes would prove to be.

Life throughout the early medieval period had been based upon the simple agrarian existence of the self-sufficient manor house. Little trade had existed; exchange of goods was limited to barter. But as the Middle Ages drew to a close, money came into common use, bringing with it the development of urban life, commerce, and industry. As this capitalistic society emerged, a gigantic economic alteration of society was brought about.

These economic changes brought with them equally basic social changes. The town became the center of European culture and society. No longer did cultural life or social life revolve around the manor house. As one historian has expressed it, "The age of the Renaissance was an age of towns and urban life."

The shift in economic and social patterns caused equally basic political changes. The feudal society of the Middle Ages had depended heavily upon personal relationships. But the development of coined money and the growth of trade and industry disrupted this personal relationship which was at the root of medieval political life, producing a shift in political loyalties. The growing urban communities tended to support the rising group of national rulers in an effort to achieve relief from the turbulence of the feudal warfare state. The new princes thus could depend on the rising economic and social framework as they consolidated power and crushed the older feudal nobility. Because of their ability to collect taxes in the new money economy, they possessed a standing army far more loyal and far more powerful than the small groups of personal retainers who had carried on the warfare of the feudal age. The administration of justice was also a centralized and standardized function of the new political state. Thus the new age brought with it new politics, destined to lead to nationalism, and before it was through, to the age of absolutism.

A time of such great economic, social, and political change naturally brought with it a major cultural revolution as well. It is to this cultural revolution that most people refer when they use the term Renaissance. This was a time of splendid development in literature, art, and architecture, as well as scientific and geographic discovery. This was the age of Shakespeare, da Vinci, Michelangelo, Columbus, Magellan, and Copernicus.

The key transitional figure from the Middle Ages to the Renaissance era was Dante Alighieri (1265–1321). Greatest of the Italian poets, he was immersed in the active intellectual life of his times, and was a member of Florentine sociey, the most culturally advanced of any in Europe. His life had been repeatedly upset by the perpetual state of civil war which plagued Florence, a conflict which in miniature duplicated the struggle between the Pope and the Holy Roman Empire. Dante's *De Monarchia* was designed to meet this political question. Should the State be independent or under the control of the Church? Although deeply immersed in the theology of the Middle Ages, Dante was the first of the Renaissance political thinkers who insisted that the ruler of the state received his power directly from God, rather than from the Pope. This began to free the European state from the control of the Church, thus potentially advancing human freedom. But, at the same time, this also began the development of what would later be made explicit: Divine right monarchy, an attitude which regressed in terms of man's political freedom.

Even while Dante was thus pointing the way toward Renaissance politics, he was devoting his best literary efforts to the purification and strengthening of the older Christian society united by common ideals. It is that traditional world view which Dante's *Divine Comedy* best represents. Yet even here, in Dante's cultural attitudes, we sense a divergence from that displayed by a St. Augustine or a St. Thomas. In much of Dante's work, especially in *De Monarchia*, for the first time in Christian thought temporal concerns are regarded as an autonomous affair with their own ends, ends which are not necessarily intended to serve the interests of the Christian Church. Human culture is regarded as a separate category.

It is immediately apparent that Dante's sources were not exclusively Christian. He was largely influenced by Aristotle's *Ethics* and possessed a romantic view of the classical past which was a considerable departure from the more critical view of that society evidenced by St. Augustine and other early Christians. In all these ways, Dante looks forward to the Renaissance rather than back to the Middle Ages. Yet throughout all this, the strongly Christian emphasis remains apparent. Dante was at once a child of the Middle Ages and an early Renaissance thinker.

The strong taste for classical antiquity which Dante evidenced was developed by such later Renaissance figures as Petrarch until it became one of the dominant characteristics of the Renaissance. It has since affected virtually every aspect of European culture, and all literary and philosophic channels. For the first time, men began to view history as at least partially man-centered, rather than exclusively God-centered.

HUMANISM

"Immortal God, what a world I see dawning! Why can I not grow young again?" So wrote Erasmus of Rotterdam in 1517. This gentle soul with such a zest for life and learning sensed in developing events what he called "the near approach of a golden age." He was right when he predicted a current of revitalization and reform in learning, but wrong in his prediction that a "public and lasting concord of Christendom" was about to be achieved.

The new fact which Renaissance thought attempted to amalgamate with medieval belief was the developing idea of an immense and uniform universe. During the Renaissance the idea that nature was a great machine whose secrets might be discovered occurred with ever-increasing insistence. Pious Christianity and Humanism merged in such men as Erasmus, producing the hope that perhaps this machine-like nature of the universe, in the same manner as a watch, was itself the expression of an Idea. They hoped to bridge the growing chasm between science and religion in this manner.

If the older scholastic approach no longer seemed to meet the new scientific realities, a new faith might be required, a faith in the methodology of science, to revitalize the truth in the depleted world of metaphysics. This attempt to make metaphysics "scientific" was to prove extremely difficult. It seemed that God could not be discovered with a telescope nor the soul discovered with a microscope. But the new discoveries of science swept on and on, exerting a compelling logic of their own. The discoveries of Copernicus seemed to imply materialistic and mechanistic conceptions of the universe. Thus, the Renaissance tended to produce a wave of reaction against medieval thought, particularly against the Schoolmen and against the Schoolmen's favorite authority, Aristotle. Some of this revulsion against the teachings of the past reached ridiculous proportions, as in Pierre de la Ramée's theses in which he set out to prove that "everything taught by Aristotle is false."

Of course, most Humanists were better able to retain their balance. Francis Bacon, as one of the outstanding philosophers of science in the new Renaissance era, sought to generalize the principles that the practicing scientists were employing. These new scientific principles, he felt could be applied to man's world view. The scientific method, the accumulation of "factual" evidence from which *a priori* reasoning was to be excluded, led to the development of what has become known as the inductive method.

"Experiment is the true interpreter between nature and man. Experience is never at fault. What is at fault is man's laziness and ignorance. Thou, O God, dost sell us all good things for the price of work." In these words, one of the greatest of the Humanists, Leonardo da Vinci, set forth the faith of the new age.

Thus, there arose throughout Western Europe a new attitude toward life which has been termed Humanism. Humanism was a reaction against the ideal of a transcendent spiritual order, an attempted return to the finite and the human. In the process, the Humanists rediscovered nature, not as a mysterious power ordered by a divine authority, but as a reasonable and predictable place which man could, by scientific method, come to know and ultimately control. These new leaders of Western thought thus placed their faith in applied science, rather than speculative knowledge. Still, for most people, no sharp break was made with the past, the majority remained faithful to the older religious tradition. In fact, most of the Humanists themselves were torn between a wholehearted adherence to naturalism and their older Christian tradition. It is this characteristic reaching backward while also reaching ahead that is most typical of Humanism.

Humanism and the Renaissance flowered first in Italy. All the necessary ingredients were present there: a strong tradition of classical learning, prosperous urban centers, wealthy patrons both within and without the Church who understood the new style of life and could afford to further those attitudes. To these people it seemed that man had inherited a vast new world and was no longer bound as a mere creature of God, no longer restricted by the older medieval idea of hierarchy, but now able to rise to great heights bounded only by his own ambition. Mirandola, a brilliant fifteenth-century Platonist who died in his thirty-first year, could write:

> Constrained by no limits, Thou, Man, shalt ordain for thyself the
> limits of thy nature . . . As maker and molder of thyself, thou mayest
> fashion thyself in whatever shape thou shalt prefer. Thou shalt have
> the power to degenerate into lower forms of life, which are brutish.
> Thou shalt have the power, out of thy soul and judgment, to be
> re-born into the higher forms, which are divine . . . .

At first glance, such assumptions seem rather startling even
to our own age. Yet, these must have been exciting times. Gio-
vanni Pico, Count of Mirandola, who lived from 1463 to 1494, was
the perfect example of the brilliant young intellectual who espoused Humanism. Mirandola spent years traveling in Italy and
France, gathering a library while learning Greek, Latin, Hebrew,
Chaldee, and Arabic. When twenty-four years old, he publicly
offered to defend against all criticism some nine hundred propositions summarizing his conclusions in theology and philosophy!
Like many other Humanists, Mirandola took all knowledge
as his province and, with his great ability and his zest for life,
seemed a perfect example of the ideal toward which Humanism
strove.

Another of the Renaissance Humanists, Leon Battista Al-
berti, described himself in *Self-portrait of a Universal Man:*

> In everything suitable to one born free and educated liberally, he
> was so trained from boyhood that among the leading young men
> of his age he was by no means the last. For, assiduous in the science
> and skill of dealing with arms and horses and musical instruments,
> as well as the pursuit of letters and the fine arts, he was devoted to
> the knowledge of the most strange and difficult things. And finally
> he embraced with zeal and forethought everything which pertained
> to fame. To omit the rest, he strove so hard to attain a name in
> modeling and painting that he wished to neglect nothing by which
> he might gain the approbation of all men. His genius was so ver-
> satile that you might almost judge all the fine arts to be his. Neither
> ease, nor sloth held him back, nor was he ever seized by satiety in
> carrying out what was to be done.

One nineteenth-century observer of the Renaissance, Walter
Pater, has summed up the Humanist spirit:

> To burn always with this hard gemlike flame, to maintain this
> ecstasy, is success in life. . .

One of the more generally known of these Renaissance figures was Leonardo da Vinci (1452–1519). He was the literal realization in the flesh of the multi-sided man who was the ideal of Humanism. For over three centuries his tremendous abilities as a painter had caused his admirers to think of him chiefly in this connection. In fact, we now know that painting was scarcely more than a sideline for him. He was engaged in numerous activities, including among others, astronomy, botany, sculpture, architecture, town planning, hydraulics, military engineering, geology, mechanics, and physical geography. Like the Humanist society in which he played a prominent part, Leonardo da Vinci was endlessly curious about the natural world, about man and his environment.

The list of names of such men is a long one indeed, and the accomplishments of the Humanists almost produce disbelief when one reads a catalogue of their activities. Although the Renaissance began in Italy, it was not limited to that area. In fact, some of the most outstanding Humanists were not Italian. Among the most important of these would be Desiderius Erasmus of Rotterdam, who lived from 1466 to1536. He dominated the European world of letters in the early sixteenth century. Although he remained a priest and a loyal Christian throughout his life, Erasmus was more a scholar than a priest. He traveled widely to visit all the areas where men seemed most interested in learning. While visiting England to lecture on Greek at Cambridge, he became a close friend of Sir Thomas More, the English Humanist. Erasmus has generally been conceded to be "the prince of Humanists."

Just as some Humanists were close to the Church, others were close to political affairs. Sir Thomas More (1478–1535) had been a successful lawyer and later became Lord Chancellor for King Henry VIII. In the case of both Erasmus and More, their subsequent involvement in the affairs of the Reformation makes abundantly clear the close Humanist connection between the Renaissance and the Reformation.

Often those who view the Renaissance and Reformation as the precursors of a "modern" age and who will allow no appearance of virtue or intelligence to be attributed to the Middle Ages will then attempt to read into the new Humanist glorification of individual human personality a direct lineage with modern democracy. Nothing could be more misleading. In fact, the Humanist was almost totally out of harmony with the so-called "common man." The new elite of Rennaissance Humanists believed in a frankly privileged class of intellect and ability. The Jeffersonian ideal of an aristocracy of talent is cast in the same mold. When Friedrich Nietzsche followed Jakob Burckhardt as a professor at Basel in the nineteenth century, he viewed the life lived by the Renaissance Humanists, as catalogued by Burkhardt, as the closest possible realization upon earth of his "Superman," a concept far removed from "democracy."

By this time it should be evident that Humanism was indeed a coat of many colors. In Erasmus and More it had its strongly theological proponents, yet an equally strong rationalistic strain was also present in other Humanists. Perhaps the Humanist was hard to classify precisely because he wanted to be an individual. But while the Humanist wanted to be himself, he was not always entirely clear what the content of that new self was to be. He thus drew heavily upon the Middle Ages in some ways, upon classical antiquity in other ways, and yet rejected these earlier teachings in certain new attitudes about man and his world. Whatever the Humanists were, they soon built up among themselves the willingness to cite one another as authorities in what has been described as a "mutual admiration society." In their attempt to be individualistic, the Humanists thus came to substitute new standards of behavior and thought for the old standards, but came to be just as insistent that all men (if they were truly Humanists) must adhere to the new standards. This is the explanation for the remark that the Humanists became vainer and more worldly Schoolmen.

The creative artists of the Renaissance seemed closest to the attitude which the Humanists adopted toward life. In the work of a Rabelais, a Shakespeare, or a Cervantes, we seem to come closest to the Humanist attempt to find a middle way between the traditions of medieval Christianity and the new rationalism of science that promised to take all the mystery from a mysterious universe.

We moderns often feel most at home with the Humanists, and seem to recognize them as contributors to the way of life we now lead:

These are the heroes of the Renaissance proper, the men whose doings make good reading, even in textbooks—Cellini, murdering, whoring, sculpturing, posturing, talking with kings and popes; Leonardo la Vinci, painting, building, writing, inventing airplanes, submarines and amored battle-tanks (on paper), engineering. Then there are kings like Francis I of France and Henry VIII of England who not only looked kingly, who not only had the athletic and hunting skills, essential to esteemed position in the upper class of Western society right down to the present-day United States, but who were also learned in the ancient tongues, witty, capable of turning out a poem or an essay, and, of course, great lovers. There are whole families like the Borgias, full of the most fascinating, immoral, and unconventional people.[33]

We moderns find soulmates in these Renaissance men, since they seemed to believe that man was the measure of all things. They appeared to be men with no stuffiness, free in the fullest sense of the word.

Rabelais again is a case in point. He loves to make fun of the monkish Middle Ages, its superstitions, its pretenses to chastity, its Aristotelian learning. He is going to free men and women from this nonsense. His Abbaye de Thélème is a very lay abbey indeed, open to both sexes, and inscribed on its gate is the pleasant command, *Fay ce que vouldras* (Do what you like).[33]

Thus the manifestation of the individual Renaissance personality has taken the name "Humanism." The component elements in this humanism were likely to be a revival of interest in the classical world, a flowering of interest in all forms of artistic expression, and the development of a new super-hero, incorporating at once the skills of the soldier, courtier, patron, scholar, and artist. One final element in the Humanist personality tended to be the rejection of Aristotelianism and the substitution of a redefined Platonism.

Aristotle came to be viewed as being too constricting, as being tied too closely to formal logic, and being too closely associated with the Schoolmen. Remember, that in the High Middle Ages Aquinas had based his system of reasoning upon Aristotle, and it was the whole spirit of Humanism to be in rebellion against that theologically based view of society. Thus, Plato, in his new form of "neo-Platonism" and with his emphasis upon ideas as the only true reality, seemed to offer an escape from the restrictions of the old system of thought. In a sense, this might appear to be a contradiction, since the Humanist placed his emphasis upon the affairs of this world (as Aristotle did, at least partially, in his view of this world and material reality). So, it would seem at first glance that Plato's view of the world and its reality, which placed its emphasis entirely upon abstract ideas, would have been less to the earthy, physical Humanist's liking.

However, the formal philosophic thought of the Humanists was never one of their strongest points. The point to remember is that while these men left one authority, Aristotle, they did so only to take up another authority in Plato. So it was Plato's approach to reality that became popular in the Renaissance. Why? Aristotelian logic plus St. Thomas' use and adaptation of that point of view was so bound up in the theological view of the world that Thomas had brought forward from the Middle Ages, and presented such a massive world view and such a complete system, that the Humanists had to turn to other approaches to build their own systems of thought and their own world view. The combination of Aristotle and Aquinas presented a road block that the Humanist had to detour on his way to the modern world. The detour by way of Plato (despite all its contradictions) offered the Humanist the escape from the past that he was looking for, and offered it at a lower price than would have had to be paid to attempt to dismantle the enormous and solid edifice St. Thomas had erected. In this, the Humanists were typically modern. As George Santayana phrased it a number of years ago, "We nowadays no longer refute our predecessors, we pleasantly bid them good-bye."

The Humanists were also very modern in their sense of being in revolt against their fathers—in their case, the men of the Middle Ages. The Humanist hoped to place his emphasis upon finding man's happiness and achievement in this life, rather than hoping that problems would become more understandable in the next. In this *secular* emphasis, Humanism pointed the way toward another of the common intellectual characteristics of the modern world.

Humanism is thus really a peculiar mixture of the old and the new. It takes much from the past and is less new or different than it pretends. It not so much rejects Aristotle and Aquinas as refuses to discuss them. Yet for all this, there is a new emphasis on this world and on the revival of many classical values that are well worth having. This tends to lead toward modern thought, as well as producing a great deal of literature, art, science, and new ideas. Humanism, however, is not really a new system of thought. It is rather a new emphasis, working within old forms and ideas.

MACHIAVELLI

One of the areas where the new Renaissance mentality was to have its most clear-cut application was in the political thought of Machiavelli. He completely ignored the medieval idea that God stands behind a fixed moral order. Displaying the curiosity of the Renaissance, Machiavelli set out to discover how men actually behave, rather than how they should behave. He thus displayed the Renaissance penchant for collection of facts and inductive reasoning as the basis for his political thought.

Niccolò Machiavelli (1469-1527) was a Florentine politician who served the Medicis in various capacities while producing *The Prince* and his less well-known *Discourses on Livy.* Properly to understand the man and his work, it is necessary first to understand something of the political situation amidst which he lived. The feudal system was breaking down and was being increasingly replaced by an urban framework. Meanwhile, as we have seen, a new middle class was arising to side with the new nation-state in its struggle for power with the feudal nobility. Furthermore, this new national state was already well advanced in a trend toward absolutism as all the old institutions fell under the control of central administration through taxation and military control. Machiavelli saw perhaps more clearly than any other man of his age the direction which politics seemed to be taking. He understood, far better than most, the large role that coercion, unlimited by any moral consideration, was destined to play in modern politics.

By the time of Machiavelli, the Papal state had become a cross between a universal monarchy and an Italian city-state. The constant warfare between Naples, Milan, Venice, Florence, and the other Italian city-states, was actively participated in by the

Renaissance Popes. The result was an anarchy which prevented this sort of centralization of national power which was occurring elsewhere throughout Europe. This lack of centralization was leaving Italy increasingly open to plunder by its new national neighbors. The age required power, and power required centralization.[35]

Looking about him, Machiavelli saw a moral degradation even more destructive for Italy than the political decentralization of which he complained. The age of the Renaissance was not a pretty era in its code of personal conduct. Moral anarchy grew apace with political anarchy. It was a period truly called the age of "bastards and adventurers." Italian society and politics were in an advanced stage of institutional decay. While intellectually brilliant and artistically creative, Renaissance Italian society was a party to the worst political and moral corruption. Cruelty and even murder had long since become the normal agencies of government, while good faith and moral scruples were regarded as forms without meaning, to be ignored, or to be given lip service. Coercion and deceit were king. It was natural enough that in such a society a political theorist such as Machiavelli would come forward, finding no limitation upon the action of the individual except that applied by his own self-interest and egotism.[35]

Both *The Prince* and *Discourses on Livy* examine the reasons for the rise and fall of political states. The more famous *Prince* deals with the type of society in which Machiavelli found himself in his own time, while *Discourses on Livy* is concerned with the process of expansion experienced by the Roman Republic over 1000 years before. Both works show the typical Machiavellian approach: the endorsement of immoral means for political purposes and the insistence that successful government depends on coercion and deceit. But it is also true that, while Machiavelli's ideal prince is a despot, the *Discourses on Livy* demonstrated genuine enthusiasm for popular government, when such a government could be founded upon a virtuous citizenry. In fact, Machiavelli felt that the more virtuous society evidenced by the Roman Republic was impossible to duplicate in the decadence of Renaissance Italy. He therefore tended to set aside such attitudes, and advocated instead the frankly amoral domination of society by his ruthless and powerful prince. For such a prince, the purpose of politics was to preserve and further increase political power. Power itself became both the means and the end and would brook no moral scruple in its path.[35]

Prior to Machiavelli, all political theory from Plato to the Renaissance addressed itself to a single question, the end of the state. Machiavelli's importance lies in his assumption that power is an end in itself. Thus Machiavelli separated power from any moral, ethical, or religious consideration. Political power thus divorced from morality and made an end in itself ultimately makes the state an end unto itself, an agency for the determination of whatever values it chooses to pursue. Thus, all value and all morality came to be engulfed in political power. In the process, Machiavelli released government from the restraint of law. This paved the way for the consummation of the royal absolutism which was already developing in Machiavelli's time. More important, and more dangerous, Machiavelli's theory also provided the rationale for the modern displays of power which have come to press so heavily upon mankind in the mid-twentieth century. In the political realm, Renaissance man was indeed the precursor of the modern world.

THE AUTONOMOUS INDIVIDUAL
AND
THE MAN-CENTERED UNIVERSE

A close connection exists between the Renaissance and Reformation and the Modern World in a number of areas besides politics. The older medieval framework was disintegrating, life was moving at a faster and faster pace, while emphasis was increasingly on this world rather than the next. The world of absolute values was tending to dissolve into a world of increasing relativism. Yes, modern society was beginning to come into existence. One of the Renaissance concepts pointing most clearly to the Modern World was the idea of individuality. Rooted in a belief in the greatness and uniqueness of man, this concept naturally carried with it an implication of the necessity for liberty to achieve that greatness and uniqueness. Free will and the free exercise of will were thus a problem of primary interest to the thinkers of the Renaissance.

In this emphasis upon individual conscience, the Renaissance was clearly pointing the way toward the Protestant Reformation.

Yet the Renaissance also carried with it a new view of man as a totally autonomous individual. This view of human nature went far beyond the Christian ideal adhered to by the Protestant Reformation, which only made an appeal against the authoritarian attitudes of the Catholic Church. To go beyond that, as Renaissance man in fact intended to go, to suggest that man is the molder of his own destiny and the master of his own fate, was to take the first steps in an increasingly secular outlook which would come to bear bitter fruit in modern politics and philosophy. At the time, Renaissance man and the Protestant reformers surely did not entirely appreciate the full implication of the doctrine. The self-consciousness of the Renaissance which began to chafe against the medieval unity was prompted at first by a sincere and beneficial desire for increased self-understanding, but in the modern world the result has become not self-understanding but ego-centrism.[4] The first steps were being taken in man's modern attempt to dismiss God and put man in His place.

THE REFORMATION

It is in the area of individual conscience and individuality that the Renaissance and Reformation have both their greatest truths and most dangerous possibility of error. It is also in the matter of individual conscience that the Renaissance and Reformation, for all the differences which we will discuss, have their closest affinity.

As in the case of the Renaissance, the changes of the Reformation were not only religious, but social, economic, and political as well. Again like the Renaissance, these changes stemmed in large part from earlier developments reaching back into the medieval period. The Renaissance also contributed its share to the Reformation. While most of society was composed of poorly educated priests and even more poorly educated laymen, many practices needing reform could pass without comment. But as the Renaissance provided an increasingly more sophisticated middle class, demand for such reform tended to grow. Of course, when the Humanists subjected the entire body of religious thought to such severe criticism, the whole problem of faith itself suffered badly in the process.

Much of the religion as then practiced in society did need reform by the time of the Reformation. The idea of witchcraft was still widely accepted, as were other superstitions. In such a state, it was impossible for the Church to adjust itself rapidly enough to the needs of the new age. An internal struggle was going on between the Pope and the Conciliar Movement, thus stifling any possibility of reform between them. It appeared that nothing short of revolution could redirect the tendency of the Christian Church. That revolution was to be the Protestant Reformation.

Most of the Protestant reformers viewed themselves as revising Christianity backward toward its original impulses, rather than seriously modifying the doctrine of the Christian Church. The criticism of the Church as it developed was directed less toward fundamental error, it appeared, than toward the Church's decadence. As medieval culture itself declined, as Gothic architecture became excessively flamboyant, so the Church itself had tended to become more worldly, losing the careful balance and self-control of the Church in St. Thomas' day. Undoubtedly, the Church of the Renaissance period was by no means as immoral as it has been made to appear by some Protestant reformers. Everybody likes a good story. Unfortunately, some of us seem to like it better as it paints a worse and worse picture. Many priests undoubtedly retained sincere vocations and were practicing Christians and Churchmen in the fullest possible sense. Yet a decline did seem to be occurring, and with it criticism, demands for reform, and even outright revolt became more and more common.

Even the gentle Erasmus wrote a diatribe attacking the excesses of the Renaissance Popes. He pictured the soul of Pope Julius as it was greeted at the gate of heaven by St. Peter who asked what the Pope's credentials were for admittance. Julius responded that he had produced a great Papacy, since he had captured Bologna.

"Why did you capture Bologna? Was the ruler a tyrant, or a heretic?"

"O, no!" responded Julius.

"Why then?" asked Peter.

"I wanted Bologna for my son."

Shocked, Peter asked, "Popes with wives and sons?"

Julius responded. "You don't understand. Not wives, just sons."

Peter again demanded to know what the Pope had done to deserve admittance to heaven and was given an account of the splendors achieved by the Renaissance Pope. Peter retorted that in his day the Papacy had not been run in such a manner, to which Julius responded that in Peter's day the Papacy had not been worth having!

Coupled with this decline in spirituality, the medieval Church organization was also clashing with the newly created absolute states of Europe. The Church owned immense estates which gave it economic independence. It possessed vast political privileges granted it during the feudal anarchy of the Middle Ages. It possessed its own court system in rivalry with the jurisdiction of national, civil courts. The Church maintained that ecclesiastical privilege and patronage within the various countries were also subject to its control. The Church attempted to exclude Church lands from taxation by the secular state. Thus in the political realm, the Church and the dominant political form of society were approaching a clash.

Decadence within the Church, patriotism in the rising national states, conflict of interest with the economic and political affairs of the absolute monarchs, the secular spirit of the Renaissance . . . together these set the stage for revolt.

Erasmus himself had become painfully aware of the corruption within the Church. His translation of the Greek New Testament had given a scholarly emphasis to reform. He was also an outspoken critic of many existing beliefs and practices. Erasmus was voicing the discontent of the leading intellectuals of his age with the Schoolmen who had apparently ceased to be a meaningful intellectual force. The common people felt many of the same discontents, but found their spokesman not in the highly intellectual Erasmus, but in the more fundamental Martin Luther.

For all of his criticisms of the Church, Erasmus viewed revolt against religious authority as a step toward religious anarchy. Unwilling to break from the Church, he advocated reform from within. Such a position placed such Humanists as Erasmus and Sir Thomas More in the difficult position of being unwilling to defend the Protestants and yet unwilling to be an unqualified supporter of the orthodox views of the Church. True to their own conscience, they were often heartily disliked by both groups. As the religious disputations of the age mounted in intensity, Erasmus and other internal reformers of the Church found themselves the object of bitter attacks.

Martin Luther charged, "Erasmus is an enemy of all religion, he is the true adversary of Christ, a perfect replica of Epicurus and Lucian. Whenever I pray, I pray for a curse on him." It seems clear that the age of the Reformation, while an era devoted to a type of freedom of conscience, in practice espoused more a "freedom to agree" than a freedom to disagree.

MARTIN LUTHER

Criticism of the Church and the currents of revolt stemming from it had already produced several comparatively minor eruptions of disobedience before the time of the Reformation, especially in the teachings of Wycliff and Hus. But the religious revolt began in earnest in Germany. The traditional medieval faith was most firmly entrenched among the Germans. It was a German mystic, Thomas à Kempis, who had written the *Imitation of Christ,* so widely studied by the sincerely religious German population. The corruption of the Renaissance Papacy, coupled with the new Humanist translations and the widespread use of the printing press, provided both the occasion and the means for a rethinking of religious attitudes and allegiances.

Of equal importance in the Germanies was the political question. Under the so-called Holy Roman Empire, Germany was divided into innumerable tiny principalities, producing disunity and weakness at a time when such rising national states as England and France were making great strides toward political unification. Not only did the German religious zeal go hand in hand with German patriotism, but German hardheaded business sense was also involved. The pious and patriotic German burgher was also conscious of the financial world around him and had come to resent the constant drain of German revenues to support the grand manner of living indulged in by the Renaissance popes. The times were pregnant with the possibilities of change.

As fate had prepared the ideal situation for the outbreak of the Reformation, it had also prepared a leader capable of making such a radical break. Martin Luther was of middle class German stock. Much to the disgust of his family he had become an Augustinian monk. His talents in religious disputation had made it possible for him to rise to the position of Professor of Theology at the University of Wittenberg. He began to probe deeply into the teachings of the Church concerning man's salvation. The Church, of course, had taught that at least a portion of man's salvation could come from the performance of good works. The deeply introspective Luther had come to feel that man was so sin-ridden that no amount of good works, nothing short of God's grace, could save him. One day in his study he reread a passage in St. Paul's Epistle to the Romans: "For therein is the righteousness of God revealed from faith to faith: as it is written, the just shall live by faith."

Salvation by faith alone! If each man could be saved by an act of faith within his own heart, then what need would there be for an interceding priesthood or for a Church hierarchy? At first the radical impact of such an idea was not fully apparent to Luther. It was to require an economic crisis to bring this implicit religious crisis to the fore.

One of the Renaissance Popes of the times, Leo X, of whom it has been said that he would have made "an excellent Pope if he had only been a little religious," had sent financial agents throughout Europe at just this time to raise money for the completion of St. Peter's in Rome. The high-pressure approach pursued in raising this money caused Luther to post his famous Ninety-Five Theses on the door of the Wittenberg Cathedral. As the dispute developed, it became clear that the religious thinking Luther had been doing in private for a number of years was causing him not merely to attack the method of raising the funds for St. Peter's, but actually to raise the question of the whole Church philosophy of good works. At first the affair was dismissed as "a squabble among monks." But as Luther continued to insist that an individual could have a relationship with God without need of the Church's intercession, the stage was set for a radical religious departure indeed. By 1520 the break between Luther and the Church had become complete. In December of that year, Luther publicly burned the papal bull which had warned him to cease from his heresy. Suddenly the religious, political, and economic discontent of the German population crystallized around this teacher of theology.

At first, Luther had advocated the right of private judgment and dissent. His own position required such a stand against the Church. But as time passed and other schisms grew from his original stand, among the Anabaptists and the group following Zwingli, Luther began to falter in his insistence upon the right of private judgment. When the Peasants' War erupted in Germany as a revolt harmful to the political authority of the Protestant princes who were backing his religious position, Luther ended all discussion of private judgment and dissent. As Lord Acton has commented:

> In consequence of this fact, Ranke affirms that the great reformer was also one of the greatest conservatives that ever lived; and his biographer, Jurgenns, makes the more discriminating remark that history knows of no man who was at once so great an insurgent and so great an upholder of order as he.[19]

In practice, Luther came to advocate the doctrine of passive obedience. "Neither oppression nor injustice excuses revolt; the only liberty for which you should care is spiritual liberty; the only rights you can legitimately demand are those that pertain to your spiritual life." Despite this final stand of Luther's, it is still clear that his work did contribute to the breakdown of authority in the last analysis. The idea of justification by faith alone broke the hold of the Church hierarchy and paved the way for the Reformation principle of the "priesthood of all believers." As Luther put the matter in his typical manner: "When you lie upon your deathbed you cannot console yourself by saying, 'The pope said thus and so.' The devil can drill a hole through that assurance. Suppose the pope were wrong? Then you will be defeated. Therefore you must be able to say at all times: 'This is the word of God.' "[4]

Martin Luther was a born leader who had no shade of hypocrisy or cant in his nature. His entire life is a demonstration of a man so absolutely sure of himself that his very intolerance takes on a certain grandeur. Placing his total trust in faith, Luther actually is representative of a return to the earlier Christian Church, rather than of the Humanism represented by such men as Erasmus.

HENRY VIII

Though the revolt in Germany had contained economic and political connotations, its primary impetus had been religious. Such was not the case in England. There the revolt was more frankly political in nature. Indeed, the man who became head of the English Church after its break with Rome never regarded himself as a Protestant and gloried in the title which an earlier Pope had given him: "Defender of the Faith." The centralization of power which had begun under the Tudors, and which had reached fruition in the era of Henry VIII and Elizabeth, tended to be directly opposed to the universalist ideas of the Catholic Church.

Here again, the Humanist with sincere intentions of reform without separation was in a dangerous and difficult position. Sir Thomas More, Lord Chancellor under Henry VIII, had actually resigned his post in an effort to avoid involvement in the political and religious quarrel stemming from Henry VIII's break with the Papacy. But he was not to be allowed the luxury of obscurity. Forced into the position of taking an oath of loyalty to the King which would involve rejection of the authority of the Catholic Church, More examined his conscience and decided that he must refuse. He was tried, found guilty of high treason, and beheaded.

JOHN CALVIN

John Calvin was almost totally independent of the political considerations which played a part in the decisions of the other Reformation figures. He had no concern except for how his religious doctrine could best be realized. Acton has summarized Calvin's attitude quite well in his assertion that:

> There was nothing in the institutions of men, no authority, no right, no liberty, that he cared to preserve, or towards which he entertained any feelings of reverence or obligation. His theory made the support of religious truth the end and office of the State, which was bound therefore to protect, and consequently to obey, the Church, and had no control over it.[19]

In the case of Calvin, the interest seemed to be less in favor of individual conscience than in the implementation of a new set of religious views. In pursuit of such an implementation, Calvin was perfectly willing to impose severe limitations upon the actual freedoms of the individuals within his control.

The system which John Calvin desired to erect was based upon his *Institutes of the Christian Religion,* certainly one of the key books ever produced in Christian theology. Calvin was quite willing to punish those holding different religious views from his own. One man found himself placed in the rack twice a day for an entire month for writing "all rubbish" on a piece of Calvin's literature. The theocracy set up in Geneva kept close watch upon the actions of every member of the community. The theater, bright colors in dress, and dancing were all treated as punishable crimes. In fact, no one was allowed to sit up in the inns of Geneva after nine P.M. (except the spies placed there to see that no one else did so). While we want to be clear that the Reformation thus in practice did not provide an enhancement of personal freedom, we also should understand that in the long run the political and economic and social freedom of the individual which was implicit in the revolt against the Church did have the ultimate effect of paving the way for a freer society. As well, the Calvinist insistence upon Bible reading implied a literate populace and a greater emphasis upon education, an education offered to all children in Geneva regardless of birth or wealth.

Many passages in the *Institutes* actually paved the way for democratic regimes to follow, as for example in Calvin's argument that:

> The vice or imperfection of man therefore renders it safer and more tolerable for the government to be in the hands of many, that they

may afford each other mutual assistance and admonition and that, if anyone arrogate to himself more than is right, the others may act as censors and masters to restrain his ambition.

Not only did the Protestant Reformation thus tend in the long run toward the possibility of greater individual freedom through fragmentation of political authority; it also retained the Christian view of a God-centered universe in which man's importance was derived not from his humanity, but from his association with a Higher Power.

THE COUNTER-REFORMATION

Though the Church had waited too long to initiate reforms which might have averted the fragmentation of Christendom, the processes of the Reformation finally brought about reform and a heightened sense of piety and purpose within the Church as well as without. One of the leaders in the Counter-Reformation was St. Ignatius of Loyola (1491–1556). Loyola had been a soldier until his thirtieth year when, while recovering from a wound, he had undergone a spiritual experience which had caused him to turn to the Church. At the University of Paris he had gathered together a small group of fellow students who bound themselves to poverty, chastity, and obedience to act as the spiritual troops of the Pope. Loyola had thus founded the Society of Jesus, destined for widespread activity in missionary and educational work. Thus the Reformation, both within and without the Church, had produced a heightened sense of piety, reform, and return to the earlier spiritual dignity of human nature.

THE INDIVIDUAL v. AUTHORITY: ECONOMIC IMPACT

One of the great changes which marked the beginning of modern times and this period of the Renaissance and Reformation was the growing spirit of curiosity and adventure, as seen in the outburst of exploration which occurred during the fifteenth century. It was in the fifteenth century that the Portuguese extended their explorations further and further down the coast of Africa until in 1485 Diaz rounded the Cape of Good Hope and opened the route to India. It was the fifteenth century which saw Columbus' discovery of the Western Hemisphere.

And while man discovered the world around him, bringing with that discovery economic changes of great import, economic changes of another sort were taking place at home. A theory which is commonly advanced suggests a close connection between the religion of the Reformation, especially Calvinism, and the rising spirit of capitalism. A distinction should be made, however, between the structure of capitalism and the spirit of capitalism. The structural elements of capitalism, such as bookkeeping, banking, credit, and a money economy, had actually been developed well before the time of the Reformation. But it is true that the *spirit* of capitalism has a close connection with the doctrines of Calvinism.

Whether the new doctrines of capitalism were stemming from structural changes which had taken place during the Renaissance, or changes in attitude which had occurred during the Reformation, the rise of capitalism was one of the elements pointing toward the modern world. The discovery of the advantages resulting from the use of capital was to revolutionize the world. One of these revolutionary changes was this redistribution of power within society. A new class, whose interests and attitudes were completely at odds with the older feudal nobility, now came into existence. This new middle class used its capital in the burgeoning economic and social framework common to the Renaissance and Reformation to revolutionize trade and commerce.

Yet, here again, we would be mistaken if we viewed the period of Renaissance and Reformation as a sudden change which did not have its roots in medieval times. Consider the matter of teachings on the taking of interest. Contrary to the commonly held view that medieval thought branded the taking of interest as sinful, St. Thomas had taught that a contract binding two parties to mutual risk was perfectly acceptable. That is to say there was nothing wrong with taking profit from loaned capital, so long as the risk was equally shared and a loss might also be taken should the venture fail. Medieval thinkers, like the Reformation moralists who followed them, still tended to place limitations upon the manner in which interest might be taken. Some objective standard of value was always being searched for and expounded. In the case of Luther, a rate of "fair" interest was assumed not to exceed five per cent. Luther also subscribed to the Thomistic idea of a contract of mutual risk. Calvin generally took the same position. In fact, the Reformation teachings on matters pertinent to the rising capitalistic ethic were in many cases produced from the traditional Christian mold.

Much the same might be said about the so-called Calvinistic ethic concerning the necessity of hard work for success in business. I think that most of us would discover that such "Christian virtues" as hard work and thrift have begotten prosperity for all people in all ages. This is scarcely a discovery of the Reformation.

Still, changes were occurring in the rise of the middle class. A new capitalist era was dawning, an era peculiarly well suited to the Calvinist discipline of hard work and to the rapid social revolution which occurred simultaneously with the Renaissance and Reformation. In many ways, the consequences of the political, social, and religious changes of the Renaissance and Reformation lent themselves to the new economic dispensation. This does not mean, as Karl Marx was later to assert, that the bourgeoisie merely seized upon the ethical standards stemming from the Reformation to feather their own economic nests. It does suggest, however, that the motivations lying behind the birth of the modern epoch were extremely complex and touched all levels of society in their inter-relationships.

THE INDIVIDUAL v. AUTHORITY: RELIGIOUS IMPACT

The connection between the rise of capitalism and the Protestant Reformation (with its revolt against authority) sometimes misleads people into a confusion between the individualism of the Reformation and nineteenth-century individualism. Actually, a great gap exists between the two. To understand the development of the modern world, it is extremely helpful to remember that Luther and Calvin were not of the same spirit as modern man. Protestantism as a religious ethic is actually quite medieval, even a return to a pre-medieval Christianity. It has been said in fact that Protestantism turned modern in spite of its motivation and its leadership, not because of them. "Protestantism was in nature and purpose a last medieval, a last great purely Christian, effort to justify in action God's way to man."[33]

Still, it is true that what began as a rather authoritarian assertion of several varieties of Protestant Christianity came in the long run to be an assertion of individualism which spread into other fields. The publication of the Bible in the vernacular and the wide distribution of the word of God, in a religious framework placing a premium upon individual reading of the Bible, dovetailed nicely with the mass production made possible by the printing press to further a highly individualistic variety of religious interpretation.

The Bible, after all, is itself subject to interpretation. Thus the Protestant appeal to the Bible as the final authority, only moved the matter of interpretation one step further, from the decision of the Catholic Church to the decision of some new authority, an authority able to interpret the meaning of Biblical passages. It has been suggested that "the Reformation superseded an infallible Pope with an infallible Bible . . ." But the promise of an implicitly individual interpretation concerning the meaning of that infallible Bible wrought a profound change on the inward ethical life of the individual. Both inside and outside the Church the marked increase in piety left the individual in a heightened relationship to his Creator. Especially in the Protestant sects, the individual was left in an almost naked confrontation with God.

The vast number of new Protestant sects which came into existence during the Reformation makes clear the emphasis upon individual conscience which did exist. Yet, as we have seen, the idea of "revolt" can be overemphasized. Remember, each of the Protestant sects went out and set up its own system, expecting and indeed forcing the people within their control to conform to *their* ideas. What began as freedom *from* the Catholic Church soon turned into "freedom to agree" with some particular Protestant sect. Both Protestant and Catholic burned heretics.

A more subtle religious point is involved in the era of the Renaissance and the Reformation which gave rise to the birth of the modern era. The Renaissance and Reformation are two separate historical entities, for all their similarities, two separate entities which at times are mutually contradictory. The Renaissance opposed the Catholic Church's control of cultural life on the grounds that autonomous human reason was sufficient unto itself. This view, when pursued far enough, was destined to divorce man entirely from any meaningful conception of God. It opened the door to an assumption that perpetual progress is possible as man's reason becomes self-sufficient. The Reformation, on the other hand, while it also opposed the authority of the Church, did so on the grounds, not that man's reason was sufficient unto itself, but rather that man's reason and all of man's institutions were insufficient to achieve salvation. Salvation to the Reformation Christian could be accomplished only by faith. The Renaissance thus looked toward a perfectible and totally self-sufficient man, while the Reformation assumed that such a development was impossible. What the modern world has seen for the last three centuries is the triumph of the Renaissance view of reality over the view held by the Reformation. Certain special circumstances have contributed to this victory. The parallel advance of science and the tremendous increases in wealth and comfort which have accompanied the technological, geographic, social, political, and economic changes of the modern world have tended to lull man into the assumption that perpetual progress is somehow his due. Modern man has tended to turn from the historical record as a discussion of "the bad old days" from which he has now permanently escaped. The assumption that such an escape from history is possible is a child of the Renaissance, not the Reformation.

As the Renaissance mind suspected, human history is indeed filled with endless possibilities. But as Reinhold Niebuhr has suggested, those endless possibilities which fill history are possibilities for both good and evil.

It [the Renaissance] believed that the cumulations of knowledge and the extensions of reason, the progressive conquest of nature and (in its last developments) the technical extension of social cohesion, all of which inhere in the "progress" of history, were guarantees of the gradual conquest of chaos and evil by the forces of reason and order. It did not recognize that every new human potency may be an instrument of chaos as well as of order; and that history, therefore, has no solution of its own problem.[4]

THE INDIVIDUAL v. AUTHORITY: POLITICAL IMPACT

One of the changes produced by the developments of the Renaisance and Reformation was the creation of a new political framework, the nation-state. Unfortunately, the Renaissance had produced Machiavelli's theory of power unlimited by moral concerns and the Protestant Reformation and Catholic Counter-Reformation had provided the excuse for the application of those doctrines on the European political scene, thus setting the stage for the age of absolutism.

The medieval political framework had been obviously dead or dying throughout Europe before the end of the sixteenth century. The regional and institutional pattern of cities and guilds and local controls retained its form but not its substance. Thus a new unit of political authority was gradually gathering all power unto itself: the state. Such was the state of affairs when Bodin published his *Six Books of the Commonwealth* in 1576. In Bodin the new age of absolutism had found its theorist. Machiavelli had favored the accumulation and exercise of power for its own sake but had never developed this concept of power to include the state as a sovereign entity in its own right. Such a development awaited Bodin and the centralized, absolute French monarchy. Bodin utilized the old concept of the Natural Law, divorcing God and morality from it and substituting the state in their place. Thus robbed of its legitimate meaning, Natural Law was perverted by Bodin into the bulwark of the new, absolute, sovereign state.

The rise of "Divine Right" and the absolute state, although beginning in France, was soon paralleled throughout Europe, even in the European nation most suspicious of power: England.

The Bourbons, who had snatched the crown from a rebellious democracy, the Stuarts, who had come in as usurpers, set up the doctrine that States are formed by the valour, the policy, and the appropriate marriages of the royal family; that the king is consequently anterior to the people, that he is its maker rather than its handiwork, and reigns independently of consent. Theology followed up divine right with passive obedience . . .

The clergy . . . were associated now with the interest of royalty . . . the absolute monarchy of France was built up in the two following centuries by twelve political cardinals. The kings of Spain

obtained the same effect almost at a single stroke by reviving and
appropriating to their own use the tribunal of the Inquisition, which
had been growing obsolete, but now served to arm them with ter-
rors which effectually made them despotic. One generation beheld
the change all over Europe, from the anarchy of the days of the
Roses to the passionate submission, the gratified acquiescence in
tyranny that marks the reign of Henry VIII and the kings of his
time.[19]

Once in the seat of power, the age of absolutism became
difficult to depose. Resistance to kings became a sin against religious faith. Worse yet, the political philosophers strongly supported this unholy union between religion and politics:

Bacon fixed his hopes of all human progress on the strong hand of
kings. Descartes advised them to crush all those who might be able
to resist their power. Hobbes taught that authority is always in the
right. Pascal considered it absurd to reform laws, or to set up an
ideal justice against actual force. Even Spinoza, who was a Republican and a Jew, assigned to the State the absolute control of religion.[19]

Thus, the Renaissance mentality in Machiavelli's development of the theory of power unlimited by morality, coupled with
the Renaissance philosophers' desire to remake society toward the
goal of perpetual progress, merged with the religious enthusiams
of Protestant and Catholic alike during the Reformation to produce a greater exercise of political power than anything possible
during the Middle Ages.

It is undoubtedly true that the Reformation was far less responsible for this turn of events than was the Renaissance. John
Calvin consistently held to the Pauline definition of sin as pride
rather than ignorance. He would surely have been suspicious of
the modern assumption of the possibility of perpetual progress, to
be achieved through political power exercised in remaking the
world. In all probability he would have suspected that such an
attempt was the most dangerous form of the sin of pride: "They
worship not Him but figments of their own brains instead." To
Luther also, the worst sin was pride, the pride that divorces man
from God in an imagined self-sufficiency.

Whether the Renaissance or the Reformation is primarily to

blame, the point remains that the collective will of man as embod-ied in the nation has achieved heights of that sin of pride never before equaled. The result?

> If you set up a polar contrast between authority (compulsion) and liberty (spontaneity), then in the balance the new state *in all its forms*, even when those forms are democratic, belongs on the side of authority. There are, of course, great historical and geographical variations, and some states can be put nearer the absolute pole of authoritarianism than others. But all of them have more political control over most individuals than was common in the Middle Ages.[33]

For good or ill, the modern age had dawned.

9

The Age of Reason

AS WITH MOST OTHER PERIODS IN MAN'S HISTORY, PRECISE
dates are difficult to assign to the Age of Reason. The period,
sometimes called the Enlightenment, is generally bracketed between 1650 and 1800. During that century and a half, Western
man developed a faith not merely in reason (Western man had
long had a faith in the human capacity for thought), but, more
specifically, believed that he had discovered an infallible method
to which human reason might be joined. That infallible method
was to be the methodology of natural science, which posited a
mechanical natural universe, a universe which contained within its
mechanism the secrets of all nature, including human nature.
What began as a scientific revolution soon led to a revolutionary
view of politics, religion, and society.

The Enlightenment brought with it a rapid cultural change
and a host of new institutions. These institutions ranged from such
political innovations as the nation state, democratic government,
and absolute monarchy, as well as such social innovations as the
numerous and widely diverse Christian sects and commercial capitalism. The medieval world view could have been characterized as
an attempted union between faith and reason, taking place in a
universe of absolute values, and conducted by men who recog-

nized themselves as a part of a system larger than any man or any combination of men. That framework was about to change radically as the Enlightenment brought with it new patterns of thought.

Much of this current of change probably stemmed originally from the Renaissance. Beginning in Italy, and then spreading rapidly throughout Western Europe, this new attitude seemed to be a reaction against any concept of a transcendent spiritual reality. Man was urged to turn from the absolute and the infinite, to a contemplation of the relative and the finite. He was urged to view nature as a realm which human beings could turn to their own uses, unlimited by any higher authority.

The search for a meaningful human existence grounded *exclusively* in human experience within the natural order, although anticipated in the Renaissance, came into its own in the Age of Reason. The new means by which the problems of the universe were to be solved was through the discovery of the appropriate "laws of nature." The most effective means of unlocking the secrets of these "laws of nature" was felt to be the science of mathematics. Thus evolved the tremendous effort to subject all aspects of the universe to quantitative, mathematical analysis.

As the Age of Reason developed, it became clear that this new emphasis broke with the past in several important respects. For the first time, men began to think of happiness on this earth as the primary goal of human existence. More important, men began to pay heed to the rationalists when they insisted that the universe was not as conceived by traditional Christianity, but was instead the Newtonian world-machine, composed *exclusively* of measurable materials and energies subject to discoverable "laws of nature." Men had always worked toward the discovery of such laws and had assumed their existence. The great change of the Age of Reason lay in the fact that the rationalist "laws of nature" were now regarded so all-pervasive as to leave no room for any transcendent values. Perhaps Man was indeed sufficient unto himself. Such a flattering possibility was to revolutionize man's view of himself and his society.

RATIONALISM

The objection could be made that a description of the Age of Reason in such utilitarian and worldly terms is an oversimplification. In one sense, this is true. In Kant and Spinoza, the Age of Reason had philosophers as concerned with ultimate values as any men have ever been. Even in the empirical, this-worldly tone of John Locke, it is clear that the Age of Reason still was quite moderate by modern standards. The rationalists in most cases still believed in God. But the central feature of their philosophy remains: a new emphasis upon *this world* was destined to have tremendous influence on modern society.

How did the Age of Reason define "reason?" More important, if reason were so all-powerful and beneficent, why was man's record as a thinking animal so badly botched? The rationalist would insist that bad law, bad environment, bad institutions, ignorance, and superstition had clouded man's thinking capacity. Thus, if man's institutions and environment were sufficiently modified to free this innate, "natural" capacity of the individual human being to reason, society could indeed be perfected.

In one sense, such an emphasis upon freeing the rational capacities of the individual human being is an exciting addition to the truly civilized ideas of the human race. Writing in 1784, in his description of the Age of Reason, *What is Enlightenment?*, Immanuel Kant raised this point:

> Enlightenment is the liberation of man from his self-caused state of minority. Minority is not the incapacity of using one's reason but is a lack of determination and courage to use it without the assistance of another. Dare to use your understanding! is thus the motto of Enlightenment.

In another sense, the rationalist faith in "immutable scientific laws" led the rationalists to assume that they could be free not only from the limiting circumstances of their human existence, but free also from all authority within the universe. In this second sort of freedom, Western man was destined to make a dangerous and ultimately destructive wrong turning. The Age of Reason brought with it the secularization of all learning, the attempt to interpret the universe and man as though mathematics, reason, and logic were sufficient unto themselves for a total explanation of human nature and the human condition. All religious value became "supernaturalism" and was viewed as an interference with tolerance and human freedom.

NATURALISM

In any examination of the history of natural science, it is abundantly clear that the Scholastics of the Middle Ages anticipated the more modern development of experimental physical science. In short, far from being the enemies of progress in this regard, the Middle Ages were already demonstrating progress in the same direction of natural science which characterizes the "modern" world. Still, it was during the Age of Reason that the great burst of development in natural sciences took place. It is this development which made possible the synthesis of the Newtonian world-machine. Considered in and of itself, this development in the extent of human knowledge concerning the natural workings of the universe in no way interfered with or *even pertained to* man's spiritual values. Unfortunately, the assumptions of natural science, quite proper when applied to the conditions of the natural universe, were also applied improperly in man's ethical and social realm until the "laws of nature" came to be viewed as a substitute for Natural Law.

To criticize the misapplication of the findings of natural science is not in any way to underrate the tremendous contribution which the Age of Reason made to natural science. Kepler, Bacon, Galileo, Descartes, Newton . . . such names immediately recall the tremendous advances in natural science which took place during the Age of Reason. Man was coming to know more and more about the universe in which he lived. Francis Bacon's championship of the inductive method, of applying collections of "facts" to the task of testing generalities, served the new scientific age well indeed, as did the tremendous contributions to mathematical analysis pioneered by René Descartes. Yet, even here, the modern scientist was heavily dependent upon his medieval scholastic counterpart for the development of those qualities of patience, accuracy, and the inquiring mind that were already the hallmark of Western scholars, long before the arrival of the Age of Reason.

Although Francis Bacon was a typical figure of the Age of Reason, the unattractive personal qualities which he demonstrated should not necessarily serve as a condemnation of the spirit of the age. Yet some connection does exist, since in many ways he epitomized the spirit of the age, at its best and its worst. Bacon was ambitious for power and wealth. His rise to Lord Chancellor of England was marked by an almost total lack of scruples. Even in the better side of his career, his scientific endeavors, some such traits are still apparent. Despite this, he was, as were many during the Age of Reason, immensely versatile and energetic, willing and eager to expand human knowledge and understanding in all conceivable areas. He epitomized the intellectual revolution which brought modern man to reject spiritual value as the final arbiter of man's affairs, substituting a faith in logical analysis. The medieval age of faith in spiritual values above man was replaced by a new age of faith in science. The entire society of Western Europe came to look for the improvement and perfection of mankind's condition through a greater knowledge of the secrets of the physical universe. This appeal was not limited to philosophers and scientists, but became attractive to rulers and scholars and bankers and clergy as well. Man's life was to be transformed through science.[33]

In modern times the expansion of the word "scientific" has reached a point at which all values not subject to the methodology of natural science are regarded in some circles as unprovable and, hence, "unscientific." Much of this tendency has its origins in the Age of Reason. In fact, most of what modern man calls "scientific facts" are really assumptions no more or less provable than those assumptions outside the laws of natural science. Yet, because of this confusion stemming from the Age of Reason, "truth" has now been replaced by "fact" and a monopoly of the ability to distinguish fact has been given to the methodology of natural science.

In largest part, this assumption of exclusive validity for "scientific fact" and the assumption of the invalidity of any truth not reached through the methodology of natural science can be traced directly to certain attitudes which had their origins in the

Age of Reason. In short, modern man has come to assume that spiritual qualities, laws, or concepts that are not measurable in terms of natural science are unprovable and therefore nonexistent. If such an asseration could be defended, man would indeed be spiritually disarmed and the builders of "heaven on earth" would have no barrier standing in their way. Actually, of course, this concept of the *exclusive* validity of the methodology of natural science, which had its origins in the Age of Reason, will not bear close examination.

To come to grips with this problem, it is necessary to understand the assumption that natural science makes about the laws of probability. Applying human reason to the problem, the philosophers and scientists of the Age of Reason concluded that it was always immensely more probable that the laws of nature would not be violated, than that they would be violated. Thus, lacking specific and tangible proof, the laws of probability would indicate that all verifiable and measurable action within the universe takes place due to "laws of nature," rather than any supernatural force which has its origins outside the natural order. Any spiritual intervention in the affairs of men is therefore of its very nature assumed improbable and, according to the laws of probability, nonexistent.

If we examine this matter of "probability" carefully enough, a peculiar sort of circular reasoning becomes apparent, a reasoning making it abundantly clear how unscientific so-called "scientific" conclusions can sometimes be when they are applied in areas where the methodology of natural science was never empowered to provide the right answers. To begin with, consider the apparently plausible assumption that, since the great bulk of human experience is with happenings within the natural order, the possibility of any human experience outside the natural order therefore becomes improbable and unlikely to occur. Think for a moment of the tremendous number of fertile unions necessary between your widely varied ancestors to produce the specific collection of physical and mental qualities which constitute your human form. If we were predicting the odds concerning the possibility of just such a particular combination of nerve endings, cells, and what-have-you of ever coming into existence, we would have to say that such a possibility was immeasurably remote. Despite the "improbability" of your physical existence in your precise form, here you are. There is nothing in the slightest way which is incredible (or improbable) about the statement that *you do exist.*[36]

Apparently then, this is not the sort of "probability" that the Age of Reason had in mind. Perhaps, instead, the philosophers of the Age of Reason, the men who came to reject the possibility of any spiritual qualities, who in fact rejected all qualities not measurable within the natural universe, were talking about historical probability.

Historical probability might be described as the idea that the more often a thing has happened, the greater the likelihood that it would happen again. The less frequent the recorded instances of an item occurring, the greater the likelihood that it will not happen again. To the philosophers of the Age of Reason, the very consistency of the "laws of nature" is supported by not merely a majority vote of past experience, but by one hundred per cent consistency.[36]

If in fact no experience so measurable and explainable by the "laws of nature" ever occurred, then we might be forced to agree that no such values exist. How do we know that all happenings within the universe are in fact the result of the *absolutely uniform* workings of the "laws of nature?" The rationalist philosopher, David Hume, in his *Essay on Miracles,* used the word "Miracle" to describe any intervention in the affairs of men having its origins outside the "laws of nature." C. S. Lewis has analyzed Hume's idea:

> . . . The regularity of nature's course, says Hume, is supported by something better than the majority vote of past experiences: it is supported by their unanimous vote, or, as Hume says, by "firm and unalterable past experience." There is, in fact, "uniform experience" against Miracle; otherwise, says Hume, it would not be Miracle. A Miracle is therefore the most improbable of all events. It is always more probable that the witnesses were lying or mistaken than that a Miracle occurred.

> Now of course we must agree with Hume that if there is absolutely "uniform experience" against miracles, if in other words they have never happened, why then they never have. Unfortunately we know the experience against them to be uniform only if we know that all the reports of them are false. And we can know all the

reports of them to be false only if we know already that miracles have never occurred. In fact, we are arguing in a circle.[36]

However this faith in the *exclusive* validity of the "laws of nature" came about, traditional Natural Law as an ethical system centered in God's being was set aside in favor of a materialistic view of the universe which placed its exclusive faith in the doctrines of the natural sciences.

RELIGIOUS IMPACT

Applied science rather than abstract, speculative knowledge set the tone for the Age of Reason. Still, no total break was made with the past. Most citizens of the Enlightenment remained faithful to the religious tradition. The great majority of society remained Christian, but took a decisive step when they separated the sphere of religion from the sphere of human reason. By the eighteenth century, this compromise broke down as the French philosophes pushed the Enlightenment on to its logical conclusion. They made an attempt to sweep away the older spiritual values of Western man, in their desire to reshape civilization on a naturalistic basis.

Despite the fact that this process took well over a century to reach its fruition, the important point is that, once the initial step was taken in the separation between man's natural universe and his spiritual ethic, the way was paved for a total rejection of man's spiritual side.

Even for those whose faith in traditional Christianity had been shaken, the idea of God seemed to linger on. Many of the distinguished thinkers in the middle years of the Enlightenment were Deistic in their religious views. And the Deist is very firm on the subject of the existence of God, although the God he posits is a distant and bloodless figure. God, as seen by the Deist, is precisely the sort of mechanical engineer we would expect to see in charge of the Newtonian world-machine. But once the engineer had set the machine running, it was unnecessary that the Deistic God should have any further concern for how his machine performed in actual operation.[33] The whole idea of a personal Creator and a fixed moral code thus came to be rejected. The Deistic God became very unlike God at all. Why would any group of intelligent men have posited such an emotionally unsatisfying and thoroughly unlikely God? Simply stated, the jump from the God of Christianity to no God at all was too great an intellectual step for most of the philosophers of the Age of Reason to take at a single bound. Voltaire's assertion that ". . . if God did not exist, he would have to be invented" may have sufficed for the transitory stages of the Age of Reason. The radicals of later generations had a different solution . . . they saw no need to invent God at all.

The tendency of rationalism thus proved to be the dismissal of God and the supernatural from its concept of the universe. Such a banishment left only the sphere of the natural universe, which the philosophers of the Age of Reason held to be regulated by a series of discoverable "laws of nature." Thus, in man's capacity to discover these laws of nature, man had gained his freedom from the supernatural and his mastery of the natural. The new director of the universe and of man's fate was to be man himself.[33]

How this process came about is a demonstration of what can happen to man's spiritual belief when he cuts himself free of all traditions and values except those verifiable by the methodology of natural science. The philosophers of the Age of Reason attempted to regard their religion as though it also were a part of the natural order. The early proponents of this idea felt that they were actually maintaining and even strengthening their religious beliefs by including those beliefs in the new system based upon the discovery of the "laws of nature."

To the philosophers of the early Enlightenment, "natural religion," the fundamental idea of the goodness and dignity of man, had always existed. These same philosophers, however, rejected miracles or religious rites or revelation as mere superstition. Thus, the new religion of the Enlightenment, so-called "natural religion," was really a new faith, a faith in the perfectibility of man on earth.

The list of men who attempted to maintain their religious convictions and yet follow the philosophic precepts of the Age of Reason is a long one. Perhaps most prominent on that list would be Descartes, Spinoza, and Leibniz, men who felt that religion must conform to reason and who strained every faculty to provide a version of religion which was able to conform. The story of how these men tried to remain simultaneously sons of the Age of Reason and sons of God demonstrates the perils faced by men who place all their values and find all their "facts" in the methodology of natural science.

Descartes made the attempt to harmonize traditional religious beliefs with a mechanistic universe in which everything could be explained by mathematics. To do this, he excluded the concept of God and the concept of the human soul from the realm of science. Through this philosophic dualism, Descartes was able to keep God and yet retain the inviolability of his scientific system. But in the very act of separation between the systems of man's spiritual universe and man's material universe, the process of the expulsion of God from the affairs of men had already begun.

Spinoza did not accept the dualism of Descartes, substituting in its place the idea that God and the material universe are one and the same. Spinoza thus kept God within the system, but at the price of making God a part of the natural order, thus making divine power subject to the same immutable "laws of nature" that man could discover and apply in the natural universe. This had the effect of making man and not God the ultimate authority in human affairs.

The German mathematician and philosopher, Leibniz, rejected the ideas of both Descartes and Spinoza and developed the idea of an ultimate reality composed of innumerable individual force centers. These monads, as Leibniz called them, were each a universe in miniature, constantly emanating from God. Thus what man distinguished as the physical universe and its workings ("laws of nature") was thought by Leibniz to be only the rational organization for the centers of force as provided by God. As in the case of Spinoza, Leibniz found himself the creator of a system in which God consisted of a measurable physical quantity, discoverable by human reason according to the laws of natural science, and therefore subject to total understanding and manipulation by man for man's own interest.

While such figures as Descartes, Spinoza, and Leibniz were trying to retain traditional religious concepts within the new rationalist idea of the universe, the Deists were intensifying their attacks on traditional Christianity. While this offensive was quite moderate in America and England, the French philosophes, as self-appointed guardians of the conscience of mankind, were unwilling to allow such "superstition" to continue. To Voltaire, the Bible was a collection of ignorance, Christ a religious fanatic:

> Every man of good sense ought to hold the Christian sect in horror. the great name of Deist, which is not revered sufficiently, is the only name one ought to take. The only gospel one ought to read is the great book of Nature, written by the hand of God and sealed with His seal. The only religion that ought to be professed is the religion of worshipping God and being a good man.

Like Voltaire, most of the French philosophes and encyclopedists ridiculed that traditional religion of Western man and substituted their new "religion of humanity" in its place. Rousseau proposed to establish Deism as the national "civil religion" of France.

The Age of Reason had tempted men to make God a part of the natural universe, leading to the Deistic break with traditional religious concepts. In the same manner the inconsistencies and shortcomings of a denatured, bloodless Deistic God, in time, produced skeptics who were unwilling to accept the truth of any religion or the existence of any God. Thomas Hobbes could describe religion as "accepted superstition," miracles as "impossibilities," immortality as "wishful thinking," and theological writing as "noise."

Thus, in time, some rationalists came to deny categorically God's exixtence. A totally mechanistic universe was said to explain all the "realities" of this world. Baron d'Holbach, a German chemist and philosopher living in France, insisted that nothing existed in the universe except matter in motion. There were only two categories in this world:1) knowledge (science) and 2) ignorance (religion). When man had finally substituted knowledge for ignorance, that is, rejected religion in favor of science, man's perfection on earth would finally be attained.

The process of gradual conversion from religious belief to atheism was the common tendency of the intellectuals of the age. In miniature, the encylopedist Diderot serves as a demonstration of this progress. He began his intellectual career as a Deist, but in time was converted to outspoken atheism. Thus was completed a process implicit in rationalism—the tendency to substitute nature for God—with disastrous historic and philosophic results for mankind. Relative morality, with a total absence of any traditional or institutional sanction for man's moral framework, was destined to become the dominant theme.

PROGRESS

The Renaissance conception of individual and historical fulfillment carried within it the seeds of the idea of progress which were to reach fruition in the seventeenth and eighteenth century age of rationalism. The idea of growth and progress, stemming from the optimism of the Renaissance, was destined to become one of the motifs of the Age of Reason and the modern world. For the rationalist, this idea of progress brought together under a single heading several concepts of particular import to the Age of Reason. The new "faith" of the rationalists was totally utilitarian. It was interested in the promotion of the happiness and welfare of men on this earth. The rationalists were also highly optimistic and were quite confident that they could discover the laws of nature, and then perfect society by living in accordance with those laws.[4]

One of those most influenced by the new concepts was Thomas Hobbes. He attempted to explain man and society by the same mathematic and scientific approach that the rationalist used for natural phenomena. He accepted the Newtonian world-machine and Descartes' mathematics and viewed man as exclusively of the natural order, concluding that what is called man's "soul" is not spiritual substance but the product of the material organization of the body.

To Hobbes, man himself functioned like a machine. Before the speculations of John Locke, Hobbes had already developed the theory of sensationalism, the idea that the organizing principle of human existence was to be found in matter in motion. Thus, the only reality in the entire world was felt to lie in the existence of matter or the occurrence of motion. When this matter in motion contacts man's sensory system, sensations take place which give man what he calls knowledge, Thus, man has no capacity for knowledge or thought except that derived from sensory perception of matter in motion.

In Locke's famous *Essay Concerning Human Understanding*, he built upon Hobbes' theory of sensationalism. According to Locke, man's mind at birth is a total blank upon which sensory experience writes throughout his life.

Building upon the ideas of sensationalism as developed in Locke and Hobbes, Helvetius reached the conclusion that all beings at birth must have precisely the same mind, since it is perfectly blank in every case. He also decided that since all knowledge acquired by men was the result of their environment (matter in motion), and since proper education and environment could be provided for all these "equal" men, social progress would become possible, even inevitable. Endless improvement in environment could be followed by endless improvement in the quality of the men produced. Thus, perpetual progress and perfection on earth!

What changes would the architects of this perpetual progress need to induce within society to achieve their goal? If man in the past had been perverted by the failure of his institutions—then sweep away those institutions! Religion and all the other restraining, retarding influences upon human development must be destroyed. Man had only to understand the "laws of nature" and eliminate all "unnatural" hindrances standing in the way of human perfection in this life.

Condorcet, one of the French philosophes, traced man's development in his *Progress of the Human Spirit*. Writing in 1794, Condorcet believed he was witnessing in the French Revolution the final fulfillment of the destruction of old institutions which was the necessary prerequisite for that human perfection. Indeed, he finished the book while under the sentence of death by the revolutionary tribunal of Robespierre. Awaiting execution, he looked forward to the day when the world would see "an earth of none but freemen, with no master save reason; for tyrants and slaves, priests and their stupid or hypocritical tools, will all have disappeared." To such a genuine enthusiast of the Age of Reason, not even death itself seemed an obstacle to the deification of mankind which was to come. Reason was to provide men with an understanding of how to control their environment and themselves.

POLITICS AND RATIONALISM

Discover and apply the "laws of nature," sweep away everything interfering with that "natural order," and achieve heaven on earth! What a bright promise. Thus it happened that the Age of Reason came finally to move from the realm of science to the realm of politics. The philosophes were assured that the laws of nature could be applied to man and his society as well as to nature.

One of the political ideas which grew from this faith in the reconstruction of society was the idea of "enlightened despotism." Many philosophers of the Age of Reason were willing to accept political control by a king, if he exercised his authority in such a way as to provide social and political progress. Thus, there appeared throughout Europe such "enlightened despots" as Frederick the Great of Prussia, Joseph II of Austria, and Catherine II of Russia. In practice, of course, these "benevolent despots" were usually a good deal more despotic than benevolent.

For all the shortcomings of benevolent despotism, Frederick the Great and others of his ilk probably did far less harm to the continent of Europe than did the rationalist ideas of popular rule. Those who would remake the world are dangerous because of their willingness to exercise such power, whether that power is in the hands of a "benevolent despot" or some other political figure ruling in the name of "the people."

The rationalists were dangerous because of their desire to sweep away existing institutions and the fabric of society, with the intention of replacing it with a master blueprint of their own design. In the process, they did irreparable harm to the society on which they imposed their ideas. In the words of Bertrand de Jouvenel:

> Community of beliefs was a powerful factor in social cohesion; it was the stay of institutions and the keeper of folkways. It assured a social order, complementary to and bulwark of the political order; its existence, as shown by the independence and sanctity of the law, discharged Power from a vast measure of responsibility and set up

against it an almost impassable barrier. Can we fail to note the coincidence of the breakdown of beliefs from the sixteenth to the eighteenth centuries with the elevation of absolute monarchies during the same period? Is it not clear that they owed their elevation to this breakdown? Is not the conclusion this: that the great period of rationalism was also that of enlightened and free-thinking despots, all assured of the conventional character of institutions, all persuaded that they both could and should overturn the customs of their peoples to make them conformable to reason, all extending prodigiously their bureaucracies for the furtherance of their designs, and their police in order to smash all opposition?[37]

It would then appear that considerable connection exists between the rationalist philosopher and the tyrant. Again, in the words of Jouvenel:

> Authority can never be too despotic for the speculative man, so long as he deludes himself that its arbitrary force will further his plans. Proof of this is the attraction, seen time after time, which Russian despotism has had for the intellectuals. The approach of Auguste Comte to Czar Nicholas is but a repetition of Diderot's waiting for Catherine the Great to promulgate by ukase the Encyclopaedist dogmas. [In a broadcast review of this book, Mr. Max Beloff compared the attraction of Catherine for Voltaire and Diderot with that of Stalin for the Webbs.] Disillusioned with the weapon proper to itself, persuasion, the intelligence admires those instruments of Power which are swifter in action, and Voltaire found it in himself to admire Catherine's ability "to make fifty thousand men march into Poland to establish there toleration and liberty of conscience."[37]

The political implications of rationalism in the modern world are thus readily apparent. Before the end of the eighteenth century these implications were to bear their bitter fruit in the French Revolution. The political idea stemming from rationalism and resulting in the French Revolution are best seen and understood when contrasted with the tradition of British and American political liberty. That comparison between the underlying philosophies of the French and American Revolution is the subject of the next chapter. Let it suffice at this point to re-emphasize that the political implications of rationalism centered on a willingness to use all necessary power to sweep away existing institutions and control the society which was to take its place. In a very real sense, the evils of modern politics stem from that decision to elevate man, or at least some men, to that position as arbiter of the universe once occupied by God.

THE HERITAGE OF THE ENLIGHTENMENT

Much of what we are and the values we hold have come from the matrix of the Age of Reason. Scientific inquiry and the tremendous developments in the field of natural science are due primarily to the new patterns of thought which developed in this age. Yet, like all men, the rationalists also had their weaknesses. Their insistence upon the perfectibility of mankind was to open the door to some of the tragic errors of modern politics. That is not to say that the philosophers of the Age of Reason lacked a passion for justice and truth and humanity. It is to say that the means which the philosophes felt justified in using to attain such goals were destined to produce far more injustice, untruth, and inhumanity in the modern world than Citizen Robespierre would have dreamed on June 8, 1794, when with a bouquet in one hand and a torch in the other, he launched the new "religion of humanity" by which the philosophes hoped to rid the world of ignorance and vice forever.

10

The Age of Revolution

❦❦❦❦❦❦❦❦❦❦❦❦❦❦❦❦❦❦❦❦❦❦❦❦❦❦❦❦❦❦❦❦❦❦

THE RENAISSANCE MENTALITY AS REFLECTED IN MACHIAVELLI'S theory of power unlimited by morality, when coupled with the Renaissance philosophers' desire to remake society toward the goal of perpetual progress, produced an age of absolutism in which far more political power was used than had ever been exercised throughout the Middle Ages. This entire generation of despots was epitomized in the reign of the "Sun King," Louis XIV. In the France of that day, the slightest disobedience to the royal will was a crime punishable by death. Even while the subjects were completely bound to the ruler, no reciprocal obligation of any kind was recognized. No guarantee of property or person was considered defensible. The impact of such unlimited power upon the crowned heads of Europe was disastrous for the rulers as well as the ruled. One answer of the philosophers had been "benevolent despotism," but good intentions and reigns in the "interest" of the people, though much discussed, were little practiced. Edmund Burke, writing his *Thoughts on the Causes of Our Present Discontents*, warned: ". . . many of the greatest tyrants on the records of history have begun their reigns in the fairest manner. But the truth is, this unnatural power corrupts both the heart and the understanding."

ENGLISH CONSTITUTIONALISM

Though the age of absolutism further darkened the shadow of centralized power spreading across Europe, there remained some encouraging exceptions. In early seventeenth-century England, Sir Edward Coke, greatest of the English parliamentarian lawyers, led the struggle against the absolutist pretensions of the Stuart monarchy. Coke renewed the principle that both ruler and ruled were subject to Natural Law. Coke was primarily responsible for the renewed emphasis upon Magna Charta and upon traditional limitations to the exercise of royal power.

Before the end of the century, the Glorious Revolution of 1688 was to complete the rejection of unlimited royal power in England. The perils of unlimited democratic power remained to be faced in the modern world, but at least royal power based on divine right had begun its decline. That decline which began in England in the seventeenth century was destined to spread throughout Europe within the next one hundred years.

ANGLICAN LIBERTY OR GALLICAN LIBERTY?

The assault upon divine right of kings was destined to produce sweeping changes in the eighteenth century. Friedrich Hayek points out in *The Constitution of Liberty:*

> This development of a theory of liberty took place mainly in the eighteenth century. It began in two countries, England and France. The first of these knew liberty; the second did not.

> As a result, we have had to the present day two different traditions in the theory of liberty: one empirical and unsystematic, the other speculative and rationalistic—the first based on an interpretation of traditions and institutions which had spontaneously grown up and were but imperfectly understood, the second aiming at the construction of a utopia, which has often been tried but never successfully.[2]

Just as the English system had been deeply rooted in the tradition of common law, equally binding on all elements within society, including government itself, the French tradition, stemming from the Enlightenment, viewed centralized political authority, acting in the name of the people, as the one element of society which should not have its power limited in any way. There are other differences between the two approaches as well. As J. L. Talmon has written in the *Origins of Totalitarian Democracy:*

> One finds the essence of freedom in spontaneity and the absence of coercion, the other believes it to be realized only in the pursuit and attainment of an absolute collective purpose; . . . one stands for organic, slow, half-conscious growth, the other for doctrinaire deliberateness; one for trial and error procedure, the other for an enforced solely valid pattern.

The English concept of liberty understood that what Western man has called political order is due less to particular political schemes imposed upon society than to the steady growth of institutions and ideas which have proven successful in the test of time. Thus, the evolutionary political tradition of Anglican liberty has rested upon a view of freedom which allows society to formulate and modify its own patterns of growth and habit as the members of that society individually and privately see fit. It is precisely this emphasis upon a freely evolving society which Gallican liberty, as developed in the Enlightenment by the philosophes, was destined to attack.

Oddly enough, the first development of the planned, centrally controlled concept of "freedom" which came to characterize the Gallican view of liberty during the Enlightenment had its origins not in France, but in England. The turbulent politics of seventeenth-century England provided the background for one of the philosophers of the new ideal—Thomas Hobbes. It was clear from the beginning that young Hobbes was destined for an unusual career. His father had been an English churchman of a peculiar sort, who on one occasion, after a long Saturday night devoted to the card table, dozed in his pulpit during his own Sunday sermon, only to awake with a start and distinctly announce, "Clubs is trumps." The congregation was understandably startled; but young Hobbes would break intellectual ground in a direction even more startling for all Englishmen, and indeed for all Western men.

Hobbes developed the idea of the "social contract" in his

book, *Leviathan*. In his view, the life of man had traditionally been "nasty, brutish, and short," until men had conceived the idea of social contract, bringing order and stability to society. In Hobbes, the social contract was used as a justification for absolute monarchy, because men had presumably contracted their rights irrevocably to their sovereign, thus empowering an absolute monarch with ironclad authority to rule for that society. Despite this emphasis, the idea of social contract which Hobbes launched was to have great impact during the Age of Revolution in the next century. There is a direct road from the *Leviathan* of Thomas Hobbes to *The Social Contract* of Jean Jacques Rousseau.

The long English tradition of the subject's liberties, which had developed throughout the centuries, was severely tested in the seventeenth century. Civil war, the Stuart Kings, and Cromwell imposed great strains upon that traditional fabric. Before the end of the century, the Stuart absolutist pretensions had become so galling to Englishmen that some major change seemed indicated. That change was the Glorious Revolution of 1688 which deposed the Stuarts and erected a genuinely constitutional monarchy in their place. As might be expected in an evolutionary, traditional society, the "Glorious Revolution" was scarcely revolutionary. Despite its great constitutional significance, it was virtually a peaceful "change of administrations."

The philosopher of the Glorious Revolution was John Locke. In 1690 he wrote *Two Treatises of Government*, once again developing the idea of social contract. Locke felt Hobbes had been right, as far as he had gone. Men indeed had originally lived in a state of nature, and life had been "nasty, brutish, and short." As Hobbes had also suggested, Locke felt that a social contract between the rulers and the ruled had been entered into to solve this problem by bringing order to society. But Locke now added another dimension to the idea of contract, insisting that the social contract was binding not only upon the ruled, but also upon the ruler. Locke reasoned from this that, though the individual contracting members of society had given a measure of their sovereignty to the ruler, they had retained their "natural rights." Thus, when the terms of the contract were violated by the ruler, when the natural rights of life, liberty, or property were endangered, the individual citizens retained their "natural right" to end that contract and enter into a new contract with a new government. This, Locke argued, was the import of the Glorious Revolution.

The revolutionary implications of the social contract idea were only implicit in Locke and the Glorious Revolution. Locke was a child of the Enlightenment, but he was far from being a philosophe. As one wag has suggested, "Even Locke's God was a Whig." Thus, the fully revolutionary aspects of the social contract doctrine were not developed until 1762, with the publication of Rousseau's *The Social Contract.* Building upon Hobbes and Locke, Rousseau insisted that man had originally been free, but had accepted the authority of government as an expedient to produce order in society. What had been implicit in Locke became explicit in Rousseau: If the ruler rejected the sovereignty of the people, thus breaking the contract, the people had the authority to overthrow such a government. What might be erected in place of a deposed government? It was here that Rousseau added his radical new dimension to the development of the idea of social contract. According to Rousseau, a "general will" existed within society, forcing each citizen into a dual role, as an individual, and as a member of the collectivity. According to Rousseau's idea of "general will," each individual could only attain his freedom within society by living in consonance with this "general will." In other words, the individual within society was henceforth to have his freedom protected against invasion by a king; and the means of that protection was the subordination of individual will to "general will."

In Rousseau, the idea of social contract was perverted into the realm of political propaganda. Rousseau's argument was never, not even at its best, free of serious flaws. But political propaganda need not be political philosophy. Liberty, Equality, Fraternity, the catchwords of Rousseau's propaganda effort, were to become the watchwords of the approaching French Revolution.

THE PHILOSOPHES

The entire eighteenth century was for the French people a race between reform and revolution. The French peasant was far better off than any other in Europe. And the Revolution came in France not because of spontaneous popular discontent, but rather because of the challenge of the philosophes as they carried the ideals of the Enlightenment to their logical fruition. As the century progressed, political critics became more and more outspoken. The age of the Encyclopedists, of Diderot, Holbach, Helvetius, Turgot and the rest, was an age in which the ideas of the philosophes were espoused by the French ruling classes as "enlightened" and "progressive." Everyone in the upper classes wished to play at politics, little dreaming what the disastrous results of that game would be.

The philosophes were a widely diverse group of men, yet they possessed certain common intellectual traits. They tended toward a naturalistic philosophy, an agnostic theology, and a strong faith in rationalism and the scientific method. They firmly believed that man could achieve perpetual progress and ultimate perfection exclusively by his own efforts with the "laws of nature." Running through these assumptions was a tendency toward pessimism concerning the individual and optimism concerning the collectivity. This can be clearly seen in Rousseau's insistence that man's genuine freedom is reflected not in the individual will, but in the "general will." For Rousseau, no distinction existed between society and the state. At least Locke had stopped at this point, making the distinction between private society and the public state. But with Rousseau's General Will, the state comes to absorb society, since no distinction is made between them. It was Rousseau's idea that the individual must give up his freedom to the collective will if he is to be truly "free." Once the General Will has achieved a literal "equality" among men, everything can then be done in the name of "the people." In such a framework, obedience to the General Will is the highest expression of the "moral freedom of the individual." At last, we have come full circle. In Rousseau's own words, "This means nothing less than that he [the individual] will be forced to be free."

Man can be forced to be "free." This doctrine has been in wide use during the past two hundred years by more than one worshipper of the state. Several generations of upper-class Frenchmen read Rousseau and approved of his novel and attractive ideas, never dreaming of the disaster which lay ahead. Rousseau and the philosophes were to launch a political revolution which had all the aspects of a religious revolution, not only transforming France, but overflowing the boundaries of France to proselytize and propagandize throughout Europe and the Western world.

Describing the changes which this doctrine of the philosophes was to bring to France, Alexis de Tocqueville wrote in *The Ancient Regime and the French Revolution:*

> It functioned in relation to this world, in precisely the same manner that religious revolutions function in respect to the other: it considered the citizen in an abstract fashion, apart from particular societies in the same way that religions consider man in general, independently of time and place. It sought not merely the particular rights of French citizens, but the general political rights and duties of all men. [Accordingly] since it appeared to be more concerned with the regeneration of the human race than with the reformation of France, it generated a passion which, until then, the most violent political revolutions had never exhibited. It inspired proselytism and gave birth to propaganda. It could therefore assume that appearance of a religious revolution which so astonished contemporaries; or rather it became itself a kind of new religion, an imperfect religion it is true, a religion without God, without a form of worship, and without a future life, but one which nevertheless, like Islamism, inundated the earth with soldiers, apostles, and martyrs.

Robespierre and the other leaders of the French Revolution strongly believed in the existence of a judgment day in which good and bad would receive their final rewards, but as Carl Becker has phrased it in *The Heavenly City of the 18th Century Philosophers,* ". . . in their theology, posterity has elbowed God out of the judgment seat: it is posterity that will judge and justify and award the immortal crown."

We begin to see at last, in this pseudo-religious view held by the French revolutionaries, the effect of viewing man, any man, as a potentially perfect creature who can afford to be a reformer since he himself does not need reformation.

Such a view of man has the effect of presuming him to be God. The changes, or revolutions if you will, which man thus induces in society are therefore not only assumed to be promulgated by those members of society most wise and powerful (most God-like), but also are promulgated with the goal of further elevating the rest of humanity. If this rationale be accepted, why indeed should not man regard himself as God, as the creature who can mold all existence and all other creatures in His own Image! The events of the French Revolution make abundantly clear how far men can go once they have lost their moral and theological bearings. In the words of Montesquieu, writing in the *Spirit of the Laws:* "Constant experience shows us that every man invested with power is apt to abuse it, and to carry his authority as far as it will go." The forces unleashed in the modern world by the French Revolution and its underlying philosophy have made Montesquieu's statement far more painfully true than ever before in recorded history.

THE IDEAS OF THE PHILOSOPHES IN ACTION

The background and events of the French Revolution are too well known to necessitate recounting them here. The overthrow of the old order, the growing terror as the new order swept on to greater and greater excess, the enthusiastic espousal of a dictator who promised to bring order out of chaos—the story is familiar to all. Once Napoleon had come to power, France looked outside herself for the solution to her problems and launched upon a decade of bloody warfare. Eventually, the dictatorial final chapter of the French Revolution seemed ended at Waterloo; but the ideas of the philosophes were not set aside so easily. In 1830 and again in 1848, new outbreaks of the revolutionary temper again erupted, each inducing further rounds of disruption, reaction, and eventual dictatorship.

How did the grandiose visions of the philosophes work in practice? Looking at the Revolution from the standpoint of a French citizen, we find the Terror, war, hardship, and an aftermath of instability alternating with dictatorship. If France has ever truly prospered again, it has been due far more to the French people than to their government and their politics. Viewing the Revolution with the eyes of "the people," in whose name the philosophes advanced their ideas, it is quite clear that the Revolution did not work in practice.

The heirs to the ideas of the philosophes, whether they call

themselves radicals, collectivists, liberals, communists, or socialists, usually insist that the ideas motivating the French Revolution
were sound. They will often admit that the Revolution was not a
success. However, they blame the failure upon the reaction which
rose up against the ideas of the philosophes. For example, the heirs
of the philosophes would insist that if Europe had not intervened
in French affairs, there would have been no war, and if there had
been no war, there would have been no dictator or instability.
They insist that the ideas were fine and would have worked, had
they been allowed to function. Similar rationales are advanced in
apology for the failures of communism, socialism, and welfare
statism in the modern world.

In fact, the French Revolution failed precisely because the
ideas motivating it were basically wrong. Viewed in that light, the
attempt to stop the ideas of the French Revolution was not "reaction," but rather a rear-guard action of humanity against the mass-
mind as manifested in an early form of *1984*.

What motives were the ideas of the philosophes based upon?
Some of the forebears of the philosophes, "realists" like Machiavelli and Hobbes, had attempted to view history in amoral
terms in which all human action was an expression of the will to
power. In the process, the so-called "realists" stripped human
history of moral content. Meanwhile, the philosophes themselves,
while using the amoral means and the "will to power" of the
"realists," applied these ideas in the pursuit of their own "idealist"
goals by which society was to be raised to new heights through the
intervention of the state. In a word, the philosophes so overlooked
the submoral character of the state that they came to view it as an
instrument of Divine Providence which would lead mankind to
perfection. The philosophes thus drew upon two traditions, one
stripping all morality from the individual and from the means that
the state might apply to the individual to achieve its ends, the
other investing that moral quality in the mystique of the state and
the collectivity. This distortion of proper moral values within society paved the way for many of the troubles which were to lie
ahead.

The philosophes believed themselves to be rational beings
capable of *total* self-direction. They felt that the final purpose of

all rational beings could be reduced to a single universal harmonious pattern. Thus, they came to feel that any behavior which was disruptive of this universal harmonious pattern, any deviation from the norm, must therefore be irrational and unacceptable and that men must be compelled to obey "rational laws." To the philosophes and to their heirs in the modern world, freedom is compatible only with rational behavior, and such "rational behavior" necessary to produce that freedom can therefore be enforced by coercion if necessary. Thus for "irrational" man (that is, for all those individuals whose actions do not conform to the universal pattern and plan) freedom can only be achieved through the loss of the individual's freedom. Individual conscience and morality are to be set aside, moral limitations upon such actions as the state deems necessary to achieve its goals must be set aside, and a new morality, a collective morality, is to be substituted in place of the traditional system. What a contrast exists between power exercised by men bound by God's will and power exercised by man-made authority which has become a law unto itself!

Once such a collective morality is the accepted standard, leaders arrive on the scene who are easily able to convince themselves that their one ambition is to serve collective humanity. Napoleon was in all probability perfectly sincere in his statement to Caulaincourt, "People are wrong in thinking me ambitious—I am touched by the misfortunes of people; I want them to be happy and, if I live ten years, the French will be happy." Unlimited by any restraint drawn from traditional morality, convinced that man is indeed the measure of all things, convinced that individual rights and freedom must give way for the goals of the collectivity, such men soon reach the point in which the exercise of political or military force is justified by the goal of the collectivity, while the goal of the collectivity is determined by those who exercise the force.

Writing as a contemporary critic of the French Revolution, Benjamin Constant warned that, however well-intended any set of governors might be, the end result of the exercise of such unlimited power would surely be oppressive. "It is not the arm that is unjust, but the weapon that is too heavy—some weights are too heavy for the human hand." Constant may have doubted that any man or any combination of men could wield such unlimited power, but the philosophes and their modern counterparts have had no such doubts about their own ability.

Viewed in this light, it is quite possible that such outbursts as the French Revolution and the tremendous accumulations of power which stem from them are the results not of a revolt against a brutal tyranny, but of new ideas which themselves provide the rationale for the exercise of great power. Simply stated, revolution may be an outburst of power at the moment when that new power senses weakness in the old system. In the words of Bertrand de Jouvenel:

> Thus we see that the true historical function of revolutions is to renovate and strengthen Power. Let us stop greeting them as the reactions of the spirit of liberty to the oppressor. So little do they answer to that name that not one can be cited in which a true despot was overthrown.
>
> Did the people rise against Louis XIV? No, but against the good-natured Louis XVI, who had not even the nerve to let his Swiss Guards open fire. Against Peter the Great? No, but against the weakling Nicholas II, who did not even dare avenge his beloved Rasputin. Against that old Bluebeard, Henry VIII? No, but against Charles I, who, after a few fitful attempts at governing, had resigned himself to living in a small way and was no danger to anyone. And, as Mazarin sagely remarked, had he not abandoned his minister, Strafford, he would not have laid his head on the scaffold.
>
> These kings died not because of their tyranny but because of their weakness. The people erect scaffolds, not as the moral punishment of despotism, but as the biological penalty for weakness.[37]

At the very time when the Revolution swept away all authority in the name of the freedom of the people, it carried the process to the point of depriving the individual of his constitutional means of protecting himself against the state. In the process, the individual, far from being freed, was enslaved more than ever before. And what of those who came to exercise power in the new revolutionary regime which promised so much to the people? Why the Terror, why the butchery, which repeatedly destroyed even the leadership of the Revolution itself? For the answer, we must return to an insight of Guglielmo Ferrero, an Italian scholar who during the Second World War came to see the problem of power in a completely new light:

And one day at last the light dawned upon me. . . . What if power acquired through a *coup d'etat* had the diabolical property of frightening the one who had possessed himself of it before it frightened the others? . . . It is impossible to inspire fear in men without ending up by fearing them: from this moral law springs the most fearful torment of life—the reciprocal fear between government and its subjects . . . We have seen that instruments of force inspire fear both in those who submit to them and in those who make use of them. We have seen that the fear of government rises to the frenzy, through the reciprocal effect and countereffect on government and subjects; that it engenders hatred and the spirit of revolt; that, terrified by the ever-present danger of a general revolt, the government attempts still further to terrorize its subjects. But if the fear of the latter increases, hatred and the spirit of revolt are also increased; on the other hand, the more fear the government inspires, the more fearful it becomes; the more fearful it is, the more it needs to inspire fear.

This inevitable sequence may lead to unimaginable horrors. Among all the evils from which mankind has suffered, this reciprocal fear on the part of a government and its subjects has been the most terrible.

No one has studied or explained this disturbing phenomenon more profoundly than Benjamin Constant, in a book he published in 1814, after the fall of Napoleon . . . Having witnessed the formation, development, and suicide of the first revolutionary government in Western history, Benjamin Constant wanted to point out its dangers to posterity. How many tragedies would have been avoided if subsequent generations, instead of neglecting it, had read and reflected upon this marvelous little book![38]

As a wielder of power who continually needed to exercise more and more power through fear of losing his position, it was Napoleon who first applied the power of government to the manufacture of enthusiasm on behalf of the state. Demonstrations, processions, triumphal arches, orders of the day, public receptions, speeches—it was Napoleon who first organized mass movements into a state monopoly.

Such is the fate of all revolutionary governments that bring tremendous power to bear on the destruction of the existing fabric of society, and then wield vast new powers in the name of the people. The further they extend their authority and their total control, the more concerned they feel about a reaction against such control on the part of the people. Those who wield power in the name of "the people" come finally to regard the people themselves as the primary enemy. Such regimes must make full use of what the modern world has come to call propaganda. Such regimes must make full use of the modern concept of total war, finding an external enemy against which the people may be united. Thus has developed the modern concept of the nation under arms, in which all individuals within the society are totally committed to defense of the "public interest." Napoleon was not the last leader of a modern state who involved his nation in foreign warfare because of sagging popularity at home.

Thus, the French revolutionaries were led by the ideas of the philosophes into an impossible position, a position which they justified through a further appeal to those same ideas. Again, in Ferrero's words, as he describes the brutality of the French Revolution:

> The Jacobins did not spill all that blood because they believed in popular sovereignty as a religious truth; they tried to believe in popular sovereignty as a religious truth because their fear made them spill so much blood. Without this inversion, the French Revolution would be nothing but a senseless tragedy played by drunken actors. Marat, who demanded 200,000 heads every day in his paper, could not bear to see an animal tortured. The contradiction is a weird one; and it has been attributed to the idiotic fallacies in the philosophy of the age. But there is a simpler explanation. Marat could suffer when he saw a dog being tortured because he was not afraid of the dog. When he was demanding 200,000 heads, he was a man crazed by fear, who from morning to night, night to morning, was terrified of being imprisoned, assassinated, or guillotined by the enemies he wanted to exterminate. Fear made him a wild animal, and the wild animal sought justification for its excesses in the absolute. It was fear and the need for an absolute that led the Revolution to make the *Contrat Social* its Bible and Rousseau its Moses. Suspended in a vacuum, unable to lean on a clear and precise principle of legitimacy, the Revolution clutched at a book, at a philosophy—a book and a philosophy that lay within easy reach.
>
> The *Contrat Social* had many advantages for becoming the Bible of the Revolution: it was short, it seemed clear and precise, though it was far less so than it seemed at a first superficial reading; it swarmed with contradictions that justified the most varying interpretations. Finally, it gave the theory of the general will the value of a religious truth. . . . It went into no details on the juridical and political procedure by which the general will, the source of legitimate power, could or should be expressed. Which was very convenient for a Revolution obliged to pack the prisons in the name of liberty, and to chop off so many heads in the name of humanity![38]

Thus, we reach a point in which the full results of the ideas of the philosophes begin to emerge. Western man's consistent emphasis upon Natural Law, upon a tradition limiting the exercise of power by man or any group of men, upon an institutional framework protecting society from its saviors, upon a morality firmly grounded in the individual rather than in an imaginary collectivity, was an approach to political and social problems which the philosophes felt they had superseded in the vision of society which their ideas promised. The result: The brutalities of the French Revolution, pointing directly to the brutalities and inner contradictions of modern totalitarianism. In the name of humanity and in the name of the French people, young and old, man, woman and child were conscripted for total war, God was abolished and man elevated to the place He had previously held, church property was confiscated by the "saviors" of society, France was made prosperous by printing worthless money enforced in value only by the death penalty, and people starved. What more damning indictment could be leveled against the ideas of the philosophes than the actual effect of those ideas when they swept away the guarantees and traditions of Western civilization?

THE DIFFERENCES BETWEEN THE FRENCH AND AMERICAN REVOLUTIONS

Since both the French and American Revolutions occurred in the late eighteenth century, and since both the French and American experiences are termed "revolutions," it is all too easy to jump to the conclusion that both events were manifestations of a single set of ideas. Nothing could be further from the truth. The French and American Revolutions are completely at variance in their widely differing attitudes toward law and order, property, the individual, the role of governmental authority, and the place for religious faith as the foundation of civil society. To clarify the point, it is helpful to recall the differences between "Anglican" and "Gallican" liberty. As Francis Lieber, the nineteenth-century German-American political thinker described the difference in an 1842 newspaper editorial:

Gallican liberty is sought in the *government* and, according to an Anglican point of view, it is looked for in a wrong place, where it cannot be found. Necessary consequences of the Gallican view are, that the French looked for the highest degree of political civilization in *organization*, that is, in the highest degree of interference by public power. The question whether this interference be despotism or liberty is decided solely by the fact *who* interferes, and for the benefit of which class the interference takes place, while according to the Anglican view, this interference would always be either absolutism or aristocracy. . . .

Phrased in other words, the French Revolution and the American Revolution are diametrically opposed answers to the same question: Is the highest value to be found in a society emphasizing the God-given integrity of individual men, or in a society emphasizing the collective will, a collective will which attributes to itself its own divine sanction?

In any comparison between the French and American Revolution, it is immediately clear that the American Revolution was primarily concerned with conserving and further enhancing an evolutionary structure of Anglican liberty. The American Revolution was turning back to previously held individual rights and governmental limitations (emphasizing the traditional rights of Englishmen); it was middle-class and property-conscious in its leadership, therefore being anything but class-oriented, as was the French Revolution; finally, the aftermath of the American Revolution produced a constitution based upon property rights, upon republican government, and upon the restriction of governmental interference in the private sector, even when that interference takes place in the name of "majority action."

The French Revolution, on the other hand, was radical and Gallican in nature in that: It demonstrated a willingness to overturn and destroy the existing order, in the Terror and in the radical legislation passed during the period; its appeal was strictly in terms of class against class; finally, its aftermath was mass-oriented in repeated rounds of dictatorship alternating with mob action, as, for example, in Napoleon, Napoleon III, the Paris Commune, and similar political aberrations.

Any comparison of the two revolutions demonstrates a basic difference in the original intent, the course, the leadership, and the aftermath of the revolutions.

BURKE

Edmund Burke was among the first to see the vital distinction between the American and French Revolutions and to sense the danger to human freedom implicit in the French experiment. Grounded in the tradition of Cicero and Aquinas, Burke understood the necessity of a religious foundation for Natural Law. He drew upon the heritage of Western man's experience in the handling of power, and warned that a society which would not recognize God as its sovereign and which elevated man to a pretension as ruler of the universe would ultimately center such terrible power in the state that individual man would be degraded beyond recognition.

Burke saw, perhaps more clearly than any other single individual of his time, the role of the American Revolution as the defender of the traditions of Western civilization, just as he saw in the French Revolution an assault upon those same traditions.

In the Age of Revolution, the battle lines became more sharply drawn between those who espoused the Western tradition, with its emphasis upon Natural Law, the individual, and limitations of governmental authority, and those who wished to destroy the Western tradition, substituting in its place the omnipotent state, exercising unlimited power derived not from God, but from man. The history of the Western world during the past two hundred years is the history of these two mutually antagonistic systems in their confrontation, one with the other.

11

The American Experiment

❦❦❦❦❦❦❦❦❦❦❦❦❦❦❦❦❦❦❦❦❦❦❦❦❦❦❦❦❦❦❦❦

THE ROOTS OF THE AMERICAN POLITICAL TRADITION

A GOVERNMENT OF LAWS, NOT OF MEN. SUCH WAS THE POPULAR slogan of the generation of Americans that produced the American Revolution. By the second half of the eighteenth century, most American colonists were convinced that the men who ran the government should be limited by law in their exercise of power. One of the leaders of the North Carlina Regulators, writing shortly before the American Revolution, made the colonial feeling quite clear: "If we are all rogues, there must be Law, and all we want is to be Governed by Law, and not by the will of Officers, which to us is perfectly despotic and arbitrary."

The two institutions through which the colonists hoped to achieve "a government of laws, not of men" were written constitutions and standing law. Though the American doctrine of constitutionalism owed a great deal to English precedents, the colonists had done much to broaden and extend the concept still further. A number of state constitutions were put into effect between 1776 and 1780, preludes to the Federal Constitution of 1787. The colonists had been trying to define the specific area of governmental authority ever since the Mayflower Compact and the Fundamental Orders of Connecticut, both already on the books fully 150 years before our Federal Constitution. Most of these numerous American efforts in constitution-making also usually included specific acknowledgment of individual liberties and immunities, a concept that would eventually produce our Bill of Rights.

If Americans emphasized written constitutions, they also emphasized standing law, usually drawn from the English Common Law. This legal heritage simultaneously emphasized two concepts: the traditional liberties of the English subject and a strong emphasis upon the rights of property. American colonial history is filled with the discussion and implementation of these concepts.

If Americans early displayed a strong interest in laws and institutions limiting the exercise of political authority, they also pioneered in the development of self-sustaining local government. Since colonial government was so *local,* it is natural that it varied widely from colony to colony and region to region. But with all the variations in form that were present within the colonies, one fact remains clear: the colonists were to a very large extent running their own affairs.

As Charles M. Andrews, dean of American colonial historians, has concluded: "In the development of American political ideas and social practices, the influence of the popular assembly . . . is the most potent single factor underlying our American system of government." What impact did this local self-government have? In the words of Clinton Rossiter, "these institutions taught the colonists one more sturdy lesson in freedom from pomp and arbitrary power."

The colonists, then, were achieving their "government of laws, not of men," first by strict legal limitation of governmental power and second by keeping the exercise of that power close to home. As England made its mid-eighteenth century attempt to tighten control over the colonies, the mother country violated both the ideals of limited governmental authority and local self-government by increasing the arbitrary power of government while moving the exercise of that power further from the colonies. The colonists thought of themselves as good Englishmen, and many of them worked to maintain their political tradition while still remaining Englishmen. This is the basis of the federal system operating within the British Empire that Franklin advocated in his Albany Plan of Union in 1756.

There need be no doubt of the vitality of the American tradition of federalism in colonial times. We need only compare the liberties of the individual and the strength of self-government in the English colonies of the seventeenth and eighteenth centuries with the centralization and arbritary exercise of governmental power present at the same time in the French and Spanish colonies of the New World. Tocqueville grasped the essence of the political heritage that gave strength and validity to the American experiment: "The general principles which are the groundwork of modern constitutions, principles which, in the seventeenth century, were imperfectly known in Europe and not completely triumphant even in Great Britain, were all recognized and established by the laws of New England: the intervention of the people in public affairs, the free voting of taxes, the responsibility of the agents of power, personal liberty, and trial by jury were all positively established without discussion. [Thus occurred] . . . the germ and gradual development of that township independence which is the light and mainspring of American liberty at the present day. . . . In America . . . it may be said that the township was organized before the county, the county before the state, the state before the union."[39]

When the British failed to see the colonial position, the American Revolution finally occurred. Yet in a very real sense Burke was right when he described the American War for Independence as "a revolution not made, but prevented." The radical change of the late eighteenth century was less in American self-government than in the Johnny-come-lately attempt Britain made to interfere with that self-government. From the beginning of the War for Independence, the colonists presented a most peculiar aspect for revolutionaries. They appealed to tradition, the common law, British custom, colonial practice, and property rights; hardly a collection of radical ideals!

The antitraditional present-mindedness of many modern scholars has produced a view of the American Revolution that overlooks the colonial American heritage of limited, constitutional government. Those who suggest that the American Revolution was only another egalitarian leveling process similar to the French Revolution must overlook the middle class and aristocratic leadership of the American Revolution, its respect for law and property rights, and its concern for maintaining a 150-year-old heritage of local self-government.

The attempt to make the Declaration of Independence into a Declaration of the Rights of Man amounts to little more than an attempt to misread a bill of indictment against the king, written in the language of British constitutionalism, until it is twisted into some sort of manifesto for the overthrow of the old order. It was precisely the preservation of the old order for which the colonists were striving. One of the pamphleteers of the Revolution, James Otis, epitomized this colonial stance in his *The Rights of the British Colonies* (1764) when he advocated what might be called "revolution by due process of law." The Declaration of Independence itself attacks usurpation and centralization of authority, calling it tyranny: "He has erected a multitude of new offices and sent hither swarms of officers to harass our people and eat out their substance. He has combined with others to subject us to a jurisdiction foreign to our constitution and unacknowledged by our laws."

Even though the colonists were drawing on 150 years of historical experience in asserting their position, they were also building upon that heritage to produce a very different sort of nation than the world had previously seen. This was the *real* American Revolution. For the first time in history, no authoritarian control would be tolerated in this new political order. "Men are endowed by their Creator with certain inalienable rights," the Declaration of Independence announced to the world.

If men are endowed "by their Creator" with these rights, it follows that God and not government is sovereign, and therefore that government must be without authority to interfere with "certain inalienable rights," such as self-government and sustenance; that is, the right to freedom, and the right to property as a means of making that freedom meaningful. What the Declaration of Independence outlined was made specific in the Constitution's Bill of Rights which placed restrictions not upon the citizen but upon the government, limiting the role of governmental power over the individual citizen in some forty-six specific instances.

The interim between the Declaration of Independence and the Constitution clearly foreshadowed the coming federal constitution in the development of state constitutions and the various bills of rights attached to them. The Founding Fathers derived their principles of limiting government and protecting individual rights from a belief in Natural Law; that is, a belief that God had ordained a framework of individual dignity and responsibility that was to serve as the basis for all human law and as the root assumption behind a written constitution.

Professor Edward S. Corwin's *The "Higher Law" Background of American Constitutional Law* has examined this basic American assumption in considerable detail.[22] Such an assumption is quite different from the "consent of the governed" theories that motivated the French Revolution and its aftermath. The difference, quite simply, is that Americans were assuming certain fixed principles that limited *anyone*, majorities included, in the exercise of their power. The Declaration of Independence had spoken of "the Laws of Nature and of Nature's God" and of a "firm reliance on the protection of Divine Providence." Thus, the liberties of the individual were felt to be inseparable from a belief in an authority above man. Viewing America several decades later, Tocqueville agreed with the American experiment when he suggested that "liberty cannot be established without morality nor morality without faith."

This deeply abiding faith in God as the ultimate source of human dignity presupposed that man was not sufficient unto himself, that some abstract blueprint for a perfect society might ultimately prove disastrous even if advocated by a majority of men. So, unlike the document of the philosophes and their French Revolution, the Declaration of Independence and the Constitution were firmly grounded in specific historical instances and carefully avoided the vast egotism always evidenced by men who would remake the world.

The distinguished group of men who came together at Philadelphia in 1787 were up against the same old political problem: freedom and order. As one of the members of the Constitutional

Convention, James Wilson, expressed it, "Bad governments are of two sorts—first, that which does too little; secondly, that which does too much; that which fails through weakness, and that which destroys through oppression."

The Confederation period had shown the new union of states that a central government was necessary, that power was required to run a nation effectively. The Founding Fathers provided that power to establish a system which has survived repeated internal and external crises in the last 180 years.

People are fond of pointing out how much America has changed. In terms of historical continuity, it is more remarkable how much America has remained the same through two centuries of existence in a world torn with violent political upheaval. We still have a President, a Congress, a Supreme Court, an Electoral College, a network of separate state and local governments, and most of the forms passed on to us by the Constitution. Surely, despite all our problems and despite the changes which have occurred within our system, great strength must be embodied within such a lasting framework.

The key to that constitutional vitality, the answer to the dilemma that all power was to be distrusted and yet had to be exercised somewhere for the nation to survive, lies in the familiar concept of "divided powers" and "checks and balances." This diffusion of power made our system a representative republic rather than a democracy. The Founding Fathers are, of course, scrupulously clear on this point, and a statement of such an assumption occurs repeatedly in both the debates of the Constitutional Convention and the later public statements of the participants.

Felix Morley has originated a valuable distinction to clarify the word "democracy." He divides the concept into *political* democracy and *social* democracy.[40] Viewed in this light, it is clear that the innumerable roadblocks thrown up in the path of the majority by the Founding Fathers in their writing of the federal Constitution and their creation of American federalism were not intended to set up a political democracy. Yet America has traditionally been the land of great social mobility and individual opportunity, that is to say, a social democracy. Thus the American tradition of federalism has deliberately limited the exercise of political power, not to suppress individual liberty, but to enhance it. Put another way, the very real success story of America has hinged upon the limitation of political power rather than its exercise.

This nation has been consistently hostile to monopoly power, whether social, religious, or political. The Constitution outlawed titles of nobility (social monopoly) and an established church (religious monopoly), and made a particular point of outlawing excessive centralization of political power,[40] as for example in the Ninth and Tenth Amendments to the Constitution:

> Ninth: The enumeration in the Constitution of certain rights shall not be construed to deny or disparage others retained by the people.

> Tenth: The powers not delegated to the United States by the Constitution, nor prohibited by it to the states, are reserved to the states respectively or to the people.

The American federal system was already quite well developed by the time of the Constitutional Convention. Thirteen colonies were separately established and by the time of the War for Independence had developed widely differing political and social customs. Only a system of federalism which recognized and protected these diversities could hope to unite the various factions and units. But that unifying effort was only one of the reasons for the American federal system. As Felix Morley explains it: "But behind the determination to keep the rights of the several states inviolate, was the even deeper determination to protect citizens of these states from centralized governmental oppression. That is why the Republic was established not only as a federation of semi-sovereign states, but also as one of balanced authority in which it would be extremely difficult to establish a nationwide monopoly power of any kind."[40]

On the whole, the system worked. The tendency of one branch of government to gather all power unto itself has usually been slowed by the inertia of the other centers of power. Critics of the system call this inefficiency, but it is an inefficiency which has created and preserved a greater productive capacity for the satisfaction of human wants and a greater area of individual freedom than any other system in the history of the world. The key to this system of American federalism has been the recognition that government is *not* the source of rights for the individual and that extension of governmental authority is therefore a potential menace to human rights.

To accept the modern statist position that the government is the source and protector of human rights is ultimately to reduce the individual to the level of a mass man, simply because it removes all qualitative distinctions between and among individual citizens. When this happens, human personality and the institutions built upon widely differing human personalities are swept away in a nameless, faceless, pointless whirl. It is just such a tragedy that the American system of federalism was designed to prevent.

In fact, American federalism has gone a good deal further than the mere structure of federalism itself requires; for example, in the horizontal as well as vertical separation of political authority. The obvious advantage of federalism has rested in its ability to avoid dangers inherent in government by remote control. So long as local affairs are reserved to the greatest possible extent for the localities themselves and so long as the people are both interested in and capable of understanding and handling their own problems, then the philosopher's stone has indeed been discovered and a large measure of both freedom and order is possible.

The weakness in federalism, its susceptibility to centralization in time of crisis, is also very much in evidence. Yet in the face of this weakness, American federalism has remained tremendously successful. Again in the words of Felix Morley: "The reason lies in a simple paradox. By the adoption of arrangements strongly negative toward the power of government, the Republic has so far permitted and encouraged its citizens to act affirmatively in their own interest. Many Americans do not realize that when first attempted this political plan was extraordinary. . . . "[40]

One might add that all too many Americans still do not understand how truly extraordinary such a system actually is, nor do they understand the nature of the American economic miracle which worked hand in hand with this American political miracle.

CAPITALISM

In the very year in which Jefferson produced the Declaration of Independence, a professor of moral philosophy at the University of Glasgow, Adam Smith, published the *Wealth of Nations*. Concerned with the problems of free choice as a necessary foundation for an understanding of moral philosophy, Smith had delved into political economy to outline a system which maintained this emphasis upon individual free choice. The work of both Jefferson and Smith coincided not only in time but in philosophy as well. Both documents summarized what the best thinkers of the late eighteenth century had come to realize: Individual freedom was both the final end and the best means to all other ends within a truly just society. The work of both Smith and Jefferson was in open defiance of George III, the English king determined to remake the world in the image of the mercantile planner. Smith provided the economic blueprint for the outpouring of human energy, while Jefferson and the rest of the Founding Fathers provided the political framework of limited government within which such an economic system could operate.[41]

In *Wealth of Nations*, a truly radical philosophy of wealth was espoused for the first time. Wealth to Adam Smith consisted of the goods consumed by *all* the members of society. Kingly treasure, mercantilist stores of bullion, monopolies for some merchants or guilds—these old definitions of wealth were swept aside by a new system in which the production and consumption of all society became the final purpose of economic life. A radical idea indeed!

And America was the ideal place for such a radical new idea to be implemented. Unlike Europe, hamstrung as it was with a long record of governmental interferences, America was virgin territory where capitalism could establish itself from the very beginning. Capitalism had been accepted morally and legally by the entire society of British America without reservation. This was the right way to do business, and the American colonists knew it.

Not even the mercantile interference of eighteenth-century England had been able to retard the process. The colonists simply ignored the fantastic web of bounties, drawbacks, tariffs, rebates, regulations, quotas, and the like which lay at the heart of the mercantile system. In the words of John Chamberlain:

> The North American colonies, too, had raised smuggling to a fine art. The colonists ignored the Molasses Acts, lured British coast-guard ships into shoal waters where they grounded, and traded in and out of the Caribbean for rum and sugar quite as they pleased. The standard of life rose in North America every time a king's agent was bilked, a tax avoided. Wages were high in New York, money earned good interest, yet the necessaries of life were cheap. Said Adam Smith in 1776: "The price of provisions is everywhere in North America much lower than in England. A dearth has never been known there." America was doing very well, thank you, without any Benevolent or Enlightened Despot's Five-Year Plan, and once the menace of the French had been removed by British and colonial successes in Canada during the French and Indian War, there seemed less reason than ever to put up with any nonsense that violated the immemorial rights of Englishmen on North American shores.[41]

Adam Smith's description of how this system works in operation was amazingly simple. Free individual self-interest to allow the members of society to pursue private gain and the result will be the production of the goods and services which society wants, in the quantities that society can use, and at the prices which society is prepared to pay. The first key, then, to Smith's system is the idea of *self-interest*. In Smith's words:

> It is not from the benevolence of the butcher, the brewer, or the baker that we expect our dinner, but from their regard to their self-interest. We address ourselves, not to their humanity, but to their self-love, and never talk to them of our necessities, but of their advantages.

However, what keeps these selfish pursuers of self-interest from gouging society? The answer is stage two of Smith's system: *competition*. In a society free from political coercion, the only means of garnering the rewards which society offers to those who serve it is to compete most effectively *in meeting society's needs*. Thus Smith's two-pronged system, simultaneously utilizing self-interest and competition, best serves the individual and his society. These two keystones of Smith's system were premised upon individual liberty, free choice, and private property, the very

prerequisites offered to capitalism in the limited-government
political framework which, together with the economic blueprint,
formed the heart of the American experiment.

Adam Smith, like the Founding Fathers, would never have
suggested that he had the final answer. In fact, one of the basic
premises of such productive and thoughtful men who would free
the individual creativity was that no one ever has the *final* answer.
The framework can be provided, the individual can be freed, but
if he is truly free and truly creative, he must work toward the
evolution of his own steadily improving "answers" within the
system. So just as Adam Smith gave the world individual economic choice, competition, and specialization in the late eighteenth century, Frederic Bastiat, writing in the 1840's, emphasized
freedom in transactions as a further necessary prerequisite of a
properly functioning marketplace. So also did Carl Menger contribute the subjective theory of value, the idea that any commodity
within society is worth no more and no less than the value it has
to a prospective buyer. Menger added his important idea in 1870,
founding the Austrian School which has been premised upon freeing the individual in his choices and value judgments, with the full
understanding that *all creative action is volitional action.* With
these refinements, the free-market, limited-government philosophy was largely in operation in nineteenth-century America.

And how did the free-market, limited-government philosophy work in action? It produced more goods and services, dis-
tributed more widely throughout larger proportions of the
population, than had any system before in the entire history of the
world. Real wages rose steadily throughout the nineteenth century. That is, the little people within American society were given
the opportunities to produce more for themselves and to enjoy the
fruits of their production. That is the way capitalism works: not
only is it the most productive system by far, but it produces those
goods and services most necessary and desirable to everyone
within the society. No more Taj Mahals—when left free to work,
capitalism serves not the rulers, but the people themselves. That
is true "economic democracy" in action!

How had society as a whole prospered under this regime of
free market and limited government? Before the First World War,

America had already become the most prosperous and powerful nation on earth. Still, we are told that this tremendous record of achievement is due not to capitalism, but to "peculiar and unrepeatable historical circumstances" connected with virgin territory, living space, natural resources, and so on. Yet Switzerland, with none of these qualities in any appreciable quantity, but with much of the same capitalistic framework, has achieved a high degree of prosperity and stability. Why? Because of "peculiar and unrepeatable historical circumstances." When unrestricted capitalism was left free to work in war-torn and prostrate Germany following the Second World War, a tremendous "Economic Miracle" took place. Why? Because of "peculiar and unrepeatable historical circumstances."When Commodore Perry opened Japan in the mid-nineteenth century, he discovered a fifteenth-century feudal society totally lacking in every modern industrial and productive capacity. In less than fifty years, Japan had moved from the fifteenth century to the twentieth century in a tremendous burst of prosperity and production. Why? You guessed it! Because of "peculiar and unrepeatable historical circumstances."[42]

We should agree with the critics of capitalism that historical circumstances are indeed "peculiar and unrepeatable." Thank goodness this is so. Nations, like individuals, have both the right and the necessity to be different, each following its own course. But to a mind not totally entrapped within the rhetoric of the day, it should be clear that, despite widely varying "peculiar and unrepeatable historical circumstances," capitalism can and does work its miracle when it is given the opportunity. When capitalism is merged with limited government and a society which places its emphasis upon the individual, as our own American society did in the nineteenth century, the results for the average citizen, the little man, in the opportunities and advantages available to him, are truly the wonder of the world.

AMERICAN POLITICS IN THE NINETEENTH CENTURY

It has become fashionable in our time to look back upon our early history and find within that history embryonic examples of the New Deals, Fair Deals, New Republicanisms, and Great Societies of our own time. This has tended to distort rather than clarify our history. Just what ideas did this country espouse in the nineteenth century? Did we truly have a consensus for limited government, individual rights, and freely working capitalism? We know that this is the system provided for America by the Founding Fathers. What did the men of the nineteenth century do with this heritage?

A number of years ago, Richard Hofstadter made the point that the differences among key American political figures have been overemphasized, thus often disguising a wide area of agreement. As American federalism has been demonstrated in action during the past 180 years, it has been shaped and modified by our political conflicts, but the real essence of our American political tradition has been revealed quite as much by the area of agreement about ends and means underlying those conflicts.

The immediate attempts at explanation and definition of our new federalism published by thinking Americans in the early years of the Republic demonstrate this consensus. *The Federalist* written by Hamilton, Madison, and Jay; *Defense of the Constitutions*, *Thoughts on Government*, and *Discourses on Davila*, all written by John Adams; *Letters of Publicola*, written by John Quincy Adams; and the *Farewell Address* of Washington—all emphasize defense of minority rights against majority dictatorship. They outline an American liberty based upon historical precedent and limited government.

Yet, the seeds of dissent were also present in the early Republic, with Americans of good will on both sides of the developing arguments. One of these arguments is best seen in the controversy between the Hamiltonian and the Jeffersonian view of the new nation. Hamilton was the prophet of the new order, a rising generation of capitalism and the burgeoning industrial revolution. Jefferson was the defender of the older agrarian order whose interests often seemed to conflict with an industrial America. The dispute between Hamilton and Jefferson is common knowledge and is extensively treated in virtually every history of our early years. What is more important, but frequently overlooked, is that Hamilton was a consistent advocate of the limitation of political power as the best safeguard of liberty, in the sense that he shared with Jefferson a distrust of excessive popular control. Our history books are often so busy telling us of the differences between Hamilton and Jefferson that they overlook the Hamiltonian fear of unchecked majorities and overlook the Jeffersonian acceptance of capitalism and the new industrial order that occurred after Jefferson became President.

Another classic quarrel of our early years also involved Jefferson. He and John Adams, both key figures in so many of the formative actions of the Republic, carried on a dialogue that embraced all facets of the new federalism. This was a bitter debate. The testy, irascible, blunt Adams wrote some letters to Jefferson that must have scorched the paper. Jefferson's response was characteristic of the sage of Monticello. He took his revenge by understating his case and by pretending that the barbs of Adams had gone unnoticed. Jefferson described Adams in a letter to a friend as "always an honest man, sometimes a great one, but sometimes absolutely mad." At the end of a friendship and feud covering well over half a century, it is symbolic of their relationship that both men were to die on the same day in 1826. It is even more symbolic that that day should have been July Fourth.

The system of checks and balances praised by Adams in 1789 in his *Defense of the American Constitutions* is largely an enunciation of our American political tradition. At the time of the French Revolution, Adams wrote a letter to Thomas Jefferson defending the American system and implying how different the American federalism was from the new system then developing in France:

> A despotism is a government in which the three divisions of power, the legislative, executive, and judicial, are all vested in one man...

How did such despotisms come about?

> Helvetius and Rousseau preached to the French nation *liberty,* until they made them the most mechanical slaves; *equality* till they destroyed all equity; *humanity* till they became weasels and African panthers; and *fraternity* till they cut one another's throats like Roman gladiators.

The doughty New England lawyer, like the rest of the Founders of the American federalism, always strongly emphasized practical concepts, based on history, common law, and a basic distrust of self-proclaimed saviors of the world. In a letter to John Taylor of Carolina he outlined his faith in human nature as he saw it:

That all men are born to equal rights is clear. Every being has a right of his own, as moral, as sacred, as any other has. This is as indubitable as a moral government in the universe. But to teach that all men are born with equal powers and faculties, to equal influence in society, to equal property and advantages through life, is as gross a fraud, as glaring an imposition on the credulity of the people as ever practiced by. . .the self-styled philosophers of the French Revolution. For honor's sake, let American philosophers and politicians despise it.

If America remains a nation where property and liberty are reasonably secure, if America remains a government of laws, not of men, much of the credit for the development and defense of such a system is due to John Adams, whose concept of "Liberty under Law" presupposes a system of constitutionally limited government, decentralized political power, and a deep and abiding faith in the American tradition of federalism, which in Adams' time was already approaching its two-hundredth birthday.

Adams once wrote Jefferson, "Whether you or I were right, Posterity must judge. . . ." He referred, of course, to the political differences that had developed between the Federalist party with which Adams had been associated and the Republican party of Jefferson. Here again the bitter dispute that took place in domestic American politics during the Napoleonic wars is a common subject of our history books. What is neglected is the wide area of consensus shared concerning American government even in the midst of these arguments. Adams and Jefferson both favored local government and institutions and suspected that good government often seemed to decline in exactly the same proportion as it moved further from the people being governed.

Our history books sometimes neglect to tell us that Jefferson as well as Adams approved a balance of power between the national and state governments, that he spoke approvingly of *The Federalist* and was sympathetic to the Constitution, even writing to Adams in praise of his *Defense of the Constitutions*. Jefferson also feared an unchecked majority rule: "An elective despotism was not the government we fought for, but one which should not only be founded on free principles, but in which the powers of government should be so divided and balanced among several bodies of magistracy, as that no one could transcend their legal limits without being effectually checked and restrained by the others."

After the passage of the Alien and Sedition Acts by the Federalists during the difficult days of the French Revolution, Jefferson and his close friend, Madison, developed the Kentucky and Virginia Resolutions, landmarks in United States federalism and in the development of the "compact theory" of the Constitution. In the Kentucky Resolution, Jefferson insisted that the federal Constitution had created a limited national government of certain definite and enumerated powers, reserving all other powers to the people and the states. In his lifetime, Jefferson repeatedly emphasized the close connection between decentralization and liberty. He placed his faith in a qualitative rather than a quantitative democracy, urging that a body of informed and capable citizens, an aristocracy in the best possible sense of the word, was infinitely superior to a mere nose count that delegated all authority to some political potentate.

The American tradition of federalism was thus soundly launched. There were differences among our statesmen and thinkers: agrarian capitalism versus industrial capitalism, Southern aristocrats versus New England professional men. Yet North and South, agrarian and industrialist, aristocrat and middle class, our Founding Fathers shared an abiding distrust of excessively centralized authority and a basic faith in the American people, with their diverse interests and attitudes, as the true vitality of the growing tradition of American federalism.

CAPITALISM ENCOURAGED

One of the dominant historical forces at work almost from the inception of the new Republic was the rapid expansion of a capitalist economy. The Industrial Revolution and the unique opportunities available to an America with great room to grow were coupled with an aggressive and optimistic American spirit of individual responsibility and initiative. The decisions of Chief Justice Marshall and the arguments of his contemporaries, such men as Justice Story and Daniel Webster, built upon the Hamiltonian vision of America as enunciated in *The Federalist*. Great stress was laid upon the sanctity of contract and of private property. It appeared vital to provide sufficiently centralized power to prevent the abuses of any of these concepts within the separate state governments. Capitalism therefore received great support from the political system. What centralization was necesssary to preserve the sanctity of contract and of private property did not, however, conflict with the American tradition of federalism as it had developed. A government of separated, limited powers, a close adherence to the principles of English common law and tradition remained very much in evidence.

Of course, Americans were still having their political arguments. The entrenched localized capitalism represented by the Charles River Bridge, or by the Southern agrarians, did not always approve of the sweeping social changes which a rapidly expanding capitalism brought to America. Some scholars of the Jacksonian era, notably Arthur M. Schlesinger, Jr. in his *Age of Jackson*, have described these domestic political and economic arguments of the time as though the Jacksonian movement were some sort of anti-capitalistic New Deal crusade against the powers of entrenched wealth. This is most emphatically not the case. It is much more nearly correct to see the political conflicts of the era as a sort of "new" capitalism versus "old" capitalism struggle. The Bank of the United States, for example, was attacked not in an assault upon capitalism, but as a complaint by a rising middle class against a monopoly situation that limited their own opportunities within a burgeoning capitalistic system.

Jackson himself was a Western aristocrat whose primary appeal to a rising middle class was equality before the law and resistance to unwarranted centralization, whether in economics or politics. Nothing could make it clearer that the Jacksonian movement was well within the dominant American tradition than the fact that upon John Marshall's death, Andrew Jackson appointed to the Supreme Court Chief Justice Taney to fill the vacancy, whereupon Taney served for nearly thirty years, from 1835 to 1864, producing a series of decisions steadily strengthening the contract clause of the Constitution.

Jackson's chief opponent in the political arena, Henry Clay, was a consistent advocate of extensive capitalistic development. Daniel Webster also advocated such developments, and yet found no difficulty in remaining close to the traditions of American federalism. As a rising young politician in the West, not too many years later, Abraham Lincoln consistently emphasized self-help, the opportunities of the growing West of his times, and the great social mobility of capitalism. All of these men, Jacksonian or Whig, consistently urged greater economic opportunity for the individual and the sanctity of property and contract as the best safeguard of that opportunity. They envisioned a government that enforced the rules of the game while leaving open the widest possible avenues for individual initiative and varied capitalistic development in a thoroughly decentralized framework. As rising capitalists building toward modern America, the generations of pre-Civil War American political and economic thinkers continued to place their faith in the growing tradition of American federalism.

SOUTHERN AGRARIANISM

While the North and the West went the way of industrial capitalism, the South, tied to the land and to its "peculiar institution" of slavery, went the way of agrarian capitalism. A different strain of political thinking, southern agrarianism is also one of the formative elements of American political thought before the Civil War.

Perhaps no purer spokesman for the Southern agrarian viewpoint could be found than John Randolph of Roanoke, an eccentric genius, unwilling to admit the slightest compromise with the new order. Randolph feared the results of excessive centralization and the impersonality of a government too far removed from the varieties of local experience. Addressing the House of Representatives, he asked: "But, Sir, how shall a man from Mackinaw or the Yellow Stone River respond to the sentiments of the people who live in New Hampshire? It is as great a mockery—a greater mockery, than it was to talk to those colonies about their virtual representation in the British parliament. I have no hesitation in saying that the liberties of the colonies were safer in the custody of the British parliament than they will be in any portion of this country, if all the powers of the states as well as those of the general government are devolved upon this House."

Russell Kirk's *Randolph of Roanoke* makes Randolph's attitude completely clear: "For Randolph, the real people of a country were its substantial citizenry, its men of some property, its farmers and merchants and men of skill and learning; upon their shoulders rested a country's duties, and in their hands should repose its government." It is John Randolph who developed much of the political framework later brought to fruition by John Calhoun. The primary emphasis in that framework as it developed rested upon the doctrine of states' rights, a position not without validity. Indeed, an earlier biographer of John Randolph, the almost equally eccentric and irascible Henry Adams, has suggested that the doctrine of states' rights was in itself a sound and true doctrine: "As a starting point of American history and constitutional law, there is no other which will bear a moment's examination."

Randolph was especially critical of the commerce clause and the general welfare clause of the Constitution. He predicted that the great extension of the power of centralized government would someday occur through these legal avenues. Time has proven him correct.

Calhoun built upon these suppositions. The "Cast-iron Man," pressured by the necessity of the growing crisis that was to produce the Civil War, early came to grips with the problem of what constituted genuine equality and liberty. In his *Disquisition on Government*, he warned that true liberty was compatible only with equality of *opportunity* and indeed was impossible if an equality of *condition* were to be enforced:

> Now as individuals differ greatly from each other in intelligence, sagacity, energy, perseverance, skill, habits of industry and economy, physical power, position and opportunity, the necessary effect of leaving all free to exert themselves, to better their position, must be a corresponding inequality between those who may possess these qualities and advantages in a high degree, and those who may be deficient in them. The only means by which this result can be prevented are, either to impose such restrictions on the exertions of those who may possess them in a high degree, as will place them on a level with those who do not; or to deprive them of the fruits of their exertions. But to impose such restrictions on them would be restrictive of liberty—while to deprive them of the fruits of their exertions, would be to destroy the desire of bettering their condition. It is, indeed, this inequality of condition between the front and

rear ranks, in the march of progress, which gives so strong an impulse to the former to maintain their position, and to the latter to press forward into their files. This gives to progress its greatest impulse. To push the front rank back to the rear, or attempt to push forward the rear into line with the front, by the interposition of the government, would put an end to the impulse, and effectually arrest the march of progress.

Liberty, equality of *opportunity*, progress—these are John Calhoun's words, yet might just as easily be the words of a Jacksonian entrepreneur. And how is the government to be kept from interfering with the balance? Calhoun's answer, well within the spirit of American federalism, was his "theory of the concurrent majority." Under other names, Calhoun's idea has long been the way we have actually run the American Republic and made our decisions. Power is to be diffused through so many separate entities that local and regional principles, programs, and interests, representing the tremendous diversity of American society, are able to work together at some times and yet check one another at other times, allowing national business to go forward, and yet avoiding suppression of anyone's legitimate action for the benefit of anyone else.

THE CIVIL WAR

Admittedly, a wide gulf existed in some instances between the industrial capitalism of the North and West and the agrarian capitalism of the South. Yet, in a number of ways the political values to which both North and South appealed before the Civil War had much in common. Both espoused limiting the sphere of governmental action, both favored diffusion of power, both favored wide latitude for individual differences and individual opportunities. In a word, both continued to do their thinking within the tradition of American federalism.

Yet, there remained a difficult road ahead for American federalism: the Civil War. The problem of slavery was being forced so far into the foreground that it could not much longer be ignored. The Southern agrarians were being driven by a small but intractable Northern abolitionist minority into wrapping the institution of slavery in the protective cloak of American federalism. Most

Northerners were also concerned with slavery, but in a very different way. The threat of the expansion of slavery into the new territories as this nation grew seemed to the average Northerner to menace his free institutions, both economic and political.

When the war finally came, the abolitionists who had done so much to bring it about were no longer in the forefront. The struggle came to be between Northerners set on maintaining their federal system as it had existed and Southerners who wished to set up an almost identical federal system within which the institution of slavery would be protected. The underlying concepts of American federalism were thus espoused by both North and South, even as the struggle of section against section was carried out.

The statements of Lincoln before and during the war epitomize the Northern insistence upon the traditional American attitude toward limited government and individual opportunity. In 1858 he commented, "As I would not be a slave, so I would not be a master. This expresses my idea of democracy." In 1861, he defined democracy as "a government of the people, by the same people." Nothing in such sentiments conflicts with the basic intent of Calhoun's concurrent majority. The great question that needed to be answered, again in Lincoln's words, was, "Must a government, of necessity, be too strong for the liberties of its people, or too weak to maintain its own existence?"

The history books often don't emphasize the fact that states' rights had a history of great strength in the North as well as in the South, as for example in the Hartford Convention of 1814. Meanwhile, the South maintained a strong sentimental and intellectual attachment to the Constitution until the very eve of the Civil War. Both sides espoused the same tradition in political theory; the trouble came rather from a sectional conflict over differing sociological concepts. As Daniel Boorstin has phrased it in *The Genius of American Politics:* "The North and the South each considered that it was fighting primarily for its legal rights under the sacred Federal Constitution . . . As often in American history, a great political conflict was taking the form not of a struggle between essentially different political theories, but between differences of Constitutional emphasis . . . The Civil War secessionist argument —like that of the Revolution, could be carried on in such a conservative vocabulary, because both events were, theoretically speaking, only surface breaches in a firm federal framework. Because of this, they both implied, win or lose, the continued acceptance of the existing structure of local government."

The Reconstruction era, for all its senseless crimes and abuses by both the North and the South, demonstrated a remarkable reintegration of the South into the American constitutional system. The Civil War had to be fought, perhaps, but both sides remained so much within the American tradition of federalism that the basic concepts of the American political fabric remained largely intact.

AMERICAN FEDERALISM AS A PROBLEM-SOLVING DEVICE

Since the American Civil War, the racial problem left as a legacy of slavery continues to plague both the South and the American federal system. In a case before the Supreme Court several years ago, Justice Frankfurter attacked "some recent suggestions that the Constitution was in reality a deft device for establishing a centralized government. . . ." Recalling Louis Brandeis' remark that the separation of powers was adopted "not to promote efficiency, but to preclude the exercise of arbitrary power," Frankfurter concluded with a suggestion we might all remember: "Time has not lessened the concern of the founders in devising a federal system which would likewise be a safeguard against arbitrary government. The greatest self-restraint is necessary when that federal system yields results with which a court is in little sympathy."

The racial problem is still with us (as are innumerable other problems as well) but it ill-behooves us to destroy the American tradition of federalism in the course of attempted "solutions" to our problems. After all, that American tradition of federalism has itself proven to be the greatest problem solver the American Republic has ever found.

Since the Civil War, a large part of American economic and political success has been the result of the wide social diffusion of power traditional in America. The churches, business, labor, agriculture, and political parties, have all exercised a measure of authority within the system, outside of governmental control.

State and local governments also serve to limit centralizing tendencies as they exercise their authority. Congress is composed of Senators and Representatives elected by localities and states and often representing national interest only in the sense that all of their separate and widely varied regional interests produce a national amalgam of opinion. It is behind this protective shelter of diffused and dispersed political power constituting the American federal system that the private individual has operated. It is this basic American tradition of an individual citizen freed from undue centralization of power that has provided the tremendous productivity and social mobility of the nation.

One example of this social mobility achieved through the decentralization of political power would be the record of the American immigrant. America is often referred to as a "Melting Pot," yet many of the various nationalities that make up our national population retain a wide variety of cultural differences with great pride. This cultural diversity is protected by the American federal system. On the other hand, in a political sense America has been a "Melting Pot." Many of the Europeans coming to these shores have brought with them some of the more radical political beliefs of their homeland, yet upon arriving here have been absorbed into moderate political life. America has shown the world that the "consensus through diversity" of political life possible under federalism opens so many social and economic doors to so many people that radical political answers are no longer either necessary or desirable.

This blend of political stability and economic and social progress made possible through the diffusion and localization of power was noted as a basic American institution by Tocqueville well over 100 years ago. He pointed out that state and local governments had come first in America and that the national government had been designed later for special purposes. In his careful study of local government institutions in the United States he found that "municipal institutions constitute the strength of free nations . . . [because] a nation may establish a free government, but without municipal institutions it cannot have the spirit of liberty. . . . However enlightened and skillful a central power may be, it cannot of itself embrace all the details of the life of a great nation. Such vigilance exceeds the powers of man."[39]

The papers of the Founding Fathers, especially *The Federalist*, are filled with approval of popular rule, so long as that popular rule is *locally* oriented. Even the national government in its congressional wing was to be a series of locally elected Senators and Congressmen, each representing a small segment of the total political body. This heterogeneous representation is still with us and has produced what Willmoore Kendall described as the "Two Majorities" within national politics. Even though the presidential majority produces a single executive authority, the congressional majority puts up the money and passes the laws that allow that presidential authority to be exercised, thus giving regional and local representation in all its diversity a powerful voice on the national scene.

Just as regional diversity and the political authority accorded it were seen by Tocqueville as the very root and branch of American self-reliance and therefore of American greatness, it has also been productive of such sentiments as that epitomized by the moral rectitude displayed in a veto message of Grover Cleveland: "The lesson should be constantly enforced that though the people support the Government, the Government should not support the people."

In our own time a student of contemporary society cannot help but wonder whether or not there may be quite a number of Americans who no longer seem to espouse such attitudes. It sometimes appears that all too many citizens seem more interested in what the government can do for them than in their own self-reliance. Certain elements within our society, especially in the late nineteenth and twentieth centuries, have gradually developed a philosophy of government quite different from the American tradition of federalism.

12

The Nineteenth Century

❦❦❦❦❦❦❦❦❦❦❦❦❦❦❦❦❦❦❦❦❦❦❦❦❦❦❦❦❦❦❦❦❦

EARLY INDUSTRIAL CAPITALISM

IN THE NINETEENTH CENTURY, CAPITALISM WAS ONE OF THE great formative influences in Europe as well as America. Yet, the capitalism of Europe has been the victim of a persuasive collective mythology in the twentieth century, until the true nature of its contribution to European well-being has been badly obscured. We are all influenced by this mythology. That is, we accept all sorts of "facts" as established, when in reality the actual effects of the Industrial Revolution were quite different than what those "facts" suggest. This mythology permeates all levels of our society, speading from politically motivated members of the academic community to the textbooks our children use in school, to our movies, to our novels, and to our daily newspapers.

The picture thus given the modern world concerning the nineteenth-century Industrial Revolution is a black one indeed. The common picture of child labor, horrible working conditions, pitiful conditions of housing and sanitation, is set forth so frequently as to "prove" the modern collectivist assumption that capitalism is exploitative in its very nature and leaves the common citizen at the mercy of the bloated capitalist. This mythology has become so all-pervasive that it is difficult to attack. The fact that capitalism has done more in the production of goods and services and the wide distribution of those goods and services throughout society than any other system before in the entire history of the world remains consistently overlooked. In the words of F. A. Hayek:

> The true fact of the slow and irregular progress of the working class which we now know to have taken place is of course rather unsensational and uninteresting to the layman. It is no more than he has learned to expect as the normal state of affairs; and it hardly occurs to him that this is by no means an inevitable progress, that it was preceded by centuries of virtual stagnation of the position of the poorest, and that we have come to expect continuous improvement only as a result of the experience of several generations with the system which he still thinks to be the cause of the misery of the poor.[43]

It was the fruit of capitalism in the nineteenth century to provide tremendous advances in health and education, while turning out inexpensive mass-produced goods and thus stimulating the enormous climb in real wealth which brought so many facets of a better life within reach of the common man.

This is not to suggest that the Industrial Revolution brought with it a new heaven on earth. All sorts of serious problems remained within society. But it is true that most of the grievances which are frequently laid at the door of capitalism were in large part a hangover of the pre-capitalist age. For example, repressive action of the British government must assume primary responsibility for keeping the new productive capacity of capitalism from spreading its benefits into housing and sanitation. As John Chamberlain has summarized these effects:

> . . . the prime reason for the lack of habitation in the Eighteen Twenties and Thirties was the 20-year cessation of building which had accompanied the Napoleonic struggles. Iron, needed for cannon to defeat "Boney," was unavailable for drain pipe; and wood from Scandinavia could not be had because of the prohibitive war duties. When peace came, the duties on building materials remained, adding a full third to the cost of a cottage; moreover, the old window taxes of the Seventeenth Century lingered on to make the luxury of light and air too costly for the poor. With the State duties added into the rent, and with builders having to resort for a period to the black market for money because of misplaced usury laws, it is scant cause for wonder that the new industrial towns were largely jerry-built. In addition to State taxes on wood, brick, and

other building materials, there were the local taxes. The builders themselves earned very little for their pains in putting up even the flimsiest of structures; and most of the blame for the disease that was periodically epidemic in the towns should properly be visited on the state authorities which continued to tax the tile and brick needed for sewage disposal.[41]

Thus, most of the charges laid at the door of capitalism are the result not of capitalism's failure, but rather the failure of its critics properly to understand their own history. As T. S. Ashton has remarked concerning one of the principal propagandists who helped spread the anti-capitalist mythology, "It [the dark view of the Industrial Revolution] is, of course, based on the writings of the Reverend Philip Gaskell, whose earnestness and honesty are not in doubt, but whose mind had not been confused by any study of history."[43]

As Dr. Dorothy George has made abundantly clear, however deplorable the state of living was in the industrial towns in early nineteenth-century England, there had in fact been a marked *improvement* in urban living conditions since the century before. The point involved is simple: Capitalism wrought a tremendous change for the better in the living standards of the common man. The confusion from which the modern mind suffers concerning the Industrial Revolution and its benefits stems from the fact that we compare the life of the common working man of the early nineteenth century with the high standards of living of our own time, rather than with the pitifully low standards of living in the centuries that preceded the Industrial Revolution. In short, we have become so accustomed to the prosperity which capitalism has provided for Western man that we now point to a time when capitalism was only beginning to work its wonders and charge it with all the depressed conditions which then still existed from previous centuries. The very reason for the "revolution of rising expectations" is simply that capitalism for the first time in the history of man has given to the common worker the opportunity to rise from the pitiful conditions of minimal existence to which he had been doomed in the pre-capitalist age.

However this mythology concerning the "failure" of capitalism has come about, the mythology continues to be actively propagandized in our own time. What our children consistently receive in the course of their formal education from our grade schools through our colleges might be compared to a book entitled *An Impartial History of the Civil War: From the Southern Point of View*. Such a view may be a number of things, but the one thing it can never be is history. Consider for example what our young people are taught in college surveys of Western civilization. Frequently the outside readings and textual references pertinent to the Industrial Revolution are based upon the 1832 Sadler Report.

The Sadler Report was based upon the work of a member of the British Parliament, Michael Sadler, who advocated investigation of factory working conditions. Sadler was appointed head of a committee to conduct this investigation and began by calling his own witnesses. It was assumed that following conclusion of the Sadler witnesses, the opponents of Sadler's prospective regulatory legislation would be allowed to testify. Oddly enough, Sadler allowed only his own witnesses to testify and then closed the hearings! Not too surprisingly, the Sadler Report demonstrated most "conclusively" the exploitative nature of industrial capitalism in England.

The outcry against Sadler's high-handed tactics led to the appointment of a second committee to reinvestigate the subject. The Factory Commission was appointed to this task in 1833. In the course of the second investigation, a number of interesting facts came to light. It became apparent that Sadler had not taken his testimony under oath, had limited his interviews exclusively to those with a grievance against the system, and had relied upon the medical testimony of London doctors unacquainted with actual conditions in the factory towns.

Many of these same witnesses, when contacted by the Factory Commission in 1833, refused to testify under oath. Among the few who did re-testify, this time under oath, numerous discrepancies of fact were detected, as in the case of the man who had testified about the low wage he had been receiving. Under subsequent re-examination, he "corrected" his previous testimony, making it clear that the amount previously described as his *daily* wage was actually his *hourly* wage.

All told, the Sadler Committee interviewed a total of only 88 witnesses, while the Factory Commission of 1833 interviewed 3,994 witnesses, with all testimony taken under oath in the actual factory towns where the alleged abuses were said to have occurred. The Factory Commission report branded the Sadler Report as a complete misrepresentation of the facts concerning the Industrial Revolution. Even such a bitter enemy of capitalism as Friedrich Engels has described the Sadler Report in the following words, "His report was emphatically partisan, composed by strong enemies of the factory system for party ends. Sadler permitted himself to be betrayed by his noble enthusiasm into the most distorted and erroneous statements."

Yet, at this very moment, in colleges throughout America, the view of early industrial capitalism being presented to students is still drawn primarily from that infamous and inaccurate Sadler Report of 1832. Small wonder that the mythology continues to grow!

The very brief suggestion of the true state of affairs mentioned here is treated in a far more detailed and fully explained fashion in an excellent collection of essays written by several distinguished scholars, essays designed to counteract the very mythology that we have been describing. This book of essays, *Capitalism and the Historians*, edited by Friedrich Hayek, is an ideal beginning for a proper understanding of the Industrial Revolution. It makes clear that the allegations of "exploitation" during the Industrial Revolution are drawn from complaints against the system, rather than from the normal workings of economic success which the system was enjoying. The deplorable conditions were caused primarily, to the extent that they did exist, by governmental interference and a hangover of earlier restrictions; but, even at their worst, they were a considerable improvement over the hardships of previous centuries. Capitalism has indeed had an unfair treatment at the hands of modern historians.

The propaganda efforts which have won such a complete victory in the modern mind were begun immediately by collectivist enemies of any system of free enterprise. Drawing many of their ideals from the philosophes and the new secular, collectivist temperament that had produced the French Revolution, nineteenth century propagandists attacked capitalism as their logical enemy.

UTOPIAN SOCIALISTS

The first of the groups to attack the newly emerging ideal of free enterprise were idealistic middle-class men who hoped to reconstruct society into a series of collectivist communities. These "Utopian Socialists" envisioned a society in which the individual members produced for the consumption of all, in essentially peaceful and pastoral surroundings which avoided all the "abuses" of the new factory system.

One of the first of the Utopian Socialists was the British cotton magnate, Robert Owen. Basing his program on the old Enlightenment idea that human nature and human behavior could be molded by changes in the environment, ("A man's character is made for him, not by him," declared Owen) he set up a colony at New Harmony, Indiana. His project was peculiarly ill-named, producing an endless round of backbiting and argument and finally collapsing completely despite generous subsidies made possible because of the success enjoyed by Owen's capitalistic textile mills in the British Isles.

Another of the Utopians was Comte Henri Saint-Simon. He built his Utopian dream on the Enlightenment idea that the concept of God was little more than a sociological convenience. In his system, religion was to be placed in the service of building a new social framework. Religion and society itself were to be secularized. This secular religion was to be what Saint-Simon called "the new Christianity." France was to be converted into a totally collective economy managed by technicians. The individual was to be disregarded in a new emphasis upon the masses. All of this new approach was drawn directly from the Enlightenment. For example, Saint-Simon's oligarchy of scholars who were to preside over the operation of the system was to be called the Council of Newton. Man and religion were to be made a part of the new scientistic universe.

Proposing his own Utopian variation on these same Enlightenment themes, another Frenchman, François Fourier, devised a scheme for a network of cooperative communities planned from his central headquarters. He actually started a number of his communitarian experiments, the best known being Brook Farm in New England. At Brook Farm, New England intellectuals of the 1840's looked forward to an opportunity to work with their hands, commune with nature, take time out for poetry and group singing, and generally evade the approaching Industrial Revolution. In practice, these schemes, like the other communitarian schemes of the Utopians, did not work out well at all. Nathaniel Hawthorne was assigned to the manure pile for one of his communitarian contributions. He soon felt the call of literary endeavor elsewhere and left Brook Farm.

In a slightly different category, Louis Blanc still reflected many of the same collectivist ideals. He insisted that the government had an obligation to provide what today would be called "full employment." He proposed a network of cooperative workshops which would eliminate the necessity of private enterprise. Much of what was later called syndicalism had its origins in Blanc's work.

The craze of such communitarian schemes was widespread in the first half of the nineteenth century. Writing in 1840, Ralph Waldo Emerson commented, "Not a reading man lives, but has a draft of a new community in his waistcoat pocket." In the United States alone, well over 100 such communities were set up. They had in common the secular, collective, essentially anti-individualistic ideas stemming from the Enlightenment. They also had in common short and unsuccessful careers. These planners of the "new order" viewed themselves as freed from the repressions of Christianity. They posited the good of a society that found its values exclusively on this earth, by limiting the scope of individual choice in the name of the total harmony of mankind.

HEGEL

While social and political thinkers were thus moving away from an emphasis upon the individual in the nineteenth century, the trend in philosophy seemed to follow a similar pattern. Easily the most influential of the philosophers of the early nineteenth century was the German, Hegel. Hegel developed the idea that the individual reached his fruition in the extent to which he was able to merge with "universal" values. This is another way of suggesting that the morality of man is to be realized in mankind's collective will. He erected a gigantic system in which all history and all mankind were alleged to find a place. The great danger to the individual within the Hegelian system lay in his complacent acceptance of the virtue of the state, a state which served as a reflection of the "universal" values which Hegel felt were present within society. Hegel's search was for the Universal Idea. In *Reason in History*, he wrote that he had found that value in the state:

> Thus the state is the definite object of world history proper . . . For law is the objectivity of Spirit; it is will in its true form. Only that will that obeys the law is free, for it obeys itself and, being in itself, is free.

Here appears the idea destined to become so tremendously popular in modern thought: the idea that freedom for the individual can only be achieved when the individual abandons his freedom to the collectivity. As Fichte phrased it, "To compel men to adopt the right form of government, to impose Right on them by force, is not only the right, but the sacred duty of every man who has both the insight and the power to do so." As Auguste Comte phrased the same idea, "If we do not allow free thinking in chemistry or biology, why should we allow it in morals or politics?"

Isaiah Berlin has summarized this view in his Inaugural Lecture at the University of Oxford:

> This argument employed by Fichte in his latest phrase, and by Hegel, and after them by other defenders of authority, from Marx and the Positivists to the latest nationalist or communist dictator, is precisely what the Stoic and Kantian morality protests against most bitterly in the name of the reason of the free individual following his own inner light. In this way the rationalist argument, with its assumption of the single true solution, has led from an ethical doctrine of individual responsibility and individual self-perfection, to an authoritarian state obedient to the directives of an elite of Platonic guardians.[44]

Much of the authoritarian political tradition of Germany has its origins in the philosophy of G. W. F. Hegel. His system embraced ethics, history, art, metaphysics, religion, and philosophy as well as politics. Yet within this all-encompassing system, the individual was to be nothing, and the state was to be all. Indeed, Hegel himself described the state as "the Divine Idea as it exists on Earth." Such ideas as this hastened the German turn toward the state socialism or welfare state of the later nineteenth century. These same ideas were also of primary influence upon Karl Marx, the next of the socialists to plan the collectivity of the future.

KARL MARX

So many Marxist sects have arisen and expounded their own varying interpretation of the original theories of Karl Marx that it is sometimes unclear what the original patron saint of "scientific socialism" proposed in his own work.

Marx and his collaborator, Friedrich Engels, originally set forth their social philosophy in a 1848 pamphlet, *The Communist Manifesto*. Despite his early association with various activist groups, Marx himself led a withdrawn existence, spending much of his adult life in the British museum. The Italian nationalist Mazzini was a close associate of Marx during the years in England and described him as a man of great intellectual power, but of almost no control over his emotions, emotions usually bitter and antagonistic toward all those around him and toward society as a whole. As Christopher Dawson has characterized him:

> The fact is that Marx was himself a disgruntled bourgeois, and his doctrine of historic materialism is a hang-over from a debauch of bourgeois economics and bourgeois philosophy. He was no great lover, no "man of desire," but a man of narrow, jealous, unforgiving temperament, who hated and calumniated his own friends and allies. And consequently he sought the motive power for the transformation of society not in love but in hatred and failed to recognize that the social order cannot be renewed save by a new principle of spiritual order. In this respect Marxian socialism is infinitely inferior to the old Utopian socialism, for Saint-Simon and his followers with all their extravagances had at least grasped this essential truth.[13]

Marx had derived many of his ideas from Hegel, especially the idea of an historical process of thesis, antithesis, synthesis, in which the status quo (thesis) was confronted with a new and challenging idea (antithesis), the two forces then producing a synthesis, or new thesis to begin the historical cycle yet another time. Marx completely accepted the idea of violent revolution based on the model of the French experience. He derived many of his economic ideas from the British classical economists, though he perverted them in application. He swept together this legacy of Hegelian statism, the violence and secularism of the French Revolution, a misapplication of the classical economists, the materialism and collectivism of the philosophes, and his own personal hatred of society into the pattern of revolutionary philosophy which is today called Marxism.

With the accustomed oversimplification so common among systems builders, Marx concluded that "all struggles within the State, the struggle between democracy, aristocracy, and monarchy, the struggle for the franchise, etc., etc., are merely the illusory forms in which the real struggles of the different classes are fought out among one another." This fundamental idea of class struggle and the exclusively economic interpretation of history became the basis of the major work of Marx's lifetime, *Das Kapital.* His economic analysis contained within it serious flaws which explain many of the peculiarities of Marxism. Marx was especially misled by the mistaken concept which he had appropriated from the early classical economists: the "labor theory of value."

Simply stated, the labor theory of value is the assumption that the value of any commodity is determined by the amount of labor present within that commodity. This is a mistaken assumption. If you choose to make mince pies and I choose to make mud pies, and the distance which I must travel for water in order to make my mud pies causes me to apply as much labor to my product as you to yours, the labor theory of value says that in the market your mince pies and my mud pies should have the same value.

However ridiculous the labor theory of value may be, if the premise be accepted that the value of a product is measured exclusively by the amount of labor present within that product, if the laboring man is therefore responsible for one-hundred percent of the value in the final price of an item, then it would follow logically that what the capitalist system calls profit is really nothing more than surplus value, rightly belonging to the worker, but exploited from him by the capitalist. Thus Marx reached the conclusion that capitalism was by its very nature exploitative of the working classes.

What Marx expected to have happen was that, under the exploitations of capitalism, the owning classes would grow progressively smaller, while the proletariat would grow continually larger and larger. Once this exploitative process had gone far enough and the few rich were fabulously wealthy and the many poor were terribly poor, Marx expected revolution to occur, sweeping away the entire capitalistic system and substituting a new collective order in its place. At that point, exploitation, competition, and all the abuses of the private, individual, free enterprise sector of society would be replaced by classless fellowship achieving paradise on earth.

Although Marx and all the collectivists who drew upon the philosophic background of the philosophes tended to dismiss God and all religious values from their systems, they were always careful to reinstitute pseudo-religious values in their new rationalistic and materialistic systems. The ideal of a Marxian paradise to be achieved as the end result of the Hegelian dialectic is just such a device. In this sense, Marxism made an essentially religious appeal. In the words of Joseph A. Schumpeter:

> Now to millions of human hearts the Marxian message of the terrestrial paradise of socialism meant a new ray of light and a new meaning of life. Call Marxist religion a counterfeit if you like, or a caricature of faith—there is plenty to be said for this view—but do not overlook or fail to admire the greatness of the achievement. Never mind that nearly all of those millions were unable to understand and appreciate the message in its true significance. That is the fate of all messages. The important thing is that the message was framed and conveyed in such a way as to be acceptable to the positivistic mind of its time . . . by formulating with unsurpassed force that feeling of being thwarted and ill treated which is the auto-therapeutic attitude of the unsuccessful many, and, on the other hand, by proclaiming that socialistic deliverance from those ills was a certainty amenable to rational proof.[45]

For this new order, Marx claimed the absolute certainty of "science." The Hegelian dialectic, the march of revolution, was sweeping mankind on toward a new collective paradise that no religious values, no individual values, no moral values would be allowed to stop. In his scientific emphasis, in his idea of "heaven on earth," in his rationalistic assumptions, in his antagonism toward the existing state of society, in his atheistic assumptions, in his bitter attitude toward the heritage of Western civilization, in his collective emphasis, in his materialistic emphasis, in all these things, Marx was a logical child of the philosophic development common to the Age of Reason.

In practice, of course, Marxism has never been borne out. The first great experiment in which Marxism had the opportunity of actually gaining control of a society, the Soviet Union, is a fine working example of such disastrous ideas when put into practice. The records of Lenin, Stalin, and the rest of the butchers make this abundantly clear.

Marx promised that the dictatorship of the proletariat would allow the common man a total control over his society once capitalism had been destroyed. Yet the Soviet Union and contemporary Marxism offer in its place what is called "democratic centralism," democratic in the sense that it is done in the name of all the people and centralist in the sense that the decisions are made by an elite. Marx promised the "withering away of the state," yet Marxism in practice has produced the most oppressive and gigantic governmental machinery in the history of the world. Marx envisioned a new society in which "the interests of the people" would be the primary concern of society. Those millions of kulaks liquidated so that collective agriculture might be achieved would perhaps have disputed this point. Some argument as to what constitutes "the interests of the people" might also have been raised by those millions within Russia who have starved and are starving (except for occasional importations of American wheat) because of the disastrous failure of this very same system of collective agriculture.

In short, the promise of Marxism has most certainly not been fulfilled. Wherever and whenever it has been tried, it has tended to reduce prosperity, not increase it. It has tended to bring great hardship to the people, to the common man. It has tended to stifle initiative while stratifying society through the imposition of a gigantic bureaucracy. While thus harming societies in which it has been tried, Marxism has been most repugnant in the tremendous inhumanities to man which the system seems to generate. It is in this area of moral decline, stemming from the loss of individual freedom and responsibility, that Marxism has demonstrated least workability. As society has become larger and larger, the individual has become smaller and smaller to the final vanishing point. Meanwhile, in those areas of the Western world where free enterprise and individual freedom have been allowed at least a partial chance to operate, what has become of Marx's promised revolution? Marx's exploited proletariat has not revolted. Instead, the American proletariat, for example, has moved to the suburbs and now drives back and forth to work in a Thunderbird. The suburbs are a poor place to look for revolutionaries.

Western man has quite properly been strongly suspicious of the systems builder. And it was not until the nineteenth century, as an aftermath of the Age of Reason and the philosophes, that the systems builders began to come into their own in the Western world. The Greeks would have suspected that anyone who, like Marx, reduced all human existence to scientifically knowable quantities and then planned how those quantities should be manipulated and altered was suffering from hubris—the kind of pride which the Christianity of the Western world had always warned came before a fall. Unfortunately, many of the same secular, rationalist, materialistic, collective assumptions lie at the root of the schemes preached by a number of other systems builders of the nineteenth and twentieth centuries who have implemented more of their ideas within Western Society than Karl Marx himself ever succeeded in doing.

SCIENTISM, NATURALISM, RELATIVISM

All of the varieties of collectivism as they developed in the nineteenth century placed their emphasis upon a collective rather than an individual morality and drew their strength from eighteenth-century rationalism, in the naturalistic, materialistic, and relative emphasis of the philosophes, in Rousseau's "General Will," in the leveling tendency to destroy the older institutions within society, in the consistent anti-religious emphasis, and in the persistent idea that "Progress" can be achieved for all mankind because the individual is essentially malleable and can be controlled by his environment in the achievement of "social" goals.

All such ideas had of course been very popular during the Enlightenment and were made to appear even more plausible when they reappeared in the nineteenth century in the form of Positivism, which alleged to provide "scientific" proof of the essentially perfectible capacities of "natural man." Auguste Comte could insist that the brain contained an "organ of benevolence." The development of limited-government philosophy and political self-rule, coupled with the material progress of the nineteenth century (stemming largely from capitalism), produced all sorts of advancement which at the time seemed to encourage this idea of progress and human perfection. Thus the ideas of the philosophes became progressively more widespread and apparently more plausible as time passed.

Yet to be written is the history of the emergence of Naturalism, of the development of the idea that *all* values within society are present within the natural order, with a reference to no higher dignity of the individual, no religious value, and no limiting factor over the "social goals" which may be imposed upon society by those who promise improvement. But when that history is fully and fairly set forth, the process of the eighteenth and nineteenth century which stripped man of his theological beliefs may well be recorded as the moment in which Western civilization made the wrong turning which led to its dissolution and destruction. In the words of Gilbert Chesterton:

> The men of science went out and took another look at the knobby nature of matter; and were surprised to find that it was not knobby at all. So they came back and completed the process with their syllogism: "All matter is made of whirling protons and electrons. My body is made of matter. Therefore my body is made of whirling protons and electrons." And that again is a good syllogism; though they may have to look at matter once or twice more, before we know whether it is a true premise and a true conclusion. But in the final process of truth there is nothing else except a good syllogism. The only other thing is a bad syllogism; as in the familiar fashionable shape; "All matter is made of protons and electrons. I should very much like to think that mind is much the same as matter. So I will announce, through the microphone or the megaphone, that

my mind is made of protons and electrons." But that is not induc-
tion; it is only a very bad blunder in deduction. That is not another
or new way of thinking; it is only ceasing to think.[34]

Unfortunately, while modern man has all too often ceased to
think, he has not ceased to act.

JEREMY BENTHAM

There were other planners of the ideal society, men perfectly
assured of their own capacity to determine man's needs and how
best to fulfill them. Jeremy Bentham founded the School of Philosophical Radicalism, or as it is more commonly known, Utilitarianism, in England in the late eighteenth and early nineteenth
century. Drawing heavily upon the works of Helvetius and other
philosophes, Bentham displayed the same optimistic attitude toward "progress," the same eagerness to translate natural science
into technology and government. In his totally naturalistic view of
human society, Bentham placed his primary reliance upon two key
elements, *pain* and *pleasure*. Writing in his *Principles of Morals
and Legislation*, Bentham urged:

> Nature has placed mankind under the governance of two sovereign
> masters, *pain* and *pleasure*. It is for them alone to point out what
> we ought to do, as well as to determine what we shall do. On the
> one hand the standard of right and wrong, on the other the chain
> of causes and effects, are fastened to their throne.

Here in a nutshell is a naturalistic view of man which treats him
exclusively apart from the idea of any Divine Creation. This is the
principle of utility, or in Bentham's phrase, *the greatest good for
the greatest number*. The only standard of judgment to be exercised within such a utilitarian society was, "Is it socially useful?"
Just as Helvetius had believed that man was perfectible if his
environment were properly controlled, Bentham took the next
step to define right and wrong within such environment as those
acts which had the greatest or the least utility respectively. Thus,
any other criterion except utility, said Bentham, could ultimately
be reduced to the personal sentiment of the individual and therefore was not worthy of consideration.

To erect such a philosophy, Bentham naturally had to display total disregard for the idea of Natural Law. In fact, as the nineteenth century was about to dawn, Jeremy Bentham, as a representative of the new naturalistic secular order, and John Quincy Adams, as a representative of Natural Law and the traditional framework of Western civilization reflected in the budding American Republic, clashed over this very issue:

> The differences between Bentham and Adams concerning Natural Law are not so much a matter of belief as of understanding. As a Christian, Adams both understood and believed in the Natural Law, and undoubtedly the utilitarian Bentham would have detested it even if he had understood it. But like secular contemporary sociologists who deny the existence of all moral norms or standards, Bentham could not even distinguish between what Natural Law was in fact, and derivations or violations of Natural Law made in its name. In denying all norms but those of social utility, Bentham was reduced to the absurdity that if men have the power to violate the imperatives of Natural Law, there is no such thing as Natural Law.[46]

In the words of a distinguished historian of Western thought, Crane Brinton:

> Bentham provides an even more typical example of the carefully contrived environment—contrived from above by the wise, fatherly authority. Bentham's basic principles are that men seek pleasure and avoid pain (note the apparent similarity to such concepts of physics as that of gravity), and that since this is a fact we must accept it as a moral good. The secret of government is therefore to devise a system of rewards and punishment such that socially and morally desirable action on the part of the individual results for him always in more pleasure than pain; and that socially and morally undesirable action should always bring him more pain than pleasure. Bentham went into great detail working out his calculus of pleasure and pain, classifying, weighing, and measuring various kinds of pleasures and pains. Of course what he did was to assign values such as a kindly, philosophical, serious-minded English gentlemen would esteem. His ethics, like those of most Westerners in revolt against Christianity, turn out to be most Christian. But Bentham would not trust the ordinary institutions of society to measure out pain and pleasure properly. Somehow society was rewarding the actions that did not bring the greatest good to the greatest number, penalizing the actions that would do so if given a chance. But mere freedom wouldn't bring that chance. Men like

Bentham would have to sit down and work out new devices, a new society . . .

Bentham's psychological detail seems to us nowadays rather naive, and the elaborate plans he makes, unworkable. But the reforming spirit we know well. Much of what Bentham and his followers tried to achieve in the reform of institutions has indeed been put on the statute books. No one is now hanged for stealing a sheep. We cannot quite hope for the sweeping results Bentham hoped for, but we continue to use many of his methods; and we continue, good democrats though we may be, to pin much of our hopes on institutional changes planned from above. The New Deal and the New Frontier both had a good deal of old Bentham in them (and note the typical implication that new is good).[33]

The idea of utilitarianism was far from new, but Bentham elevated the entire concept to the level of "science," and made it into still another secular religion. All economics and politics were now to be dealt with in the same impersonal manner that one solved a mathematic equation. Much of the utilitarian doctrine appeared to be on the right track. Drawing from classical economics, Bentham called for low taxes, efficient government, unlimited competition, and free trade. In politics the utilitarians looked toward civil liberty and limited constitutional government. Yet, the difficulty with Bentham's philosophy of utilitarianism lay in the fact that if the government might exercise its control in terms of the greatest good for the greatest number, with all values strictly utilitarian in nature, the end result would be a tendency to dehumanize man in the materialistic search for the greatest good of the greatest number. By 1870, utilitarianism as an active philosophy was dead, but the idea that the government could labor in behalf of the greatest good for the greatest number and was limited only by its own utilitarian concepts of how best to achieve those goals was destined to linger on into the twentieth century.

HERBERT SPENCER

The mid and later nineteenth century saw new thinkers rise in opposition to the utilitarianism of Bentham and the idealism of Hegel. By the mid-century the new ideas of Charles Darwin had largely upset Hegelian idealism and new philosophies were being expounded in terms of the Darwinian interpretation. Best known and most widespread of these was the work of Herbert Spencer, the founder of what came to be called "Social Darwinism." Spencer was critical not only of the total state implications of Hegel, but also saw much to complain of in the increasingly welfare statist tone which came to dominate the utilitarian search for the greatest good of the greatest number. Building on the classical economists such as Malthus and Ricardo, Spencer insisted that the immutable laws of nature applied in the social sciences as well as the natural sciences. Taking such ideas as the Malthusian doctrine that population tends to outrun subsistence, Ricardo's idea that wages are inexorably limited by the food supply, and the Darwinian idea of evolutionary struggle for the survival of species, Spencer applied evolutionary concepts to human problems, coining the phrase, "survival of the fittest."

In Spencer's cosmology, the laws of science were to be allowed to work their way uninhibited by any pressures from government. The entire system, like evolution in the animal kingdom, was to evolve toward a higher and higher level of complexity, until it reached the point where the system hung in perfect equilibrium. Any interference with this freely working system by government amounted to an interference with society's progress.

Here at last seemed an answer to the Hegelian idealization of the state and to the Benthamite idea that man could perhaps have his affairs manipulated by some beneficent planner in the name of the greatest good for the greatest number. Unfortunately, Spencer still drew his ideas from the same fatal Enlightenment doctrines of materialism, determinism, naturalism, and secularism which characterized the intellectual roots of those with whom he was most, on the surface, in disagreement. Because his system sprang from the same polluted source, Herbert Spencer was disarmed in his struggle to avoid the very disastrous interventions which he opposed.

Spencer quite rightly had recognized that the exercise of power within society was the negative, limiting factor which had to be curbed. But he had mistakenly assumed that the ideas which he espoused would lead toward the gradual diminution of that power. In building his system, he had looked forward to a time when the system would hang in perfect equilibrium without the necessity for any power being exercised. (Note the similarity between this idea and Marx's "withering away of the state.") Spencer himself lived long enough to see the collapse of his dreams. As the nineteenth century and Herbert Spencer grew old, they witnessed the gradual centralization and development of greater power over men than had ever been exercised before. What Spencer, and indeed most of the thinkers since the time of the philosophes, had forgotten was that Natural Law, because it limits interference with individual rights, tends to restrict power. But a theory, any theory, which rejects Natural Law and which discusses the end rather than the source of power (e.g., Spencer, Bentham, Marx) opens the door to a situation in which ". . . society forges and can modify at will [a standard of objective right], and the only subjective rights are those which it deigns to grant."[37] Thus the door is open for the gradual minimization of the individual and the maximization of society's control over the individual, whatever the system might be called.

MILL, DE TOCQUEVILLE, AND
THE APOSTLES OF FREEDOM

Some of the greatest minds of the nineteenth century perceived the dangers apparent in divorcing man's affairs from God. The Swiss historian Jacob Burckhardt warned that the idea of progress which the nineteenth and twentieth centuries have so taken to their heart was a false dream, a dream in no way borne out by the history of the human race, a dream, furthermore, in whose name the greatest repressions of the individual might be pursued.

A young Frenchman, Alexis de Tocqueville, visiting the United States in the 1830's, had sensed the tremendous creative capacities of human freedom unlocked by the American experiment and had warned that if the ideals of the philosophes and the French Revolution ever came to replace that emphasis upon human freedom, if America ever came to believe in Man in place of God and to emphasize all the secular, material, naturalistic values involved in such a substitution, the light of freedom might one day be extinguished here as well. In 1848, de Tocqueville warned the French Constituent Assembly:

> Democracy extends the sphere of individual freedom, socialism restricts it. Democracy attaches all possible value to each man; socialism makes each man a mere agent, a mere number. Democracy and socialism have nothing in common but one word: equality. But notice the difference: while democracy seeks equality in liberty, socialism seeks equality in restraint and servitude.

When de Tocqueville's analysis of the American society, *Democracy in America*, was first published, he took time to write a personal letter to John Stuart Mill, whom he felt, of all the book's reviewers, had best understood the meaning of his work. The two of them became fast friends and frequent correspondents for the remainder of their lives. It is natural enough that de Tocqueville and Mill would have been attracted to one another's ideas.

In Mill we see an important political education taking place during his lifetime. Raised in the Benthamite circle of his father, James Mill, John Stuart Mill lived on into another generation in which the high hopes for Benthamite utilitarian reform had already begun to fail as the system revealed its shortcomings. Mill had both the opportunity and the intellect to recognize that a democratic society had within itself the power to practice a tyranny even more formidable than any of the earlier repressions of the human spirit which had been practiced. He warned that robbing the individual of God-given dignity was the first step in the suppression of all dissent. As he phrased it: "All silencing of discussion is an assumption of infallibility." He wrote *On Liberty* shortly before the dawn of the century the political history of which has been a living demonstration of his warning. He already knew what the twentieth century apparently still must learn:

> A state which dwarfs its men, in order that they may be more docile instruments in its hands even for beneficial purposes—will find that with small men no great thing can really be accomplished; and that the perfection of machinery to which it has sacrificed everything, will in the end avail it nothing, for want of the vital power which, in order that the machine might work smoothly, it has preferred to banish.

In the twentieth century, the warnings of the Burckhardts, de Tocquevilles, and Mills have evidenced a painful accuracy. The systems builders of the collectivist, secularist, naturalist stripe were to have ample opportunity to replace God with Man and to work their will upon the human race. The heirs of the philosophes were soon to have their day in the sun.

13

Twentieth Century Collectism

❧❧❧❧❧❧❧❧❧❧❧❧❧❧❧❧❧❧❧❧❧❧❧❧❧❧❧❧❧❧❧❧

MANY OF THE PATTERNS OF THOUGHT STEMMING FROM THE Renaissance and the Enlightenment re-emphasized sound values centering on the individual and his capacity to reason. Unfortunately, the Renaissance and Enlightenment also had the effect of cutting us loose from our traditions, from our past, and from all definite standards by which we might judge or defend our position. As the result, the modern world has come to emphasize that other, less attractive, heritage—collective solutions, centralization, anti-traditionalism, anti-individualism, and a society so equality conscious that it becomes increasingly intolerant of our differences.

Some will say that these are the results of a changed social and economic system: modern technology, the Industrial Revolution, new social problems, mass democracy, and so on. The emphasis in such thinking is on *change*, rather than on the remarkable sameness of human nature and the human condition over the centuries. And as modern man has rushed to pursue change and to depart from his traditions and his heritage, he has produced a chapter of history which displays more inhumanity to man in the twentieth century than ever before. We see increasing material prosperity. We see more technical advance and achievement in scientific knowledge than the mind can readily grasp. Yet, we also see the steady constriction of man's freedom, an increasing nihilism toward any and all traditions and values, and a threatened destruction of civilization. The problems of man in many ways seem to be worse than ever in our time. How can a society which promises so much deliver so little? This great gap between promise and performance has plagued us since the time of the French Revolution and the terror and destruction it let loose upon the world in the name of the good of man. The debate concerning man, his institutions, and his values has continued unceasingly since then. One answer, the answer adopted by the great majority of men in the twentieth century, is the collective solution, the centrally planned society.

In our public utterances, we heirs of Western civilization speak critically of the totalitarian solutions of the Russians or the Chinese, implying that our values are less collective and more individualistic than theirs. We thus refuse to see the extent to which we have adopted the collective ideal within our own society. One of the seminal thinkers of the New Deal, Professor Rexford G. Tugwell, was a bit more honest with himself than are many Americans as he described the new value system in *Our Economic Society and Its Problems:*

> The real challenge to America . . . is the challenge of the planning idea. Russia has silenced forever the notion that economic affairs are governed by adamant natural laws. She has demonstrated that men have it in their power to set up the system they want and to make it obedient to their wishes.
>
> With Russia as an example, intelligent people in America . . . will want to plan and act.

It is this very planning ideal which our society has so completely espoused in the twentieth century. How has this come about, and how has the planned economy worked in practice?

By the second and third decades of the twentieth century, many American intellectuals had become persuaded that capitalism afforded neither economic prosperity nor freedom. They placed their hopes upon a future in which great political authority would be exercised over men's economic affairs, somewhat as proposed by the newly established Communist society in Russia. At that time, the planned society was an ideal concept, a blueprint of how men might order their affairs according to human reason by experts. This theoretical ideal was contrasted with the realities of capitalism as it had developed in the Western world with all the imperfections of any human system. Thus the real was contrasted with the ideal. Not surprisingly, the real came off second best when contrasted with a utopian state of affairs as seen on the drawing board.

The planned society is no longer in the blueprint stage. The plans have long since been applied within our own society and throughout the world. It is no longer necessary to compare the real with the ideal. Now the realities of competitive capitalism may be compared with the realities of the planned economy. Their respective records speak for themselves.

If the intellectuals of the twentieth century had to have this fact demonstrated, other political economists of higher capability had long ago perceived what sad results to expect of the planning experiment. As Adam Smith predicted in his eighteenth-century *Wealth of Nations:*

> The statesman who should attempt to direct private people in what manner they ought to employ their capitals, would not only load himself with a most unnecessary attention, but assume an authority which could safely be trusted to no council and senate whatever, and which would nowhere be so dangerous as in the hands of a man who had folly and presumption enough to fancy himself fit to exercise it.

The Bible might well have been describing the modern intellectuals who still cling to the planning ideal despite its disastrous consequences when it referred to *those who believe a lie unto their own destruction.* The failures of the planned society become steadily more apparent with the passage of time. More and more excuses are needed for the failures of this planning ideal. One cartoonist has depicted two Russians scanning the heavens shortly after the launching of the first Russian satellite, one commenting to the other, "Glorious 'Sputnik' is like glorious food production, and glorious consumer goods production. Is not visible to naked eye, comrade stupid."

It is the Russian variety of the planned economy which offers the most graphic examples of failure, simply because it has progressed furthest down the disastrous road of planning. The Russian economy has had its collective troubles with incentives. In an effort to get people to produce effectively, communism has had to institute piece work incentives that it decried as "brutal" and "exploitative" when used 150 years ago in the early capitalist economies.

Perhaps a more pressing problem for the Communist state has been its attempt to solve the problem of pricing. Price in the free market is the communication device by which goods, resources, and skills are automatically sent to the point of their most economic use within society. Free market pricing works automatically to eliminate shortage and surplus and to allocate everything of value within society to the most productive use. However, central planning perverts or totally destroys the function of price in its planned and totally regulated economy. It relegates to its planning authority the function performed in the free society by price. The planner must then allocate goods and services, must determine production costs, must ration scarce materials, must decide how much should be produced, and of what precise size, quality, shape, and other specifications. It is in this area of pricing that the Russian planned economy has suffered some of its most disastrous shortcomings.

Consider a Russian nail factory, operating not by price but by planned "quotas." In such a nail factory, a quota can be set for production of nails by weight. This of course places a premium upon large nails, few in number, since they are most easily produced to reflect high quantities in weight. Such a nail factory produces railroad spikes in an effort to satisfy the quotas placed upon it. But soon the complaints begin to pour back from the other planners who are consuming the fruits of this planned production. It is discovered that railroad spikes are peculiarly unsatisfactory for laying carpet. The planner immediately adjusts to the new situation, setting the quota in terms of *number* of nails, rather than *weight* produced. This has the effect of stimulating production of the smallest possible nails, thereby solving the problem. That is, the problem appears solved until other planners within society try to meet their quotas in the laying of railway track. It seems that carpet tacks are unsatisfactory for attaching rails to ties!

Consider the strange plight of various Russian embassies and public buildings throughout the world when their ceilings came crashing to the floor. Actually, there was nothing mysterious about this. The production quotas for a Russian chandelier factory had been set in terms of total weight of chandeliers produced! Such examples sound absurd in the Western world. We are so used to price automatically allocating goods and resources to give all customers the quantity, quality, and variety of goods most economic for their situation that we have difficulty appreciating the disastrous consequences faced by a society in which the planners attempt to take the market's place. Perhaps the classic example of the failure of planning has been that of collective agriculture. In an age when the Soviet Union has brought tremendous political power and "planning" to bear in an effort to increase agricultural production, it has produced famine. At the very same time, the United States has brought tremendous political power and "planning" to bear upon American agriculture to reduce production, thereby producing a surplus.

Socialism largely depends upon material achievements which can never be created by the planning ideal itself. At best, the planned society can only distribute and manipulate the fruits of a production which it can never duplicate. Under "planning," the ultimate consumer finds his choices restricted by the planner's definition of what he "should" have. Thus, pricing and all systems of measurement, as well as consumer sovereignty, are swept aside by a system sterile in nature, a system with great power to disrupt and stultify and virtually no power to produce. What production is still achieved is not because of, but in spite of, the planner.

The response in the Western world to this totalitarian planning ideal has been the so-called "mixed economy." "We will continue to utilize the market in all transactions where it meets with success, but will intervene with the planning ideal at those points where free enterprise does not work properly." So goes the rationale, a rationale destined to have disastrous results for our own society and the Western world.[47]

The story has been told of an Indian maharajah who maintained an elaborate hunting preserve on his estates. On one occasion, years ago, a young English woman visited the maharajah and was sent out with a Hindu guide to try her hand at bird hunting. All morning long, the maharajah heard occasional shotgun blasts from his preserve. Upon the return of the young lady and her guide, the maharajah inquired as to what success the morning had brought, to which the tactful Hindu replied, "The beautiful lady shoots divinely, but Providence is merciful to the birds." The modern planners within our society, those who advocate the "mixed economy," may not be doing their work "divinely," but at least they have been doing plenty of shooting at their selected targets for intervention within our society. The problems that have so occupied the planners have not only resisted solution-by-government-intervention, but in the process have been further aggravated so that the planners are now planning "solutions" to new problems arising from previous plans and interventions!

We were told that regulation of the transportation systems of this nation would protect the consumer from exploitation by a few monopolistic or oligopolistic giants; yet the principal effect of the Interstate Commerce Commission or the Civil Aeronautics Board has been to restrict the entry of competition into the field of transportation and almost totally to eliminate market pricing. It is just such semimonopolistic lack of competition from which the planners promised relief for the ultimate consumer.

More recently we have been told that Urban Renewal would sweep away the slums, thereby improving housing for the poor and achieving various side benefits such as the reduction of juvenile delinquency. Yet the high-rise apartment houses erected in urban renewal projects are not offered at a rent which the slum dweller is capable of paying. As Professor Martin Anderson, author of *The Federal Bulldozer*, makes abundantly clear, the principal effect of Urban Renewal upon the slum dweller is to move him to more crowded, higher-priced slum areas, thus aggravating housing conditions and such related problems as juvenile delinquency.

In the 1930's we were told that a system of planned interventions in the agricultural sphere of the American economy was needed to "save the family farm." After decades of milking the taxpayer to support the agricultural program, the principal result of agricultural price supports has been the conversion of agriculture to big business. Anyone who doubts that agriculture and the milking of the agricultural support program has become big business should consult the *Congressional Record's* yearly publication of the long, long list of recipients whose yearly "benefits" from the program are in five figures or more. Meanwhile, whatever happened to the family farm? The answer, of course, lies in the simple fact that so many of the small farmers whom the program was designed to protect are not eligible for or benefitted by the bulk of payments and are thus driven from the land by the plan. In this area, government intervention can create tremendous agricultural surpluses and fiscal deficits, to the delight of a Billy Sol Estes, but apparently it cannot solve the problem which the planners originally set for themselves.

We are told of the efficiency of planning; and every failure of the planners is immediately defended as "due to insufficient authority to deal properly with the problem." Yet it would be hard to envision a situation in which more total monopolistic control could be in the hands of the planners than in the case of the United States Post Office. Costs rise higher and higher as service sinks lower and lower. Not long ago in Chicago the backup of undelivered and unsorted mail reached such proportions that it became a national scandal even in an era used to the failures of the post office. A group of planners analyzed the problem and came up with a very sensible solution: Destroy the mail in question and get a fresh start. At least this solution, unlike so many suggested by the planners, had the merit of solving the problem, albeit in a temporary fashion and at a high cost.

We were told that the intervention of government in monetary affairs through the Federal Reserve System would prevent future banking panics. Yet, in the early 1930's this very system played a major role in producing the most severe banking panic in the history of this nation. The same government intervention in monetary affairs contracted the currency more than 40 per cent in the time of recession between 1929 and 1931, thereby assuring a full-scale depression.[53] Yet this very failure of government intervention was so disastrous that the Great Depression itself became the basis for further planned intervention! There apparently is no point at which the principle of "planning," of "government intervention for the good of society as a whole," is ever called upon to prove its effectiveness. The disasters of planning only generate new appeals for even greater authority, for even more "planning."

But planning doesn't work, whether in the totalitarian framework, or in the "mixed economy." Not only does the system fail in operation, but it brings with it such dangers as inflation. The constant expansion of the money supply by the planners is pursued as a panacea to help temporarily ameliorate all the dislocations which previous planning had introduced into our economic life. In the process, "temporary" government projects become institutionalized. Meanwhile, the savings and pensions of our society are eroded as the lifeblood of our economic circulatory system is steadily diluted. Such problems and dislocations multiply within a society until one day it ceases to function. On that day, the planners who produced the debacle will still be telling us that it is a "failure of capitalism." The common man is beginning to suspect those who congratulate themselves on their ability to control what everyone does within society. Meanwhile, the advocates of the mixed economy continue to propose all sorts of further intervention: Warming the economy, cooling the economy—each new proposal contradicting the others.

Despite the disagreement among those who advocate their various plans for our salvation, the one underlying thread of common consent remains: Planning the economy and backing those plans with the coercive force of government is a viable solution within society. This attitude is still dominant, despite the bad record of the planning ideal in practice. This may be what Professor Frank Knight had in mind: "It is not that so many know so little about economics. The trouble is that so many know so much that is wrong."

Why does the planned economy fail in actual operation? Ultimately, economics is only another expression of an underlying moral order, a moral order premised, as all moral choice must be, upon the individual. We have forgotten that units of *one*, the individual consumer and individual producer, make up an economy. There always remains a great gap between plan and performance in the "planned economy" because individual human beings will not stay charted on a graph as the modern planner would have them. The basic fact of economics is finally the relationship of constantly shifting human judgments and choices. The failure of the planning ideal is reassuring proof that you and I are more than lines on a chart or raw material to be molded at some planner's whim.

Despite this fact, the idea of "let the government intervene" as a solution to every problem within our society continues to dominate our leadership thinking. Thus, the planner continues to plan and to produce a network of interventions and controls that stifle dynamic free enterprise. The modern planners of the "mixed economy" have answered Hayek's classic question, "Who plans for whom?" with the self-assurance that they and they alone should have the power to order the lives of everyone else. This reveals the terrible fallacy involved in the planning ideal. No man knows what another man's abilities or opinions are worth. And any coercion exercised over those abilities and opinions must thus be exercised in ignorance. The planner's state is not only dependent upon force but is dependent upon *blind* force. What's more, this blind force presses hardest upon those whose productive and creative capacities would best serve society if they were allowed free play. In the words of Edith Hamilton:

> Indeed, any attempt to establish a uniform average in that stubbornly individual phenomenon, human nature, will have only one result that can be foretold with certainty: it will press hardest upon the best, as everyone knows who is driven by large numbers to use mass methods.[25]

ECONOMICS AND POLITICAL FREEDOM

The truly destructive aspect of the planned economy lies not in the fact that it doesn't work, that it fails to confer material benefits. The great danger lies instead in the underlying *reason* the system doesn't work: it gives too little to the individual, his freedom and his personality as a human being. In the planner's quest for centralization and organization, human freedom finds no place.

A common defense of the planning ideal suggests that the power of government is to be brought to bear to "help individuals." Various humanitarian goals are suggested as those which all men favor—surely to intervene in behalf of such goals is a worthwhile and fruitful program! Yet it is precisely the use of *coercion* which is the sticking point, no matter what reform may be intended. In the words of Richard Weaver:

> There is a difference between trying to reform your fellow beings by the normal processes of logical demonstration, appeal and moral suasion—there is a difference between that and passing over to the use of force or constraint. The former is something all of us engage in every day. The latter is what makes the modern radical dangerous and perhaps in a sense demented. His first thought now is to get control of the state to make all men equal, or to make all men rich, or failing that to make all men equally unhappy. This use of political instrumentality to coerce people to conform with his dream, in the face of their belief in a real order, is our reason I think, for objecting to the radical. As an individual he may think about molding the world to his heart's desire. He may even publish the results of his thinking. But when he tries to use the instrumentality of the state to bring about his wishes, then all of us are involved, and we have to take our stand.[8]

Controls, however well intended, are interferences with individual decision-making and free choice. This can extend to very "small" items. A farmer prevented from growing wheat to feed the animals on his farm, or a businessman jailed for selling Alka-Seltzer below the "Fair Trade" price,[53] is a person who has lost the freedom of choice in the work he will pursue or in the disposal of his own property. It is because of this close relationship between property rights and basic freedom that the planners have so assaulted the concept of private property in their eagerness to substitute the planned state for individual free choice. We need not look to the works of Marxist theoreticians to find examples of this tendency. Professor John Kenneth Galbraith, one of the popularizers of the new order, has made abundantly clear his view that the individual's purchasing power should be curtailed and the same moneys spent upon various collective projects of one sort or another. The underlying assumption of all such plans is that the private citizen is unreliable and incompetent to handle his own affairs and must abandon his self-direction to a government which determines for citizens what they *should* want.

Hilaire Belloc warned as he saw the approach of the planned society, "The control of the production of wealth is the control of human life itself." Despite this self-evident connection, it remains a dominant idea of our times that politics and economics are separate entities, allowing any sort of planned economy to be imposed without effect upon individual political freedoms. Thus the Russian brand of totalitarianism can be criticized for its political degradations of the individual at the very time when many aspects of the planned economy are being applied within our own society. But political liberty and economic freedom are so closely related that they defy separation. As Lawrence Fertig phrased it:

> Any system which deprives the individual of his economic freedom —by controlling his job, or how much he can earn, or what he should buy, or how he should live—takes away his basic freedom. And it is important to remember that throughout history, whenever bureaucrats controlled people's economic lives, they soon came to control their political freedom as well. It is essential for the survival of democratic government that economic power be separated from political power. This is the *sine qua non* of democracy. It is the reason why the preservation of private capitalism is essential for the maintenance of a free society.[48]

The failure to understand this particular issue has led many intellectuals within our society to espouse the planned economy. In so doing they have undercut the very intellectual freedom which they have been most vocal in defending. A society unfree in its economic life will soon become a society without freedom in any sector.

It is this gradualist approach of the Western intellectual, favoring the planned state but insisting that such an economy can be derived within democratic political institutions, that has been epitomized by the Fabians in England and by what goes under the name of "Liberalism" in the United States. The point remains, however, that freedom is no less severely attacked in a Fabian approach than in a Marxian approach. Gradual collectivism, after all, amounts to gradual reduction of freedom. Planning without coercive force to put the plans in operation is nothing more than a sand castle. As one straightforward planner, Maurice Dobb, phrased it, "Either planning means overriding the autonomy of separate decisions or it means nothing at all."

This underlying theme of coercion is present in even the most high-minded of the new economic planners. No less a prophet of the new order than John Maynard Keynes quite frankly based large portions of his theories upon mercantilist ideals. He himself credited as one of the primary sources of his ideas on "full employment" and monetary policy the mercantilist theoreticians of the eighteenth century. Mercantilism, as you recall, was precisely such a system of tight regulation on the part of all elements within society, regulation in which the individual was consistently sacrificed to the collective interest.

This willingness to use force to achieve social goals surfaces repeatedly in Keynes. His solution for depression situations and unemployment had been centrally planned and controlled expenditure, if you will, compulsory expenditure, divorced from individual choice. Less well known was a little book that he wrote during the Second World War entitled *How to Pay for the War*. In it he urges "deferred savings" as a means of financing the war effort. A portion of all British wage earnings was to be compulsorily invested in government bonds not redeemable until after the conclusion of the war. This would finance the war and fight inflation at the same time. Following the war, just when government spending would be falling off, the savings bonds could be cashed, thus stimulating the economy when most needed. Compulsory saving! Quite the opposite from his earlier plan for compulsory expenditure. Yet, one key word remains in both economic plans: *compulsion.*

There is some sign that Keynes, before his death, had come to fear how this tremendous planning power might be exercised. When Friedrich Hayek's *Road to Serfdom* appeared in 1944 as a challenge to this very planning ideal, Keynes wrote to Hayek:

> I should . . . conclude rather differently. I should say that what we want is not no planning, or even less planning, indeed I should say we almost certainly want more. But the planning would take place in a community in which as many people as possible, both leaders and followers, wholly share your own moral position. Moderate planning will be safe enough if those carrying it out are rightly oriented in their own minds and hearts to the moral issue. This is

in fact already true of some of them. But the curse is that there is also an important section who could be said to want planning not in order to enjoy its fruits, but because morally they hold ideas exactly the opposite of yours, and wish to serve not God but the devil.

(Robert L. Heilbroner, *The Worldly Philosophers*)

Apparently, Keynes was beginning to suspect that this tremendous planning power might fall into "the wrong hands." Whatever Keynes might have felt, since his death his disciples as advocates of the "mixed economy" have pushed the ideas of coercively enforced planning further and further. The mixture of freedom and intervention seems to contain a steadily larger proportion of coercion and a steadily shrinking proportion of freedom as the years pass. So, at least, seems to be the Western experience in the mid-twentieth century.

THE GROWTH OF UNCHECKED POWER IN THE MODERN WORLD

One of the great intellectual currents of modern times which has seriously interfered with and displaced individual choice has been the perversion of the concept of "democracy." Initially, the coming of democracy was viewed as an end to entrenched power, as a permanent emasculation of the social agencies and spiritual authorities thought to be standing in the path of man's liberty. Once the authority of church, king, and aristocracy were swept away, the reign of all men was to begin. What may have happened is less an end to power than its realignment.

Hobbes had defined political power as political liberty and insisted that man would be free when he possessed a share of political government. Yet the democratic fragmentation of political power into numerous bits and pieces may have afforded the individual no more freedom than it did sovereignty—both illusory. As long ago as 1870, Proudhon warned in his *Theory of the Constitutional Movement in the Nineteenth Century:*

It is no use saying that an elected person or the representative of the people is only the trustee for the people . . . in despite of principle, *the delegate of the sovereign will be the master of the sovereign.* Sovereignty on which a man cannot enter, if I may so put it, is as empty a right as property on which he cannot enter.

The democratic ideal did not originally intend to substitute the arbitrary will of the citizenry for the arbitrary will of the King. But, as Georges Clemenceau wearily observed as he contemplated the condition of democratic Europe in the early twentieth century, ". . . had we expected that these majorities of a day would exercise the same authority as that possessed by our ancient kings, we should but have effected an exchange of tyrants." The fragmentation of sovereignty occurring in mass democracy thus proved a feeble shield for individual liberty.

Both of the traditional guarantees of limited power, *decentralization* and *Natural Law,* had been subverted in the process. Decentralization of power throughout the private, institutional framework of society had been replaced with the comparatively meaningless fragmentation of sovereignty among vast numbers of individuals. The idea of Natural Law, of limitations placed upon ruler and ruled alike, had been replaced by the dangerous and totally incorrect *vox populi, vox dei.* The stage was set for the confusion of the "power of the people" with the "liberty of the people." And the power about to be exercised in the name of the people was destined to make all previous exercises of power throughout history seem pale by comparison.

Throughout the nineteenth century, Tocqueville, von Mohl, Burckhardt, and Acton shared these serious doubts about unlimited democracy. They prophesied that the very democracy which had originally been conceived for the emancipation of the individual could itself become the means of a new enslavement.

A recent television comedy sketch conveys the place of power in the new democratic era perhaps even more effectively than the thoughtful essays of social critics. In the scene, Jackie Gleason and Art Carney are trying to decide which of them will occupy the master bedroom at a hotel they are visiting. Carney delivers a lecture about "democratic processes" and "the American way," prompting a series of votes which, naturally enough, always produce a one-one tie. Carney proposes, "I'll vote for you, if you'll vote for me," again producing the same result. They then decide to flip a coin. Gleason calls "heads," and Carney then challenges Gleason's right to make the choice, insisting, "That's undemocratic."

The comedians exploit the ridiculous situation to its fullest extent, proposing various devices to solve the problem and yet always coming up against Carney's assertion that Gleason's choice of a means to settle the dispute is "undemocratic." Gleason finally loses his temper, and gives the answer which majorities often give in the process of decision making: "See the size of this fist? It's bigger than yours, isn't it? *That's why I get my choice!*"

The current of reform in the eighteenth century which swept away monarchy and promised a brighter day for the common man through democratic processes was quite properly directed against abuses of power by those who operated the political processes of the state. The reforming current was equally correct in its opposition to power when exercised in the private realm through monopoly situations (situations usually stemming from political grants of power by the state).

This reforming zeal began to go astray when it mistook the close connections between the clergy and royal absolutism for a connection between religion and morality on the one hand and political power and exploitation on the other. Bodin and other apologists for Divine Right had so interwoven Natural Law and Divine Right that the reformers rejected moral restraint when they rejected monarchy, thus throwing out the worthwhile with the worthless and opening the door to a tremendous centralization of power because they discarded one of the two great bulwarks against power, the assumption of a law limiting ruler and ruled alike.

Though power had been distrusted when in the hands of church, monarch, and aristocracy, the reformers came to feel that power could be safely entrusted to the people. Even such a staunch advocate of personal liberty as John Stuart Mill came to believe that power was no longer a decisive factor in politics, since the rule of the people would lead to the equitable solution of all problems through free discussion in a common marketplace of ideas.

Other nineteenth-century advocates of freedom also saw power as a declining force which would no longer trouble the modern world. As we have seen, Herbert Spencer reasoned from organic analogies patterned after Darwinian theories of evolution within the animal kingdom, and attempted to demonstrate that an abatement of power was to be the natural result of evolution and progress.

The First World War made clear that free discussion and popular sovereignty had, in fact, not done away with power at all. Yet, the reformers were not fully convinced. The rhetoric of the World War I era is filled with statements placing blame for that outburst of raw power on a last desperate reaction of the old nondemocratic order. What solutions did the reformers offer for this new outburst of power? More democracy, of course: "Open covenants openly arrived at," "self-determination of peoples," and a League of Nations extending discussion and democracy to a truly international level. Thus, the democracies put on the greatest display of raw power exercised up to that moment in history, in the name of "making the world safe for democracy."

It might be argued that a monarchical Germany started the war, not the Western democracies. Yet even if such a thesis could be demonstrated (and the facts would indicate that all the major nations, democracies and monarchies alike, played their part in bringing on the war) it would still be true that even the most democratic of Western nations soon came to copy the Prussian methods of mobilizing the private sector and the individual citizen for "total" war efforts. Even in England and the United States, the two nations in which the individual citizen had been most successful in preserving his liberty against the encroachment of governmental power, conscription became the means of providing an army, while great pressures of borrowing and inflation, amounting to a form of economic conscription, provided the war chest.

The "good cause" justifying this extension of power was the preservation of "democracy." Under the new democratic regimes, the warfare state pointed the way toward the welfare state since both were to give endless and often irresponsible power to the few while degrading the many, all in the name of an abstract equality of men. Oddly enough, this "equality" is only to be achieved, its proponents tell us, through a tremendous inequality in the exercise of power, giving some men the right to act for others.

If the First World War had only shaken the dogma that

democracy meant an end to the dangers of power, the Second World War ended such a notion once and for all. Since the late 1930's, we have seen the unrestricted play of power on our society and the world, limited effectively by neither political theory nor moral principle. The traditional safeguards of *decentralization* and *Natural Law* have both been undercut by democracy, only to have democracy itself provide a fertile field for the most unchecked reign of power in world history. Apparently Lord Acton was right about the corrupting capabilities of power. Surely, Hitler and his gang should be sufficient proof of that fact.

For a time, some of the reformers still argued that such power was not harmful so long as it worked toward "humanitarian" goals. We all remember the years when the totalitarian regime of Stalin was viewed by many in the West as morally superior to the totalitarian regime of Hitler. But, in practice, the Poles, Latvians, Lithuanians, Estonians, and any number of other subject peoples could scarcely distinguish between the Red totalitarianism and the Brown.

Meanwhile, how did power fare in those Western democracies which prided themselves on being most nontotalitarian? In the words of one of the most distinguished students of power:

> Whereas the Capetian kings made war with a few seignorial contingents whose service was for no more than forty days, the popular states of today have power to call to the colours, and keep there indefinitely, the entire male population. Whereas the feudal monarchs could nourish hostilities only with the resources of their own domains, their successors have at their disposal the entire national income. The citizens of medieval cities at war could, if they were not too near to the actual theatre of operations, take no notice of it. Nowadays friend and foe alike would burn their houses, slaughter their families, and measure their own doughty deeds in ravaged acres. Even Thought herself, in former times contemptuous of these brawls, has now been roped in by devotees of conquest to proclaim the civilizing virtues of gangsters and incendiaries.
>
> How is it possible not to see in this stupendous degradation of our civilization the fruits of state absolutism? Everything is thrown into war because Power disposes of everything.[37]

So much for the modern warfare state. What of the modern welfare state? The same era which saw the rise of democratic reformism in the eighteenth and nineteenth centuries also saw the widespread acceptance of the principles of natural science and the unfortunate accompanying tendency to apply the methodology of science in the political and social realms. As quoted earlier, Auguste Comte's remark, "If we do not allow free thinking in chemistry or biology, why should we allow it in morals or politics?", and Fichte's assertion, "To compel man to adopt the right form of government, to impose Right on them by force, is not only the right, but the sacred duty of every man who has both the insight and the power to do so," epitomize the assumption at the root of the subsequent "social planning" which has come to dominate modern society. Men are now to be made free from their own ignorance and inadequacy. Power used to coerce is thus supposed to be beneficent power, power exercised "for the good" of the many.

Throughout history, the greatest vice of power had generally been thought to be the restriction of individual liberty which the exercise of such power entailed. But once modern man began to recognize no restriction of Natural Law upon his capability to know what is "best" for people and know it better than the individual citizen himself, the modern statist was in a position–

> ... to ignore the actual wishes of men or societies, to bully, oppress, torture them in the name, and on behalf of their "real" selves, in the secure knowledge that whatever is the true goal of man (happiness, fulfilment of duty, wisdom, a just society, self-fulfilment) must be identical with his freedom—the free choice of his "true," albeit submerged and inarticulate, self.[44]

As Friedrich Hayek has made abundantly clear, it is only modern man that has confused freedom from coercion (the traditional use of the word) with an illusory freedom from obstacles, implying a physical ability of man to be in complete control of and beyond the limitations of his natural environment. In this way, individual freedom has been corrupted until it implies a "right" to any material benefit which the social order can procure for him.

Hayek continues:

Once this identification of freedom with power is admitted, there is no limit to the sophisms by which the attractions of the word "liberty" can be used to support measures which destroy individual liberty, no end to the tricks by which people can be exhorted in the name of liberty to give up their liberty. . . .

This reinterpretation of liberty is particularly ominous because it has penetrated deeply into the usage of some of the countries where, in fact, individual freedom is still largely preserved. In the United States it has come to be widely accepted as the foundation for the political philosophy dominant in "liberal" circles. Such recognized intellectual leaders of the "progressives" as J. R. Commons and John Dewey have spread an ideology in which "liberty is power, effective power to do specific things" and the "demand of liberty is the demand for power," while the absence of coercion is merely "the negative side of freedom" and "is to be prized only as a means to Freedom which is power."[2]

It is instructive that the great proletarian revolutions of modern times, those in France and Russia, both promised a revolt *against* power. Shortly before assuming authority, Lenin wrote that it was the task of the Revolution to "concentrate all its forces against the might of the state; its task is not to improve the governmental machine but *to destroy it and blot it out.* The revolutionaries acting in the name of the people have moved against power with the avowed purpose not of assuming that power but of *destroying* it. Despite this, those who assumed temporary power to destroy other concentrations of power have usually proven unwilling to relinquish that authority once the revolutionary process is brought to completion.

Before the rapids, there was the rule of a Charles I, a Louis XVI, a Nicholas II. After them, that of a Cromwell, a Napoleon, a Stalin. Such are the masters to whom the peoples that rose against Stuart or Bourbon or Romanov "tyranny" find themselves subjected next. . . .The Cromwells and Stalins are no fortuitous consequence, no accidental happening, of the revolutionary tempest. Rather they are its predestined goal, towards which the entire upheaval was moving inevitably; the cycle began with the downfall of an inadequate Power only to close with the consolidation of a more absolute Power.[37]

In both the nontotalitarian Western world and in the more frankly totalitarian experiments, the same pattern holds true. The initial assault against power is followed by a more complete and all-pervasive power structure of its own. The danger of such structures is all the more enhanced by the fact that such despotisms are erected in the name of "the people."

In the words of Henry Mencken:

> It [the state] has taken on a vast mass of new duties and responsibilities; it has spread out its powers until they penetrate to every act of the citizen, however secret; it has begun to throw around its operations the high dignity and impeccability of a State religion; its agents become a separate and superior caste, with authority to bind and loose, and their thumbs in every pot. But it still remains, as it was in the beginning, the common enemy of all well-disposed, industrious, and decent men.[49]

If the modern state has indeed become so all-pervasive in its exercise of power, why is there not more organized resistance? It is the pretext that such power is wielded by and for "the people" which in effect has delivered the people, the individual citizens, into the hands of this new despotic power.

This power now exercised in the name of "the people," whether in the welfare state pattern or the frankly totalitarian form, is tremendous in scope. Worse yet, such power tends naturally to accumulate still more power to itself. An Italian scholar who witnessed the rise of the fascist state in Europe, Guglielmo Ferrero, has made the shrewd observation that a government of great power tends to suspect that the citizens being governed would like to throw off the yoke which they bear. It is Ferrero's thesis that this fear of the government against the governed, thus engendered, tends to rise to a greater and greater level as more power is exercised—thus the more totalitarian a government, the more dictatorial, oppressive, and brutal it is likely to become.

Thus power breeds appetite for more power, until not only obedience, but enthusiasm is expected from the subjects of that power. It was Napoleon who first made wide use of deliberately contrived propaganda techniques to win enthusiasm for the regime in power. Since then, virtually every wielder of great power has further perfected the same technique. "Public image," a desire to be at once powerful and popular, seems to be a common goal in such societies. Often the pursuit of this goal has produced suppression of facts which might prove unpopular. We have all come to expect such suppression from the modern totalitarian state We are also learning that a "credibility gap" can exist in our own society as well.

Thus, the powerful state comes to fear the subjects over whom it exercises power, while the individual citizen comes to fear the increasing repressions and interferences of the all-powerful state. It is to this that Ferrero refers:

> It is impossible to inspire fear in men without ending up by fearing them: from this moral law springs the most fearful torment of life —the reciprocal fear between government and its subjects.[38]

The root of this fear in both the governing and the governed is the fear of power, rampant and unchained from Western civilization's traditional limitations of power, *decentralization* and *Natural Law*. Power in such a society is finally embraced because of its capacity to produce discipline. The exercise of power thus becomes an end in itself, rather than a means.

Finally, under whatever political label, a new agency has come into being in the modern world:

> Throughout the world, a new revolutionary theory and system seem to be taking substance: what Tocqueville predicted long ago as "democratic despotism," but harsher than he expected even that tyranny to be; in some sense, what Mr. James Burnham calls "the managerial revolution"; super-bureaucracy, arrogating to itself functions that cannot properly appertain to the bureau or the cabinet; the planned economy, encompassing not merely the economy proper, however, but the whole moral and intellectual range of human activities; the grand form of *Plannwirtschaft*, state planning for its own sake, state socialism devoid of the sentimental aims which originally characterized socialism.[50]

PHILOSOPHIC DECLINE IN AMERICA

As the planning ideal has invaded the economic and political life of the Western world in the twentieth century, the United States of America has tended to lag behind on that disastrous timetable. This is due directly to the long tradition of individuality and limited government with the widest possible range of free enterprise that Americans have grown accustomed to throughout their long history. Still, the change has gradually occurred as America has slipped down into the same morass which has claimed most of the thinking of the world by the mid-twentieth century. One way to understand how this change came about in America is to understand the new philosophy dominating our academic heritage in the present century.

Several generations of American historians and philosophers have been dedicated to the proposition that the necessary precondition for "reform" is the destruction of the existing legal system and the traditional political, economic, and social fabric. Drawing heavily upon the attitudes of the Renaissance and the Enlightenment, with large portions of modern scientism and naturalism added for good measure, these intellectuals have attacked the existing traditional framework of moral, political, social, and economic society in their quest for progress and "the dignity of man."They have produced instead a collective age, a secular age, an age of great unrest, exemplifying unprincipled institutions, as well as emphasis upon material goals and collective rather than individual views of reality and morality. Perhaps never in history has man more graphically traded his birthright for a mess of pottage.

It should be recalled that several of the systems builders of the nineteenth century, such as Hegel, Marx, and Spencer, stressed a deterministic view of the world. To one American philosopher, such systems seemed to leave no room for free will or individual moral choice. William James thus came to break with Herbert Spencer, though he earlier had been a disciple. James complained of absolutes, whether of Hegelian idealism or Spencerian materialism, and steadfastly refused to accept either type.

The new system which James proposed as a substitute was that of Pragmatism, a blend of Darwinian evolutionary concepts, the idea of progress, and a new view of looking at the mind as a physical rather than a spiritual entity. His new philosophy was destined in the twentieth century to become both the product and the molder of the American mind.

The three principal figures in the origin, development, and application of the ideas of Pragmatism were Charles Peirce, William James, and John Dewey, Charles Peirce had been influenced by Chauncey Wright. Wright was a thorough-going naturalist who saw *nothing* spiritual in man. Teaching at Harvard, he had written the *Evolution of Self-Consciousness* and had attacked even this last citadel of spirituality. Peirce (1839–1914) was a close friend of William James and largely a free lance, although he occasionally taught at Harvard. Most of his philosophy lies outside Pragmatism. Yet, he originated the Pragmatism that James was later to set forth. Peirce developed the concept that ideas are really rules for action, that thinking stems from "an agony of doubt," and that man examines what are the practical consequences of an idea in action, thus testing the "*clarity*" of an idea. These concepts proved to be the basic elements of Pragmatism: 1) Test ideas in action; 2) Never accept a final idea. It is this that James seized upon, although taking it much further and applying it much more widely than Peirce had ever intended.

William James was of a famous family. He and his elder brother, the novelist Henry James, had earlier been immersed in Swedenborgianism, a form of religious mysticism, which they later rejected. Some biographers insist that William James ended his life a mystic, but George Santayana, a close personal friend of James and a fellow philosopher at Harvard, insisted that James actually had no beliefs. Perhaps the best known of the biographers of James, F. O. Mathieson, insists that all of the James family were neurotic since they lacked deep intellectual or religious roots. James staggered through many interests, in philosophy, physiology, and psychology, producing the famous *Principles of Psychology* in 1890. But his first love was always philosophy, within which he was apparently groping for a satisfactory religious faith.

William James became famous following his delivery in 1898 of an address on philosophy at the University of California. He took Peirce's forgotten principles and applied them to religion. James broadened Peirce's concept and began to test the *truth* of ideas, rather than merely testing their clarity. From then on Pragmatism and James were famous. He produced a number of works going far beyond the original concept, including *The Will to Believe* as well as *Pragmatism* and *A Pluralistic Universe*.

In psychology, James stressed the *active* role of the mind. To him, a thought was itself a form of action. This idea, coupled with his rejection of absolutes, whether of the Hegelian idealistic sort or of the Spencerian materialistic sort, produced the philosophy of Pragmatism. His philosophy was heavily dependent upon the Darwinian evolutionary concept and yet, James felt, left room for a higher striving of man through the utilization of Peirce's testing process. It was this testing process which served as the heart of Pragmatism, that is, the idea of testing the truth of an idea by finding out if it works. To James, the truth of an idea was established by 1) Practical results; 2) No conflict with more important previously established truths.

A religious idea to James was true to whatever extent it gave personal mental peace—no more. After having had so much trouble establishing his own personal beliefs, James decided to "will" himself to believe. It is this search for belief and the inability ever fully to satisfy that search that best characterizes William James and his version of Pragmatism.

The problem of always testing ideas and yet never achieving a final test contains within it a dichotomy. The idea of "never a final test" implies that an absolute principle can *never* be reached. Yet the whole idea of *"never* an absolute principle" is itself an absolute principle. James emphasized that man must make a continuing effort to find ultimate truths, and refuse to accept a completely deterministic world. For his emphasis upon individual will and human personality, James is much to be congratulated. But in his eagerness to avoid determinism, James went so far as to insist that no final principles or ultimate values could indeed exist at all within the system as he had set it up. Such a rejection of ultimate value was to bear bitter fruit in the twentieth century.

With its emphasis upon practicality, democracy, and every man a philosopher, the new philosophy of James became immediately popular and identified with America. People with the traditional American impatience with established authority were especially attracted to a philosophy that in practice denied content to any philosophy and insisted that each individual, in each concrete situation, had to make his own formulations, quite apart from any system. It is this philosophy of Pragmatism which has come to be such a great influence in the twentieth century. Indeed it proved to be the dominant philosophy of the whole reformist, antitraditionalist approach typical of the New Deal and its several successor deals.

Pragmatism in its later forms has certain easily recognizable characteristics, readily apparent in the political, economic, social, and religious thought of our times. It is immediately identifiable with the dominant collectivist mentality of our age. Pragmatism as adopted by the American collective mentality emphasizes relative values, with an absence of definite standards, definite morality, or definite right and wrong. Pragmatism implies a turning from spiritual belief to material belief and epitomizes an eagerness for change and experimentation, an impatience with established institutions, customs, and values. Most of these attitudes stem not from William James, who insisted that his ideas were intended only for the *individual* testing of ideas. In all probability, he would have been horrified at the application of his ideas in the twentieth century. It is another philosopher who followed James and expanded the ideas implicit in Pragmatism to whom its later development should be primarily attributed.

John Dewey took up where William James left off. Since approximately 1910, Dewey and his followers have come to dominate Pragmatism, calling their social adaptation of Pragmatism by the new term *Instrumentalism*. Simply defined, Instrumentalism is a socialized version of Pragmatism. While James had been concerned primarily with the individual, Dewey came to broaden the concept until it became a comprehensive social philosophy. He systematically applied pragmatic thought to all areas of philosophy, leaving no aspect of the discipline unexamined. It was his conscious intent to improve society. Ideas were still to be tested, as in the earlier attitudes of Charles Peirce and William James, but now they were to be tested by and within society at large.

Dewey emphasized the unfinished nature of society and the universe. He insisted that man could mold his society. In Dewey's conception of an evolutionary philosophy, man could dominate the process through the role of the human mind. These ideas can easily be traced in twentieth century American politics, in the Progressive reform movement and in the New Deal. Such projects as the N. R. A. and T. V. A. were carried out by administrators who were clearly Instrumentalists in philosophy and approach. In fact, since Dewey's time it is difficult for anyone to escape his ideas in social or governmental occupations.

What did Dewey advocate? He placed an emphasis upon a thorough-going philosophy of experience, feeling that man should rely primarily on experience to evaluate what needed to be done. This is very optimistic when compared to European thought and was typically American, Dewey was also very much American and very modern in his emphasis upon science and technology as the solution to man's problems. He felt that science and technology had progressed to a point where man could use and control them and thus cope with his present and his future. Dewey felt it was experience that had improved science and technology and which would govern the application of science and technology in the new, planned society brought about through the use of human reason.

Radical new methods of education can also be traced to Dewey. The progressive school experiment of the mid-1890's at the University of Chicago became a widespread movement throughout the world. His book, *Democracy in Education*, written in 1916, had a great impact in Mexico, Turkey, China, and Russia during the 1920's. Part of Dewey's teaching was beneficial. He made it clear that learning was not a passive process, that much interaction between pupil and teacher does have value, and that thought and action are inseparable. He tended to break down the rigid formation of the old school. But as Dewey's thought spread throughout the educational system, there was a watering-down process. Much of his subtlety was lost. The simple fact remains that in many areas school cannot perform the functions of the family. As the theory was watered down, the distinction between child and adult was increasingly lost, until Dewey himself could not recognize his original ideas. In fact, the system could never have worked except in very special conditions and was vastly overidealized. This was a good example of "freedom" from the old forms so common in modern times, a freedom which does not replace the old forms with any other standard and which therefore sinks into the morass of no standards at all.

Dewey also studied aesthetics, as a special version of evolutionary theory. He did not rule out art as an end in itself. In fact, he wrote a book in 1929 entitled *Art as Experience.* But again, the disciples outran the master, ruling out art for art's sake, and deeming it only a technique to mold society in a sort of perpetual postoffice mural. This is readily apparent in the art so common in connection with W. P. A. projects during the New Deal years.

A certain similarity exists in all collective experiments and ideas when they are centrally planned and controlled. Consider, for example, similarities between the attitudes of twentieth-century Russia and the Instrumentalism of John Dewey as we have just seen it. Both are children of the same Enlightenment values. In both instances, society is valued above the individual. There is no definite right or wrong, since all truth is relative. There is no power superior to planners and society, since in a naturalistic society there is no further need for God or Divine Authority. Such old institutions as the family are now regarded as a hindrance to proper education and proper social attitudes. Science and technology become the keys in both systems, the tools by which man will achieve his heaven on earth. If we examine education or art or social planning, we find the same consistent emphasis, not upon the God-given integrity of the individual, but upon the collective social good of the here-and-now materialistic order.

For a final example of the strong similarity between Instrumentalism and Marxism, consider the study of ethics as advanced by John Dewey. He popularized a naturalistic ethics in his 1922 publication of *Human Nature and Conduct.* He ruled out all supernatural values and again insisted that "experimental method" was the keystone of the new order. No value, even in religion, could thus be accepted if it did not benefit society. All ideas which did not benefit society should be immediately discarded. Dewey also suggested discarding the supernatural ideas of religion, thus making Instrumentalism incompatible with religion as it then existed. He stressed instead what he called "a new kind of religion" to be derived from human experience and relationships. In other words: *Make a religion out of Instrumentalism.*

Here again our parallel holds. Marxism and Instrumentalism, despite all the rhetoric about how different the two systems are, both discourage religious values, and both elevate their own system to the level of religion.

It should be made clear that the ideal toward which Dewey was working was socialized democracy, not the state socialism we see in the Soviet Union. He desired to preserve individuality and democracy. Yet it should also be recalled that much lip service is paid to "democracy" and "individualism" in the Communist experiment. It is only in practice that the system fails to achieve and protect those goals. In fact, as the totalitarian systems of fascism and communism steadily developed power in the 1930's, Dewey became disillusioned with some of his earlier values, taking refuge in the concept of democracy. Unfortunately, that concept also is subject to collectivist interpretation in the modern world.

This comparison of communism and Instrumentalism is not intended as a slur upon Dewey. It is not an exercise in name calling. Dewey clearly was not Marxist. The point is that collective, planned-from-above, naturalistic, relativistic blueprints for a perfect society seem to gravitate to similar answers to the problems they are trying to solve. Apparently the similarity of values within collective systems inclines them toward similar solutions. No more graphic proof of this fact could possibly be adduced than John Dewey's own definition of the acceptable application of collective power in pursuit of social goals, published in 1916 in *Ethics:*

> Whether [the use of force] is justifiable or not. . .is, in substance, a question of efficiency (including economy) of means in the accomplishing of ends; . . . The criterion of value lies in the relative efficiency and economy of the expenditure of force as a means to an end.

In a word, no limitation of power is to be allowed to stand in the way of the new political morality, a morality based solely upon collective utility.

THE EFFECTS OF COLLECTIVE
PHILOSOPHY UPON SOCIETY

Such concepts as *humanity, mankind, society,* or *nation* are all modern in their origin. Ancient and medieval men tended to view man as an individual unit. They usually thought of larger collections of men as being merely larger numbers of single individuals. Thus, such words as *mankind* or *society* did not, until modern times, convey a difference in meaning, but instead implied only a difference in quantity. It is instructive that our modern patterns of thought now give such words as *society* or *humanity* or *nation* a new meaning, *no longer connected directly with the concept of the individual.*

What modern society seems to have forgotten, in the words of Frank Chodorov, is that, "Society are people." Within the traditional Western framework of *Natural Law,* our forebears have generally recognized a realm of spiritual value, beyond the laws of natural science and beyond the trappings of society. It is this recognition of the spiritual dignity of the individual person which gave birth to the concept that each individual had certain rights which no other man or collection of men would be justified in violating.

Modern society, acting in the name of "the people," has been increasingly willing to override such guarantees of individual freedom. In the process, absolute power has steadily replaced absolute rights. Once we have accepted the premise that the majority should determine the rules by which each of us will live his individual life, we become increasingly defenseless in the face of the growing authority exercised by the agents of that majority. All too often, those most enthusiastic in their support of an unlimited majority are the same people who expect that they will serve as the agents of that majority. Thus the exercise of essentially unlimited power gravitates into fewer and fewer hands.[2]

Just as it is true that the fate of a book is dependent upon the reader, it is equally and painfully correct that the meaning of a political idea stems from the group that appropriates it. The meaning given to "democracy" and the application of the tremendous power unleashed by the new definition of "popular rule"have paved the way toward an exercise of power never dreamed of before modern times. Yet, 50 to 75 years ago, those most enthusiastic about modern democracy believed that all dangers from power were past, since the power of the future, represented in its most concentrated form by the modern state, was to be used only in the advancement of the material interest of the common man.

Some astute observers, such men as Nietzsche, and Burckhardt, were warning as long ago as the mid-nineteenth century of the dangers stemming from the new mass-man and the new mass-state. Social critics of our own time, of the stature of Wilhelm Roepke and Ortega y Gasset, have pointed to more and more signs of the dangers inherent in the centralized modern state. Meanwhile, the consolidation of power in the new dispensation has steadily advanced. In the words of Frank Chodorov, writing in *The Rise and Fall of Society:*

> The present disposition is to liquidate any distinction between State and Society, conceptually or institutionally. The State is Society; the social order is indeed an appendage of the political establishment, depending on it for sustenance, health, education, communications, and all things coming under the head of "the pursuit of happiness." In theory, taking college textbooks on economics and political science for authority, the integration is about as complete as words can make it. In the operation of human affairs, despite the fact that lip service is rendered the concept of inherent personal rights, the tendency to call upon the State for the solution of all the problems of life shows how far we have abandoned the doctrine of rights, with its correlative of self-reliance, and have accepted the State as the reality of Society.

Such a system makes far too little allowance for man's freedom or personality. The state swallows the individual. Even if such centralization were efficient in the satisfaction of human wants, which it is not, the means used to achieve the end would still be unacceptable simply because they are incompatible with human freedom.

Even more dangerous, perhaps, is the risk that the very concept of freedom itself can become so misused and distorted within such a society that no individual dare lay claim to any rights or dignity having a higher source than the society in which he lives. At that moment, the guarantees developed by Western civilization to protect the individual from the arbitrary exercise of power have in effect all been swept away, no matter what label that society might give itself.

Once such checks upon the exercise of power have been removed, all the internal vitality and freedom in such a society are open to destruction in the name of "order." Soon the preservation of "order" or the pursuit of the "greatest social good" is identified with whatever action the wielder of centralized power deems suitable. Resistance against the exercise of such power comes to be viewed by society not as an expression of human individuality and free choice, but as an assault upon the public good, a crime of the selfish individual against the selfless community.

A new type of personality soon comes to the forefront in such a society. Many who would tend to go largely unnoticed in a freely competing society soon begin to exercise centralized power to invade the marketplace and the private sector in an attempt to manipulate individual decisions to achieve "social goals." In a society in which officials wield such tremendous power, they come to occupy a larger and larger place in the public eye and in their own self-esteem.

The exercise of power thus becomes a gratifying and expansive experience. The wielder invariably flatters himself that he is undertaking a tremendous burden "for the good of" those over whom he exercises power. The legend of the Grand Inquisitor, who felt he had taken upon himself "the curse of the knowledge of good and evil" to achieve the happiness of "thousands of millions of happy babes" has been re-enacted time and again throughout human history, with ever-increasing frequency in our age. Such wielders of power soon lose themselves in their dedication to "service," forgetting their underlying motivation of self-aggrandizement.

Further, the manner in which the modern state opens the exercise of power to men of ambition from various walks of life tends to make the exercise of that power, and indeed its further extension, all the more acceptable to the mass of the people. In the older era of kings and aristocrats, few men had the slightest hope of achieving a share of power. But in a modern society in which any man is a potential wielder of power, many who should and perhaps do know better will still allow the exercise and extension of power on the assumption that they themselves are capable of wielding such devastating and corrupting force. It is from this complicity in the crime of power that modern democracy especially suffers, since so many among us believe that to achieve the good society we need only "throw the rascals out" and replace them with "good men," who would wield power properly.

The "intellectual" has been especially at fault. Seldom has the case been stated more clearly than by the distinguished journalist, George S. Schuyler, in *Black and Conservative:*

> It unfortunately has become fashionable for the artist in modern society to quibble over this issue of freedom. He says on the one hand that he prefers a society which emphasizes physical security for all (which necessitates in technological civilization a degree of regimentation which endangers freedom). At the same time he properly wants a society where he is free to write, paint, and compose as he wills. He fails to recognize that the artist is so influenced by the society of which he is part, that he cannot remain free when all else is controlled.
>
> The error of the intellectuals of the West for the past two centuries has been advocating a society actually slavish but paraded as freedom. This means, then, that along with free art (and indeed the very basis for it) must be free political institutions, free economic enterprises, and a society free of onerous restrictions.
>
> The tragedy of so many intellectuals in the contemporary world is that while opposing extreme forms of totalitarianism, they are themselves half-totalitarian; that is to say, they express a desire for a society which is half-controlled, half-regimented, half-planned, part capitalist, and part socialist. This strange hybrid they will find (indeed, have found) to be a Frankenstein monster which, ironically, they have a great responsibility for creating.

However the centralization of power may have come about, its existence and its exercise are painful realities in the Western world. We need not look to the Russian or Chinese totalitarians for examples of this power. Within our own society, the unchecked power of labor unions, backed by coercive political legislation, has been used against private property, the general public, and, above all, the union members themselves. The ill-concealed pressures exerted by centralized power through the large and growing numbers of regulatory agencies and their "administrative" legal decisions have left private property and the businessman literally at the mercy of forces beyond either his comprehension or his control. The levels of taxation within our society closely circumscribe the range of choice for the individual citizen in the disposal and use of his property. The end result of the use of power is always the same: curtailment of individual and social freedom.

Examples of unchecked power infringing upon the private

sector and the individual within our own society could be multiplied almost indefinitely. How does it happen that such extensions of power and curtailments of liberty have taken place with little or no public outcry? The answer is a painful one for the friends of man: most people are unaware of liberty and its benefits. Indeed, if the loss of freedom and the expansion of power are sufficiently gradual, it seems that the citizens will not rise in protest. The conversion of the private sector into the public sector, of the individual's power to make decisions into the state's power to coerce decisions, has proceeded more gradually here than in the French Revolution, the Russian Revolution, or the Fascist experiments in Italy and Germany. Yet, such accumulation of power and attrition of liberty, however unspectacular their progress, have been under way in this nation.

The process whereby power has come to dominate our society was outlined well over 100 years ago in Alexis de Tocqueville's oft-quoted warning:

> Above this race of men stands an immense and tutelary power, which takes upon itself alone to secure their gratifications and to watch over their fate. That power is absolute, minute, regular, provident, and mild. It would be like the authority of a parent if, like that authority, its object was to prepare men for manhood; but it seeks, on the contrary, to keep them in perpetual childhood: it is well content that the people should rejoice, provided they think of nothing but rejoicing. For their happiness such a government willingly labors, but it chooses to be the sole agent and the only arbiter of that happiness; it provides for their security, foresees and supplies their necessities, facilitates their pleasures, manages their principal concerns, directs their industry, regulates the descent of property, and subdivides their inheritances: what remains, but to spare them all the care of thinking and all the trouble of living?

> Thus, it every day renders the exercise of the free agency of man less useful and less frequent; it circumscribes the will within a narrower range and gradually robs a man of all the uses of himself. The principle of equality has prepared men for these things; it has predisposed men to endure them and often to look on them as benefits.

> After having thus successfully taken each member of the community in its powerful grasp and fashioned him at will, the supreme power then extends its arm over the whole community. It covers the surface of society with a network of small complicated rules,

minute and uniform, through which the most original minds and most energetic characters cannot penetrate, to rise above the crowd. The will of man is not shattered, but softened, bent, and guided; men are seldom forced by it to act, but they are constantly restrained from acting. Such a power does not destroy, but it prevents existence; it does not tyrannize, but it compresses, enervates, extinguishes and stupefies a people, till each nation is reduced to nothing better than a flock of timid and industrious animals, of which the government is the shepherd.

I have always thought that servitude of the regular, quiet, and gentle kind which I have just described might be combined more easily than is commonly believed with some of the outward forms of freedom, and that it might even establish itself under the wing of the sovereignty of the people.[39]

As the state thus accumulates all power unto itself and increasingly absorbs the private and the individual sector, a tendency to acquiesce in the situation seems to develop among the people. We can see this process at work in our own society in the tendency of each new generation to accept an ever-widening area of governmental involvement in the lives of its citizens. Today's young people are willing to accept displays of governmental power which were anathema to the youngsters of thirty years ago and were absolutely unknown to the young people of sixty years ago. As the state accumulates this power, it tends to rationalize its position, using its newly acquired controls as a tool by which the "social benefits" of the new order are advertised.

There are occasional outbursts of protest as this process develops. Even many of the advocates of centralized authority are currently alarmed about the dangers implicit in the new Federal Data Bank. They recognize that a Federal government with a computerized source of complete information concerning every citizen is indeed a potentially powerful agency, but they are really only complaining about an increased governmental efficiency. Whether or not the material was gathered in a single place, and whether or not it was computerized, the fact is that the central government has long had such information available to it. In effect, many advocates of enlarged governmental powers are now complaining because the government appears closer to the exercise of those powers.

What sort of a centralized apparatus has grown up for the

exercise of this new power? In the 89th Congress alone the extension of "domestic aid" programs was fantastic: James Reston has reported "twenty-one new health programs, seventeen new educational programs, fifteen new economic development programs, twelve new programs for the cities, seventeen new resource development programs, and four new manpower training programs" (New York *Times*, Nov. 22, 1966). In this single area of "domestic aid" programs, these new additions contribute to some startling totals: some 170 federal aid programs currently enacted into law, financed by over 400 separate appropriations within the federal budget, administered by 21 separate federal departments and agencies, assisted by over 150 Washington bureaus and over 400 regional offices. Power? Yes, indeed! Multiply these statistics by the other areas of government intervention in taxation, in land ownership, and in its far-flung regulatory activity, controlling our business, communications, food supply, money supply, transportation, housing, and nearly every other aspect of our lives, then add the additional proposed forays into our educational system and virtually every other area of the private sector, and you have a formula for total political control.

The result? As Samuel Lubell has phrased it in *The Future of American Politics:*

> The expansion of government to its present scale has politicalized virtually all economic life. The wages being paid most workers today are political wages, reflecting political pressures rather than anything that might be considered the normal workings of supply and demand. The prices farmers receive are political prices. The profits business is earning are political profits. The savings people hold have become political savings, since their real value is subject to abrupt depreciation by political decisions.

What are the prospects for freedom within such a totally politicalized society. The unlimited power of coercion present in a society so tightly tied in economic bonds has been plainly stated by one of the modern theorists of the total state, Leon Trotsky: "In a country where the sole employer is the State, opposition means death by slow starvation. The old principle, who does not work shall not eat, has been replaced by a new one: who does not obey shall not eat."

The threat to liberty produced by Tocqueville's predicted "enervation" and Belloc's "Servile State," because of the insidious quality of such gradualist, ameliorative, "humanitarian" regimes, may be most dangerous of all. Liberty is increasingly weighed in the balance against equality and is found wanting by those who offer themselves as "friends of the people." One of these advocates of the new order, Gunnar Myrdal, has written in *An American Dilemma:*

> In society liberty for one may mean the suppression of liberty for others . . . In America . . . liberty often provided an opportunity for the stronger to rob the weaker. Against this, the equalitarianism in the (American) Creed has been persistently revolting. The struggle is far from ended. The reason why American liberty was not more dangerous to equality [in the early days of the nation] was, of course, the open frontier and the free land. When opportunity became bounded in the last generation, the inherent conflict between equality and liberty flared up. Equality is slowly winning. . . .

Power becomes absolute when it becomes the agency through which society chooses to solve its problems. There are many signs that such a choice has been made in our own society. Not only has the accumulation of power proceeded dangerously far in our governmental structure, but, perhaps far more dangerous, the rationale justifying that accumulation of power has made great progress among the individuals composing our society.

What is in store for a society in which power has become so centralized?

> The social hierarchy is in ruins; the individual members are like peas shelled from their pods and form a numerical whole composed of equal elements. The state is the beginning and end of organization; it must apply itself to the task with the highest degree of authority and attention to detail. But is that to say that there are no longer any privileged persons? There are indeed; but as regards the state they are no longer privileged as men, preceding its authority. They hold their privileges in and from the state.[37]

Such a centralized authority soon comes to take upon itself the power of totally reordering society. The concept of law is stripped of a higher meaning and utilized as an enabling act for the achievement of that total reordering of society. To do all, power must be master of all.

Soon such a state recognizes no authority beyond itself. All functions, public and private, all actions, no matter how individual, are subject to mass control as a part of the exercise of total power.

> Such is totalitarianism in its essence. It is not merely an oppressive regime; indeed, in principle, it does not have to be particularly oppressive at all, at least not to large sections of the population. What is involved is something much more fundamental. The old-fashioned despot demanded obedience, taxes, and manpower for his armies. The totalitarian regime wants much more: "It's your souls they want," as someone once put it, referring to the Nazis. It's total possession of the whole man they want; and they will brook no rivals in engaging man's loyalties, hopes, and affections.[51]

The living man, the individual with a source of dignity which earlier societies had viewed as transcending the state, is scheduled to have his creative capacities, his dignity, and his personality sacrificed to the new abstraction of collective power. Bureaucracy and the statistical evaluation of mass-man become the new means of social sacrifice, making burning at the stake appear inefficient by comparison.

What Dostoevsky's Grand Inquisitor achieved through authority and mystery, the scientists of Huxley's *Brave New World* achieved through scientific control of life forms. More recently, in Skinner's *Walden Two*, behavioral psychology updates the latest vision of the controlled society, suggesting that, with sufficient conditioning, the individual will be so free of frustration or the necessity of decision as to be finally free of the responsibilities of freedom. The new society which has arisen in conjunction with the modern centralization of power has brought with it the tools of mass-conditioning necessary to bring about such a perverted view of "freedom."

Even while such concentrations of power and such a conditioning process rob the individual citizen of his liberty, thus destroying the individual's creative capacity and in effect penalizing both the individual and his society, the greatest corruptions of all are likely to occur in the very institutions and men called upon to exercise this vast new power. The subjection of other men's wills to a man's purposes, no matter how well intended, is even more dangerous to the power wielder than to those over whom the power is exercised. Coercion begets coercion, producing a greater and greater necessity for the application of centralized power in society since it simultaneously disrupts the private sector and justifies its own extension to solve the problems stemming from those disruptions. A man cannot stoop to using coercion against another man without allowing the corrupting influences of that power to work its corruption upon him. However *politically* necessary such interventions into the private sector of society may appear to the ardent collectivist, the potential wielder of such power must first of all make an *ethical* choice to violate the decision-making dignity of another individual, thus arrogating power to himself over the lives of others in an ethical area where individual conscience should be supreme.

A power-oriented society tends to become more and more monolithic, producing enmassment that removes all decision-making further from the individual citizen. Such a society produces a citizenry tending to regard the technical and social achievements which it sees around it as something stemming from the exercise of centralized power, rather than from the personal efforts of highly endowed individuals. At that point, the mass-man comes to identify himself with the state and becomes as corrupted by power as those who themselves exercise that power. In such a society, so completely divorced from the creative capacity of the individual, the way is paved for a social decline of great magnitude.

> Then everything includes itself in power,
> Power into will, will into appetite;
> And appetite, an universal wolf,
> So doubly seconded with will and power,
> Must make perforce a universal prey,
> And last eat up himself.
> (Shakespeare, *Troilus and Cressida*)

Once Natural Law and a decentralized society are no longer accepted as the bulwarks of the private sector, soon power, appetite, and will begin to find every area of society a proper sphere for a further extension of coercive authority. Intervention is piled upon intervention and power both encourages and feeds upon the strife between factions of society as they struggle to prosper through the intervention of power in favor of their particular group. As the exercise of coercive power grows steadily greater and steadily more damaging to society, the strife between factions to benefit from the exercise of that power becomes equally destructive to the fabric of a true society. Thus, the exercise of power is in the last analysis antisocial, destroying the society in which it occurs.

The individual citizen within such a society, already stripped of any higher dignity that does not emanate from the state, is offered an illusory social welfare, the promise of better things to come, for his acquiescence in the new system. All man's ills are now to be solved by the passage of the proper law, by the proper use of coercive power.

Such a society, abandoning individual dignity and responsibility for self in return for the promises of the new collective ethic, tends to breed a new form of social being. If the individual is not responsible for self, then a society formed of such individuals is also not responsible. The way has been paved for a new ethic of total irresponsibility on the part of individual members of that society. Surely we witness the results of such thinking in our own time. Every conceivable crime and failure in our society is attributed not to the individual but to some failure or another of society to care properly for the individual.

With Dr. Johnson, we might admit, "We cannot pry into the hearts of men, but their actions are open to observation." Surely the observation of an increasing number of the actions of men in our time would indicate some failing in their innermost being. The statistics are distressing: Crimes against property have increased (relative to population) by over 300 percent in the past twenty years. Crimes against persons have doubled in the same period of time. Even these alarming statistics do not reflect the wide acceptance of public immorality in areas not categorized as crime. The subsidized illegitimacy of the Aid to Dependent Children program or the wide acceptance of cheating on so many college campuses are only two of many such symptoms of moral decline.

The steadily growing trend toward moral failure seems to advance at the same rate as the older ideal of self-responsibility continues to decline.

The American has never been a perfect instrument, but at one time he had a reputation for gallantry, which, to my mind, is a sweet and priceless quality. It must still exist, but it is blotted out by the dustcloud of self-pity. The last clear statement of gallantry in my experience I heard in a recidivist state prison, a place of two-time losers, all lifers. In the yard an old and hopeless convict spoke as follows: "The kids come up here and they bawl how they wasn't guilty or how they was framed or how it was their mother's fault or their father was a drunk. Us old boys try to tell them, Kid, for Christ's sake, do your *own* time. Let us do ours." In the present climate of whining self-pity, of practiced sickness, of professional goldbricking, of screaming charges about whose fault it is, one hears of very few who do their own time, who take their own rap and don't spread it around. It is as though the quality of responsibility had atrophied.[27]

Something of such social results was predicted over 100 years ago by the British historian, Lord Macaulay, when he warned that the twentieth century would be as disastrous for America as the fifth century had been for the Roman Empire, with the difference that the Huns and Vandals who had destroyed the Roman Empire had come from outside the system, while our barbarians would be engendered within America by our own institutions.

As self-responsibility within our society has atrophied, what sort of a nation have we become? One social critic, Philip Wylie, has developed the idea that we are becoming a nation of nonpersons, engaging in "nothing education," "nothing readership," "nothing citizenship," "nothing art," and "nothing music." He describes our society as a "generation of zeros," produced by an educational system which avoids the creation of any "trauma" for the individual student, from which all competition, all discipline, and all possibility of low grades have been removed from the student's path. He cites television as the creator of a generation of nothing readers. He cites the current student population who all too often are for nothing and who often assume no role or responsibility in their society except that of criticism and nihilism as nothing citizens and eventually nothing persons. He finds the total absence of creativity in much of modern art as a demonstration of nothing art and levels much the same charge against modern music. He cites the noninvolvement of the members of our society, people who are unwilling in case after case to offer aid or even call the police in times of crisis, as for example in the Kew Gardens, New York murder of a woman, witnessed by some thirty-eight people who did not want to become "involved."

Thus the history of unrestricted power is again borne out. When the centralized power of the state reaches a certain point of concentration, the society it governs will tend to disintegrate. Individual action, the spark of creativity, and human charity, all decline as the exercise of power becomes the dominant solution to all problems. Voluntary human action is increasingly destroyed in preference for coerced human action.

Yes, power does corrupt, a fact amply borne out by the Bobby Bakers who increasingly inhabit the seats of power. Yet such men are nothing more or less than a mirror held up to the citizenry of America, a mirror all too graphically depicting the moral decay of our society. Professor Ortega y Gasset has predicted the final result of such decay:

> The result of this tendency will be fatal. Spontaneous social action will be broken up over and over again by State intervention; no new seed will be able to fructify. Society will have to live for the State, man *for* the governmental machine. And as, after all, it is only a machine, whose existence and maintenance depend on the vital supports around it, the State, after sucking out the very marrow of society, will be left bloodless, a skeleton, dead with that rusty death of machinery, more gruesome than the death of a living organism. Such was the lamentable fate of ancient civilization.[52]

The twentieth century is well advanced upon such a path.

14

Twentieth Century Alternatives to Collectivism—The Crossroads

❦❦❦❦❦❦❦❦❦❦❦❦❦❦❦❦❦❦❦❦❦❦❦❦❦❦❦❦❦❦❦❦

THE PRODUCTIVE CAPACITY OF THE FREE SOCIETY

THE PEOPLE OF THE UNITED STATES HAVE BEEN BLESSED with the opportunity of living in an essentially free society. In a sense, this is a mixed blessing, because we have become so accustomed to this situation that we have forgotten how most men have spent their lives on earth. The characterization of human life as advanced by Thomas Hobbes is quite accurate as a description of the existence of most men who have trod this earth. Life indeed has been "nasty, brutish, and short." The achievement of freedom in the economic and political sphere which has been the blessing of this nation is the exception rather than the rule.

It is always true that the free eras have also tended to be the productive eras, leading to the greatest advances in cultural as well as material pursuits. Freedom and productivity went hand in hand in the heyday of Athens, of Rome, and of Renaissance Florence. Unfortunately, it also seems true that the very prosperity engendered by freedom seems to produce a blindness to spiritual and individual values which eventually undercuts freedom itself. At the point at which freedom is undercut, the prosperity stemming from that freedom also begins to decline. At last, the civilization which has followed the path from freedom, to prosperity, to disinterest in freedom, to loss of prosperity, comes full circle. Some such pattern can be detected in Athens, Rome, and perhaps within our own society as well.

There are many facets to the case for human freedom. Surely of vital concern is the productive and creative energy for the advancement of civilization which is released by individual freedom. In the words of Milton Friedman:

> The preservation of freedom is the protective reason for limiting and decentralizing governmental power. But there is also a constructive reason. The great advances of civilization, whether in architecture or painting, in science or literature, in industry or agriculture, have never come from centralized government. Columbus did not set out to seek a new route to China in response to a majority directive of a parliament, though he was partly financed by an absolute monarch. Newton and Leibnitz; Einstein and Bohr; Shakespeare, Milton, and Pasternak; Whitney, McCormick, Edison, and Ford; Jane Addams, Florence Nightingale, and Albert Schweitzer; no one of these opened new frontiers in human knowledge and understanding, in literature, in technical possibilities, or in the relief of human misery in response to governmental directives. Their achievements were the product of individual genius, of strongly held minority views, of a social climate permitting variety and diversity.[53]

Not all the creative energies of society are reflected in the brilliant personal achievements of an Edison or a Schweitzer. In a free society, all of us participate by exchanging something of less value (to us) for something of more value to us. We operate in an area of *mutual* profit, producing in our area of greatest efficiency and exchanging the fruits of that production with other producers who are also working in their specialties of greatest efficiency. In a free nation where each is free to pursue his own profit, society itself is the final and greatest gainer.

The growth record of our relatively free society in the nineteenth and early twentieth century is a demonstration of this very fact. Think of the tremendous advances made possible in communication, production, and distribution, when men have been left free to combine their own abilities with those of others for maximum mutual benefit! In an age in which the government takes unto itself a larger and larger responsibility for the promotion of "welfare," we might ask the question, "Who really promotes the country's welfare?" One of the best answers has been provided by Lawrence Fertig:

> People and business organizations in this country who have labored for generations to save and invest in improved tools and techniques of industry should get medals for promoting welfare. Unless this capital had been saved and invested we could not now have the good life we lead. Still more wealth-producing capital investment is necessary if we are to pay for more doctors and hospitals, more educational institutions as well as churches and ministers who offer spiritual welfare.[48]

The guarantees of private property, of individual initiative and free exchange, are absolute prerequisites if this tremendous productive miracle, this genuine promotion of "welfare," is to be achieved. The argument perhaps boils down to a comparison between the public sector and private sector. Simply stated, it is the private sector that is truly productive. Does this imply dog-eat-dog competition, an atomistic individualism with every man competing for his own interest at the expense of everyone else? In a free society, the private sector is the truly *cooperative* realm. It is this very capacity for cooperation between and among individuals, the achievement of *mutual* benefit, that characterizes the system. In the words of William H. Peterson:

> ... what is the private sector? It is the competitive order of social cooperation—cooperation under freedom—freedom to choose a livelihood, to choose the means of satisfying your own needs and the needs of those you love—as well, of course, as you as a producer satisfy the needs of society, a society of sovereign consumers who also choose, i.e., make their choices of those producers best able to satisfy their needs. This is freedom of choice—freedom without coercion. Does this mean, to answer a Socialist argument, the freedom to starve? No, not unless one insists on starving—and if his fellow man should choose to give up the Judeo-Christian individual responsibility of privately serving, when necessary, as his brother's keeper. Anyway, capitalism and starvation (as well as capitalism and poverty, for that matter) seem quite foreign to each other, as the historical record indicates. Historically communism can make no such claim, as the record from Governor Bradford's Plymouth Bay colony to Khrushchev's farm failure shows.[54]

Since Adam Smith's time, it has been repeatedly pointed out that the private sector, with its capacity for providing mutual profit, with its capacity for self-adjustment to serve most efficiently the needs of society, does indeed provide as by an invisible hand, a hand which moves for the benefit of all. As Adam Smith suggested, private enterprise means public welfare.

There can be little question that free enterprise provides the most productive social organization in the history of the world. Why then do men fight this system? So many people in our time fight the idea of free enterprise simply because they do not understand the source of its vitality. As the modern world has turned increasingly from a spiritual order protected by an institutional framework, it has come to deny the validity of the free market. The political meddling in the marketplace which so dominates our own age is due precisely to an attempt to deny human dignity by denying volitional action. In short, men have lost faith in themselves and no longer judge the individual capable of dealing with his affairs without outside coercion.

> So long as effective freedom of exchange is maintained, the central feature of the market organization of economic activity is that it prevents one person from interfering with another in respect of most of his activities. The consumer is protected from coercion by the seller because of the presence of other sellers with whom he can deal. The seller is protected from coercion by the consumer because of other consumers to whom he can sell. The employee is protected from coercion by the employer because of other employers for whom he can work, and so on. And the market does this impersonally and without centralized authority.

> Indeed, a major source of objection to a free economy is precisely that it does this task so well. It gives people what they want instead of what a particular group thinks they ought to want. Underlying most arguments against the free market is a lack of belief in freedom itself.[53]

A society unwilling to place its faith in the dignity and capability of free men is a society doomed to the mismanagement of "little men playing god." These little men of course fail completely to realize that contrast and individual difference are the foundation of all genuine creativity. A situation in which an individual is left free to dispose of his property and order his affairs as he sees fit is an ideal, both for human productivity and for human freedom. Such institutions of the private sector as private property constitute an indispensable support of personal liberty. Viewed in such a light, private property becomes truly spiritual, valued less for its material complexion than for its underlying spiritual value. The Biblical injunction, ". . . seek ye first the Kingdom of God, and His righteousness; and all these things shall be added unto you," is a suggestion of how important are the underlying spiritual values, and how they serve as an absolute prerequisite for the creative capacities which are unleashed when our spiritual values and our emphasis upon individual freedom are in proper order. If we would be materially prosperous, let us begin by being spiritually healthy, by allowing a productive form of social organization, a truly free market and free society premised upon the dignity of the individual.

MORALITY AND DIVINE AUTHORITY

While it is true that freedom "works" and that it is the only system consonant with a high degree of material prosperity, it is the underlying *why* it works, the spiritually correct condition of individual freedom which releases those creative energies, to which we owe our primary allegiance. Any emphasis solely upon material goals may well prove our undoing. Such overemphasis of material concerns has undone more than one freedom-oriented civilization throughout history. There are signs, in fact, that we are already unduly concerned with material things and have come to view them not as effects of a proper moral order, but rather as replacements for any moral order whatsoever:

> . . . we are also poisoned with things. Having many things seems to create a desire for more things, more clothes, houses, automobiles. Think of the pure horror of our Christmases when our children tear open package after package; when the floor is heaped with wrappings and presents, say, "Is that all?" And two days after the smashed and abandoned things are added to our national trash pile, and perhaps the child, having got in trouble, explains, "I didn't have anything to do." And he means exactly that—nothing to do, nowhere to go, no direction, no purpose, and worst of all no needs. Wants he has, yes, but for more bright and breakable "things." We are trapped and entangled in things.[27]

Could it be possible that we have become so prosperous that we have lost sight of the true source of that prosperity? Is it possible that we no longer feel duty, obligation, or purpose in our existence? Is it possible that we have taken the Christian injunction, "All things are yours, but ye are Christ's," and have shortened it to read simply, "All things are yours."?

If so, modern man's insistence upon collective solutions is understandable, since he has divorced himself from the spiritual values which give meaning to him as an individual personality. Many people have perceived this danger. This is the basis of Kierkegaard's warning, "The crowd is untruth."

Only the freely choosing individual has the capacity to modify *who* and *what* he is. Fixed values must exist within which the individual makes his choice, but in the final analysis that choice still must rest with the individual:

> It is the moral agent who has the authority to make the moral decision. To place the authority elsewhere would be to deprive the agent of his responsibility. But the fact that the conscience must ultimately have the authority to do the choosing and must assume full responsibility for it does not imply that the decision is arbitrary or subjective. The moral decision is not right because *we* choose it but because we choose it *rightly.* The conscience decides upon, but does not constitute, the right.[55]

In an age increasingly divorced from any fixed standards or individual codes of conduct, divorced indeed from the individual capacity to choose, men of our time must take a hard look at the source from which ethical systems derive their authority. With Cardinal Newman, we might well remember, "In morals, as in physics, the stream cannot rise higher than its sources."

The decline of religious authority in Western civilization has produced such total secularism that often men will no longer acknowledge any spiritual authority. We have forgotten that separation of church and state most emphatically does not mean the exclusion of religious values from our educational systems, but instead means that religious values should be taught with a full understanding of what a number of different sects have to teach us. Instead of a broadly tolerant attitude which emphasizes the religious values underlying our civilization, our schools evidence an increasing secularism which excludes all religious value and breeds a generation of spiritual illiterates. Such spiritual illiterates, divorced from the heritage of their civilization, are exactly the sort of raw material from which collectivist experiments in the planned society can be readily constructed. A reinstitution of ethical values, of the spiritual heritage of our civilization, is an absolute prerequisite if the direction of our age is to be reversed.

What are these moral values which our civilization has to teach us? Many men of good will, unable to discern a single system of value applicable in all circumstances, therefore assume that no set of values, no ultimate "truth" exists. In fact, truth is fixed and absolute, definite standards of right and wrong do indeed exist. Individual conscience enters the scene at the point where this fixed and absolute truth is comprehended differently by each of us as we experience our own moral growth. It is the modern inability to distinguish between good and bad, to recognize some fixed authority, that opens the door to the modern collective tragedy which we are experiencing:

> Many a popular "planner" on a democratic platform, many a mild-eyed scientist in a democratic laboratory means, in the last resort, just what the Fascist means. He believes that "good" means whatever men are conditioned to approve. He believes that it is the function of him and his kind to condition men; to create consciences by eugenics, psychological manipulation of infants, state education and mass propaganda. Because he is confused, he does not yet fully realize that those who create conscience cannot be subject to conscience themselves. But he must awake to the logic of his position sooner or later; and when he does, what barrier remains between us and the final division of the race into a few conditioners who stand themselves outside morality and the many conditioned in whom such morality as the experts choose is produced at the experts' pleasure? If "good" means only the local ideology, how can those who invent the local ideology be guided by any idea of good themselves? The very idea of freedom presupposes some objective moral law which overarches rulers and ruled alike. Subjectivism about values is eternally incompatible with democracy. We and our rulers are of one kind only so long as we are subject to one law. But if there is no Law of Nature, the *ethos* of any society is the creation of its rulers, educators and conditioners; and every creator stands above and outside his own creation.[56]

Man must indeed be free to choose, free to exercise his own conscience, but he also must have guidelines within which that choice can be exercised, or the choice itself ultimately becomes meaningless. If man is to be truly free to choose, there must be some basis for his choice, some fixed standard within which he exercises his conscience. It is that fixed standard which modern society has so undermined and attacked.

The nature of the attack upon this morality has come from not one source but two. The first asserts that morality is different according to time and place. Stressing the attitudes of cultural anthropology and "comparative religion," the modern subjectivist suggests that ethical standards among different cultures differ so widely that in fact no common standard exists at all. Nothing could be further from the truth.

> If a man will go into a library and spend a few days with the *Encyclopedia of Religion and Ethics* he will soon discover the massive unanimity of the practical reason in man. From the Babylonian *Hymn to Samos*, from the Laws of Manu, the *Book of the Dead*, the Analects, the Stoics, the Platonists, from Australian aborigines and Redskins, he will collect the same triumphantly monotonous denunciations of oppression, murder, treachery and falsehood, the same injunctions of kindness to the aged, the young, and the weak, of almsgiving and impartiality and honesty. He may be a little surprised (I certainly was) to find that precepts of mercy are more frequent than precepts of justice; but he will no longer doubt that there is such a thing as the Law of Nature. There are, of course, differences. There are even blindnesses in particular cultures—just as there are savages who cannot count up to twenty. But the pretense that we are presented with a mere chaos . . . is simply false . . .[56]

The second incorrect attitude held by modern men concerning a fixed moral code is that if man should tie himself to a fixed moral framework, he would cut off all "progress" and "development."

> Does a permanent moral standard preclude progress? On the contrary, except on the supposition of a changeless standard, progress is impossible. If good is a fixed point, it is at least possible that we should get nearer and nearer to it; but if the terminus is as mobile as the train, how can the train progress towards it? Our ideas of the good may change, but they cannot change either for the better or

the worse if there is no absolute and immutable good to which they can approximate or from which they can recede. We can go on getting a sum more and more nearly right only if we know the one perfectly right answer [does exist].[56]

A fixed moral code in no way limits individual freedom of choice—rather it gives it meaningful direction. A man without a moral code is indeed free from moral problems, in the same sense that a man who has never learned to count is free from mathematical problems.

A man asleep is free from all problems. Within the framework of general human ethics problems will, of course, arise and will sometimes be solved wrongly. This possibility of error is simply the symptom that we are awake, not asleep, that we are men, not beasts or gods. If I were pressing on you a panacea, if I were recommending traditional ethics as a means to some end, I might be tempted to promise you the infallibility which I actually deny. [Instead], I send you back to your nurse and your father, to all the poets and sages and law givers, because, in a sense, I hold that you are already there whether you realize it or not: that there is really no ethical alternative: that those who urge us to adopt new moralities are only offering us the mutilated or expurgated text of a book which we already possess in the original manuscript. They all wish us to depend on them instead of on that original, and then to deprive us of our full humanity. Their activity is in the long run always directed against our freedom.[56]

Much of what is called human history, in its seemingly endless war, poverty, and suffering, can be interpreted as the human attempt to achieve some sort of happiness apart from God. But not even God can give man happiness apart from Himself, because no such happiness exists. How then do we relate ourselves to this God? We do so through conscience, through a sense of right and wrong. This is what constitutes morality:

The Golden Rule of the New Testament (Do as you would be done by) is a summing up of what everyone, at bottom, had always known to be right. Really great moral teachers never do introduce new moralities: it is quacks and cranks who do that. As Dr. Johnson said, "People need to be reminded more often than they need to be instructed." The real job of every moral teacher is to keep on bringing us back, time after time, to the old simple principles which we are all so anxious not to see; like bringing a horse back and back to the fence it has refused to jump or bringing a child back and back to the bit in its lesson that it wants to shirk.[57]

Morality, after all, is concerned with more than a sense of fair play among individuals. This is the element of morality which society always stresses, since such a morality is necessary for the smooth operation of any society. More important to the life of the individual is finding a way to bring his sense of purpose, his moral sense, in line with the direction toward which all human life is intended. There is absolutely no value in ordering a society according to so-called moral standards unless we recognize that the individual must be at peace with himself and at peace with the purpose of his Creator before he can be morally responsible toward his society.

What is the good of telling the ships how to steer so as to avoid collisions if, in fact, they are such crazy old tubs that they cannot be steered at all? What is the good of drawing up, on paper, rules for social behaviour, if we know that, in fact, our greed, cowardice, ill temper, and self-conceit are going to prevent us from keeping them? I do not mean for a moment that we ought not to think, and think hard, about improvements in our social and economic system. What I do mean is that all that thinking will be mere moonshine unless we realise that nothing but the courage and unselfishness of individuals is ever going to make any system work properly. It is easy enough to remove the particular kinds of graft or bullying that go on under the present system: but as long as men are twisters or bullies they will find some new way of carrying on the old game under the new system. You cannot make men good by law: and without good men you cannot have a good society.[57]

That is why, if the architects of the "good society" are genuinely sincere, they must look to the individual and to a fixed moral system before their institutional schemes, *whatever they might be,* can have an opportunity to work. This suggestion involves a genuine ecumenism, of the Catholic, the Protestant, and the Jew, as well as the man who finds his home in no particular church yet has a sense of religious values. Only when all such people are united in the common belief that man has a higher side, potentially in tune with a Divine Consciousness, and that man's development must be in tune with that consciousness and must be left free to develop if his humanity is to be expressed, only then can we hope to turn back from the destructive course so far advanced in the mid-twentieth century.

THE VISION OF WESTERN CIVILIZATION

If we were to attempt the summary of the root collective assumptions generally at variance with the heritage of Western civilization—assumptions stemming from rationalism, the French Revolution and the collective attitudes of the nineteenth and twentieth centuries—we would have to include relative morality, collective rather than individual values and ethics, materialism, secularism, naturalism, atheism, and a willingness to violate all traditional values and institutions. All of these attitudes, already treated at some length, can be summarized in the statement that the entrenched ideas of our time have so departed from a correct view of reality that we are no longer equipped to meet the challenges confronting Western civilization.

Most of the ideas stemming from the Renaissance and the Enlightenment have operated in opposition to the status quo, to the prevailing order of society. The modern world has been an age of change which revels in the destruction of old ideas and institutions. The push of modern history is therefore toward nihilism and destruction, destruction of the old order with all too little idea of what might be erected in its place.

Apparently this belief that modern man is a breed unique unto himself, who can reject the past, control nature, and eliminate the necessity for God, has become a very pervasive idea in our time. Witness Joseph Wood Krutch's story concerning the lady tourist who looked into the Grand Canyon and remarked, "You can't tell me it was made without human aid." One is reminded of St. Augustine's insistence that pride not only goes before a fall, but is a fall in itself, a fall of man's attention from what is better (God) to what is worse (man himself). Finally, of course, to lose faith in God is to lose faith in oneself, to be divorced from the very wellspring from which human dignity flows. Such an individual, divorced from his Maker, finally comes to lose his moral directions, as does the society made up of such men. It may well be that the ecumenism of our own time is less a triumph of the much vaunted "love" over self-righteousness than it is the triumph of indifference and lack of direction in the human search for truth.

The Western intellectual world of the nineteenth century

rushed to scientific solutions to achieve a "perfectible" world. But as the twentieth century has seen more and more of these "scientific solutions," there are signs of increasing doubt as to how "perfectible" the world actually is. Even while we bravely discuss our scientific achievements and the "final victory" over various human problems, the twentieth century turns more and more in its art and entertainment to those aspects of the nineteenth century in which the individual, rather than the societal, framework was emphasized. Consider for example the tremendous popularity which Western frontier history has achieved in our urban age. As we live through an era of enmassment, surrounded by more and more gadgetry, we seem to sigh instead for a return to individualistic values which the nineteenth century took for granted, even while it talked endlessly of the scientific revolutions to come.

The present collectivist regimes of the world exercise tremendous power, but if history teaches us anything, it should surely teach us that power exercised without a proper view of reality is doomed to go down to its own destruction. Recently a member of the Indian legislature addressed himself to the exercise of collective power in India, with the words that might be echoed by all civilized men in the mid-twentieth century: "If this Government does not go . . . it will destroy the country. It will bring down the pillars of the stability of our country, of its economic and social life . . . For God's sake go while there is some administration and some order. Do not destroy the country before you go."

Perhaps the utopian ideas of the Enlightenment, the ideas so dominant in the modern world, emphasizing the belief that man can build a heaven on earth, are destined to keep collapsing until they become totally unimportant. Perhaps the day will arrive, as Ortega predicted, when politics will cease to be man's interest, when *life* becomes more important:

> We discover at last that life does not exist for the benefit of the idea, but that the idea, the institution, the rule exists for the benefit of life, or, as the Gospel has it, that "the sabbath was made for man, not man for the sabbath."[16]

In fact, socialism and the degradation of the human spirit may follow a beneficent purpose, if they make us look into ourselves to analyze the problem and improve our own understandings. There is a difference between the city of light and the city of darkness. Unencumbered by faulty moral precepts, Western man can again distinguish the difference between the two. For brief periods in the past, he has already been able to do just that. If he has fallen off the track, he has always managed to climb back on once again. A period of pre-Greek savagery gave way to an age of Greek democracy and tremendous philosophic and cultural attainment. The era of Greek collapse produced the Stoicism which led to the greatness of Rome. The era of Roman collapse brought forth Christianity, with its tremendous Judeo-Christian heritage. The Christian heresy of gnosticism led to the emergence of St. Augustine as a great Christian spokesman. The anarchy of the Italian city-states led to the beauties of the Renaissance. In our era, we have tremendous coercion exercised over men, in one of the most stultifying eras which the human spirit has ever undergone. What will man produce to rise above this coercion?

We should recall, however, that the mere presence of a problem does not guarantee its solution. As Edmund Burke is supposed to have suggested, "All that is necessary for the triumph of evil is for good men to do nothing."

What might Western man do? Tolstoy recounts the parable of the hedgehog and the fox, categorizing the fox as "he who knows many things," and categorizing the hedgehog as "he who knows *one big thing.*" In an era filled with many foxes who know more "facts" than ever before in the history of the world, perhaps what Western man needs to do is once again become the hedgehog, he who knows *one big thing.* As hedgehogs, secure in our knowledge of one big thing, we might recall that while modern science has added a new dimension to man's understanding of his material universe, it has in no way changed the basic human dimension of life on this earth. A number of distinguished scientists are themselves coming to the realization of this very point. Professor Roger Williams, a distinguished biochemist, has made this point abundantly clear in his *You Are Extraordinary,* a study emphasizing that science itself is coming to understand the tremendous individualities and human differences which fly in the face of the stereotype of "humanity" that the modern social scientists would pass off upon us.

Not only is science itself moving toward a realization of the traditional view of man already held for two millennia by Western civilization, but it is also true that:

> There is no reason, at least I know of none, why the universe should necessarily be intelligible to the mind of a twentieth-century human being, and I take leave to remind him how late a comer he is upon the cosmic scene and how recently he has begun to think.[14]

Thus we are all at the beginning of our understandings. Human development and human perception of reality lie ahead as well as behind. We find ourselves faced with the same questions always faced by the men of Western civilization. What view of man and human nature and the universe should we espouse? Should we base our view of man on the assumption that he is a mere material animal? Or should we endow him with a soul? If we give him a soul, we have to give him a Creator, and we have to give him certain fixed rules to live by, a framework within which he may exercise his reason, or we find ourselves in the same predicament as that of the rationalists during the Enlightenment, when they confused nature and God. Either man has a heritage from his God, his experience, his tradition, within which he can find standards, or he does not. If he does, he should begin to order his world and his goals to such a system, through the exercise of his reason, giving the individual sufficient freedom to achieve the exercise of his free will. If he truly does not believe that man has such a heritage, then he should continue to place his values in materialism, collectivism, centralization of power in the state, and secularism. He should continue to eliminate individual freedom and obliterate man's heritage as he has been doing in the twentieth century.

Thus, the problem always remains the same after these thousands of years. Does God exist? What is man? What is man's nature? What standards should man adhere to in this world? In the final analysis, the answer to these questions dominates our political and social thought, as well as our very existence.

Perhaps the ethical system discussed in these pages has in some regard or another met with disagreement on the part of the Catholic, the Protestant, the Jew, and the agnostic. I hope that such disagreement is due primarily to a different perspective rather than to a basic and insurmountable difference in principle. The existence of such a framework, within which each of us must ultimately work out his own salvation (or development, if you prefer) must be the basic premise from which he proceeds. Anything less abandons the field to the coercionist without a struggle. If this attempt has outlined the outer limits within which we must all work, has described the framework that we dare not violate, it has served its purpose. The point of this heritage of ours is well expressed in a remark by the President of the Princeton Theological Seminary: "Our destiny is bound up with the rediscovery of our heritage; and the road to Tomorrow leads through Yesterday."

It is true that the great thinkers of the past were far from perfect agreement, but it is also true that they were moving toward a system of values stemming from a Creator—a direction almost diametrically opposed to the course of modern man. It is true that to be human is to be free. It is also true that the achievement of this freedom in humanity and understanding is the meaning of history. In the words of Karl Jaspers, "History is man's advance toward liberty through the cultivation of faith."

As man thus grows in understanding, he moves closer to a realization of his total meaning and purpose as a creature of God. Oliver Wendell Holme's "The Chambered Nautilus" expresses that human striving:

> Build thee more stately mansions, O my soul,
> 　As the swift seasons roll!
> 　Leave thy low-vaulted past!
> Let each new temple, nobler than the last,
> Shut thee from heaven with a dome more vast,
> 　Till thou at length art free,
> Leaving thine outgrown shell by life's unresting sea!

Malcolm Muggeridge, on the occasion of his investiture as rector of Edinburgh University observed:

The curtain, indeed, is falling, if it has not already fallen, on all the utopian hopes which have prevailed so strongly for a century or more. I personally rejoice that it should be so because I know that then, looking desperately into the mystery of things, we shall once again understand that fulfillment must be sought through the spirit, not the body or the mind, and will be realized, if at all, elsewhere than in this world of time and space. . . .

There is a chance that our country will find its way again, picking up the threads of its incomparable language and literature, cherishing its lovely countryside, being true to its splendid history and finding a different greatness in the world's changed circumstance. I may not live to see it, but it will happen.

None of us now alive "may live to see it," but at least we can understand that the problem of our time is a departure from our tradition, from our nature as human beings, and from a proper world view. We can understand that to tamper with man's traditions is to tamper with his freedoms. We can understand that the heritage of Western civilization is the development of values worthy of adherence. It is true that we have made progress, that we can continue to progress, but only if we guard and cherish our tradition and our past, our experience, our divine spark of absolute value (conscience) and thus dignify man as a spiritual as well as an animal creature, with values and integrity, with a peculiar God-given individuality that must not be stifled within any man-made heaven on earth.

It has been suggested that man has two duties on earth. He must come to know God and must make the effort to realize himself as a person. It may well be that, when our understanding has progressed far enough, we will find that knowing God and realizing ourselves as persons are different facets of the same single reality. Some men with such understanding already exist. They are the remnant to whom Isaiah was instructed to carry the message.

Bibliography and Notes

Certain authors, when they speak of their work, say: "My book, my commentary, my history" . . . They would do better to say, "Our book, our commentary, our history," since their writings generally contain more of other people's good things than of their own. (Blaise Pascal, *Pensees*)

PASCAL'S FAMOUS REMARK CONCERNING THE LACK OF ORIGINAL-ity present in most published works is especially applicable to this volume. I am under obligation to innumerable writers in political theory, moral philosophy, economic theory, and most other disci-plines that anyone would care to name. Many of these debts are acknowledged when direct quotations are credited to the author in question. Many more thoughts, ideas, and insights of all sorts have come from hundreds of books or articles written by others. These have become a part of my makeup and have been accepted by me until they form a portion of my own thought processes, demonstrating that imitation is indeed the sincerest form of flat-tery. I extend a blanket word of thanks to these distinguished authors, past and present, who have contributed their portion to this review and defense of our Western heritage.

Russell Lynes once commented, "The Literary Snob has not only read the book you are reading but takes pleasure in telling you the names of all the earlier and more obscure books by the same author, and why each was superior to the better known one that has come to your attention." I hope this does not constitute that sort of bibliography. Still, a word about the mechanics and intent of this particular bibliography is in order. It generally follows the order of first mention in the text—on the assumption that those who are pursuing some point of interest to them will wish to consult the book which served as the source for the idea. This, plus the fact that the book is addressed to a nonspecialized readership, has led me to avoid customary footnoting. Instead, the citations in the text refer only to the number of the book in the order in which it appears in the bibliography. This may not appeal to some academic commentators, but I hope it encourages further reading on the part of the interested layman.

This book and bibliography are not intended as a scholarly survey of the entire heritage of Western civilization. Rather, they are intended as an introduction and a jumping-off point for those who would wish to pursue the subject further, and the footnoting and bibliography are designed primarily with that in mind. Since the classic authors; Plato, Cicero, Augustine, Aquinas, Burke, and the rest of similar stamp are available in so many forms to the reader interested in pursuing their thought, only modern analysts of their ideas are included in this bibliography.

Finally it should be remarked that these several titles are only a helpful sample of a much larger body of literature, a body of literature to which the reader will be led by the authors here included.

1. Richard Weaver, *Ideas Have Consequences*, The University of Chicago Press, 1948. In his first major work, Weaver examines the philosophic bankruptcy of the modern world and urges a reinstitution of older, deeper values.

2. Friedrich Hayek, *The Constitution of Liberty*, The University of Chicago Press, 1960. An exploration of the philosophic foundations of freedom and an analysis of today's dangerous departures from those foundations.

3. Richard Weaver, *Visions of Order*, Louisiana State University Press, 1964. In this, his last book, Weaver attacks the democratism, presentism, and scientism of a modern world engaged in the subversion of the traditions of Western civilization.

4. Reinhold Niebuhr, *The Nature and Destiny of Man: Human Nature*, Charles Scribner's Sons, 1964. Subtitled "A Study of Human Nature from the Perspective of Christian Faith," this volume provides an excellent analysis of a number of the traditions important to the Western heritage, especially the idea of individual self-transcendence.

5. Lecomte du Noüy, *Human Destiny*, David McKay Company, Inc., 1947. A distinguished scientist stresses that the findings of science and the traditional speculations of theology do indeed move in the same direction.

6. Thomas Molnar, *Modern Art as an Expression of Our Times* (privately printed by the Intercollegiate Studies Institute). Professor Molnar renders a valuable service as he relates the declining standards in art to the declining standards within our society as a whole, tracing that decline to the philosophic concepts pervading our present civilization.

7. Antoine de Saint-Exupéry, *Wind, Sand and Stars*, Harcourt, Brace & World, Inc., 1949. One of the most perceptive analyses of human nature and the human condition, written with the impact of an excellent novel.

8. Richard Weaver, *Life Without Prejudice*, Henry Regnery Company, 1965. A posthumous collection of some of Richard Weaver's most thoughtful essays, further developing various aspects of his modern Platonism.

9. Richard Weaver, "Up from Liberalism." An essay appearing in *Modern Age* (Winter, 1958–1959) which suggests many of Weaver's ideas in summary form, thus serving as a valuable introduction to a modern author of great significance.

10. Johann Eckermann, *Conversations of Goethe with Eckermann*, E. P. Dutton & Co. Inc., 1930. In this volume, many of Goethe's attitudes are revealed by Eckermann to provide an artist's insight into the problems of the human condition.

11. Jeffrey Hart, "The Rebirth of Christ." Appearing originally in *National Review* (December 28, 1965), Hart's analysis of C. S. Lewis and his thought is a helpful introduction to the moral dilemma of contemporary civilization and the solutions offered by one of this century's most trenchant Christian moralists.

12. Helmut Schoeck and James Wiggins (Editors), *Relativism and the Study of Man*, D. Van Nostrand Company, Inc., 1961. This collection of scholarly essays examines the pitfalls of modern relativism, especially in those areas where that relativism has distorted the "social sciences."

13. Christopher Dawson, *The Dynamics of World History*, Sheed & Ward Inc., 1956. One of the distinguished Christian historians of the Western world here sets forth many aspects of the Western heritage that merit our close examination.

14. C. E. M. Joad, *Teach Yourself Philosophy*, Fawcett World Library, 1965. Professor Joad's work is especially helpful for an understanding of the Platonic tradition and the development of the rationale for a fixed moral order.

15. C. S. Lewis, *The Great Divorce*, Macmillan Company, 1946. One of the Cambridge don's articulate expositions of the Christian moral framework, stressing the ultimate necessity of individual choice.

16. Ortega y Gasset, *The Modern Theme*, Harper Torchbooks, 1961. A difficult book, not to be lightly undertaken, yet capable of providing a brilliant insight into the philosophic shortcomings of modern society.

17. Joseph Wood Krutch, "If You Don't Mind My Saying So," *The American Scholar*, Autumn, 1966. In Krutch's column which regularly appears in *The American Scholar*, he frequently offers a sound defense for the values which have produced Western civilization. In this particular column, he offers an articulate definition of the timelessness of that heritage.

18. Edith Hamilton, *The Greek Way*, W. W. Norton & Co., Inc., 1930. An excellent treatment of the contribution of Greek civilization to the Western world.

19. Lord Acton, *Essays on Freedom and Power*, The Free Press, 1948. A thoughtful analysis by a distinguished nineteenth-century historian which examines the concepts of freedom throughout history, especially the history of the Western world.

20. Henry Grady Weaver, *The Mainspring of Human Progress*, The Foundation for Economic Education, Inc., 1953. A helpful introduction to many of the ideas which have made Western civilization so uniquely successful.

21. Leonard E. Read, *Elements of Libertarian Leadership*, The Foundation for Economic Education, Inc., 1962. A graphic discussion of the limitations and potentialities of the individual who is truly committed to the freedom philosophy.

22. Edward S. Corwin, "The Higher Law Background of American Constitutional Law," Harvard Law Review, 1928. A scholarly historical study of the basic attitudes and ideas which Western civilization contributed in the development of the American Republic.

23. R. H. Barrow, *The Romans*, Penguin Books Ltd., 1949. A penetrating historical analysis of the history of Rome, peculiarly relevant for our time.

24. W. G. Hardy, *The Greek and Roman World*, Schenkman Publishing Company, Inc., 1962. Professor Hardy's survey of the ancient world is a must as an introduction to the heritage of Western civilization, especially in his treatment of the decline and fall of the Roman Empire, a treatment upon which this book has heavily relied.

25. Edith Hamilton, *The Roman Way*, W. W. Norton & Co., Inc., 1932. Edith Hamilton does the same fine job of grasping the subtleties of Roman thought as she had done earlier in her analysis of the Greeks.

26. Thomas Molnar, "Imperial America." In a thought-provoking *National Review* article (May 3, 1966), Molnar sets forth the disquieting parallels which exist between Imperial Rome and the America of our own time.

27. John Steinbeck, *America and Americans*, The Viking Press, Inc., 1966. A highly penetrating view of contemporary America, especially valuable for its thoughtful consideration of the declining standards which afflict our present society.

28. Christopher Dawson, *Religion and the Rise of Western Culture*, Sheed and Ward Inc., 1950. A careful historical analysis of the close connections between religious values and Western civilization.

29. Christopher Dawson, *The Making of Europe*, Sheed & Ward Inc., 1952. A history of the formative events which have molded European character and played such a large role in the development of Western civilization.

30. *A Monument to Saint Augustine*, published by Sheed & Ward Inc., 1945. A collection of essays examining various aspects of the "Eagle of Hippo," with particularly thought-provoking essays by Christopher Dawson and Jacques Maritain.

31. C. S. Lewis, *The Discarded Image*, Cambridge University Press, 1964. A discussion of the medieval world view and an illuminating comparison between the view held by medieval man and that adopted by modern man.

32. Rousas J. Rushdoony, *This Independent Republic*, Presbyterian & Reformed Publishing Co., 1963. A description of the elements which have constituted the genius of the American governmental experiment.

33. Crane Brinton, *Ideas and Men: The Story of Western Thought*, Prentice-Hall, Inc., 1963. A sweeping and brilliant analysis of the forces and events which

have produced the modern Western world, very helpful for an understanding of Western civilization.

34. Gilbert K. Chesterton, *St. Thomas Aquinas,* Doubleday & Company, Inc., 1956. The best possible introduction to the life and work of St. Thomas Aquinas, providing a simple yet profound delineation of his ideas.

35. George H. Sabine, *A History of Political Theory,* Holt, Rinehart & Winston, Inc., 1961. An excellent scholarly survey of the political thought of the Western world, especially valuable for its treatment of St. Thomas Aquinas and medieval political attitudes.

36. C. S. Lewis, *Miracles,* Macmillan Company, 1947. A critical discussion of contemporary naturalistic assumptions, written in a manner readily understandable by the layman.

37. Bertrand de Jouvenel, *On Power: Its Nature and the History of Its Growth,* The Viking Press, Inc., 1949. Perhaps the finest scholarly analysis of the dangers of unlimited power, together with the description of the havoc that it has wrought in the modern world.

38. Guglielmo Ferrero, *The Principles of Power,* G. P. Putnam's Sons, 1942. A highly personalized yet scholarly analysis of the problem of power, filled with flashes of insight which throw considerable light upon the subject.

39. Alexis de Tocqueville, *Democracy in America,* Sanders & Otley, 1840. The finest possible introduction to an understanding of the values which made America great.

40. Felix Morley, *Freedom and Federalism,* Henry Regnery Company, 1959. A detailed and scholarly examination of the American conception of federalism and the assault which has been made upon it since the American Civil War.

41. John Chamberlain, *The Roots of Capitalism,* D. Van Nostrand Company, Inc., 1965. A persuasive and highly interesting treatment of the underlying concepts of capitalism and their fabulously successful application in the United States.

42. William A. Peterson, *The Wonderful World of Modern Economics* (privately printed by the Intercollegiate Studies Institute). An entertaining summary of the productive capacities of capitalism and the destructive capacities of governmental intervention.

43. Friedrich A. Hayek (Editor), *Capitalism and the Historians*, The University of Chicago Press, 1954. A series of essays by noted scholars which demolishes the customarily dark view of the early Industrial Revolution still commonly held by all too many Americans.

44. Isaiah Berlin, *Two Concepts of Liberty*, The Clarendon Press, 1958. An inaugural lecture delivered before the University of Oxford in 1958, this pamphlet penetrates much of the peculiar "double think" which has come to confuse our modern concept of liberty.

45. Joseph A. Schumpeter, *Capitalism, Socialism, and Democracy*, Harper & Row Publishers, Inc., 1950. A scholarly treatment of capitalism, covering both its strengths and its weaknesses.

46. Peter J. Stanlis, *Edmund Burke and the Natural Law*, The University of Michigan Press, 1958. A careful treatment of the impact of the Natural Law philosophy upon Edmund Burke, suggesting the importance of the concept of Natural Law for the preservation of Western civilization.

47. Henry Hazlitt, *The Failure of the "New Economics,"* D. Van Nostrand Company, Inc., 1959. The best single treatment of the failure of the "mixed economy," demolishing the new economics point by point on the basis of its own theoretical and operational failures.

48. Lawrence Fertig, *Prosperity Through Freedom*, Henry Regnery Company, 1961. An articulate statement of the productive capacities of the free market and the stultifying effects of government intervention.

49. Albert J. Nock, *Our Enemy, the State*, The Caxton Printers, Ltd., 1946. An early warning to the twentieth century that the expansion of governmental authority was a disaster for all men.

50. Russell Kirk, *The Conservative Mind*, Henry Regnery Company, 1960. An extremely well written discussion of some of the men whose ideas have been the rallying point for the defenders of Western civilization.

51. Will Herberg, "Christian Faith and Totalitarian Rule." In this essay, appearing in *Modern Age* (Winter, 1966-1967), Professor Herberg sets forth the Christian ideal as the final and most meaningful bulwark against totalitarian domination.

52. José Ortega y Gasset, *The Revolt of the Masses*, W. W. Norton & Co.,

Inc., 1932. An early classic of the distinguished Spanish philosopher, in which many of the causes of modern decline are skillfully set forth.

53. Milton Friedman, *Capitalism and Freedom*, The University of Chicago Press, 1962. The proper role of competitive capitalism, as set forth by a distinguished contemporary economist.

54. William A. Peterson, *The Private Sector and The Public Sector: Which is Which and Why* (Privately printed by the Intercollegiate Studies Institute). Another of Dr. Peterson's entertaining and clear exposes of the fallacies which so dominate current thinking.

55. Eliseo Vivas, *The Moral Life and The Ethical Life*, Henry Regnery Company, 1963. A careful development of a distinguished modern philosopher's ideas concerning the individual nature of genuine moral choice.

56. C. S. Lewis, *Christian Reflections*, Wm. B. Eerdmans Publishing Co., 1967. More analysis of the modern world, written from the perspective of a deeply Christian scholarship.

57. C. S. Lewis, *Mere Christianity*, Macmillan Company, 1952. A statement at considerable length of the underlying values upon which an enduring civilization must be based.

Name Index*

*Prepared by Vernelia A. Crawford.

Subject Index